The Paradox of Spanish Foreign Policy

The Paradox of Spanish Foreign Policy

Spain's International Relations from Franco to Democracy

Benny Pollack

with
Graham Hunter

Pinter Publishers, London

First published in Great Britain in 1987 by
Pinter Publishers Limited
25 Floral Street, London WC2E 9DS

British Library Cataloguing in Publication Data

Pollack, Benny
   The paradox of Spanish foreign policy :
   Spain's international relations from Franco
   to democracy.
   1. Spain—Foreign relations—20th
   century
   I. Title   II. Hunter, Graham
   327.46   DP85.8

ISBN 0-86187-468-4

Typeset by Florencetype Ltd, Kewstoke, Avon
Printed by Biddles of Guildford Ltd.

Contents

Glossary and abbreviations

Axis: Japanese–Italian–German *entente* during the Second World War

Cámara de los Diputados: Lower Chamber of the Spanish Parliament

CC.OO: Comisiones Obreras (Workers' Commissions), Communist-controlled trade-union organization

CCPMA: Comité Conjunto para Asuntos Políticos, Militares y Administrativos (Joint Committee for Political, Military and Administrative Affairs), a US–Spanish high-level organization

CDS: Centro Democrático y Social (Democratic and Social Centre), a centre–left party headed by Adolfo Suárez, replacing UCD in the 1980s

CEDA: Confederación Española de Derechas Autónomas (Spanish Confederation of the Autonomous Right), a right-wing party during the Spanish Republic

CEOE: Spanish Employers' Organization

CEPYME: Spanish Association of Small and Medium Enterprises

Comintern: Communist International

Contadora Group: Group of Latin American countries involved in a peaceful solution of the Nicaraguan conflict

Coordinadora Estatal de Organizaciones Pacifistas: National Organization for the Coordination of Pro-Peace Action, Spain

CP: Coalición Popular (Popular Coalition), a group of right-wing parties

Cortes: Spanish Parliament

CPSU: Communist party of the Soviet Union

ECLA: United Nations' Economic Commission for Latin America

EEC: European Economic Community

Estado Nuevo: New State, autarkic stage in the development of the Franco regime, after the Second World War, characterized by inward-looking, protectionist economic policies, and social and political authoritarianism and repression.

ETA: Euzkadi Ta Azkatasuna (Basque Nation and Liberty), the Basque separatist movement

FAO: United Nations Food and Agricultural Organization

GARD: Advisory Group for Aerospace Research and Development (a NATO agency)

GDP: Gross Domestic Product

ICI: Instituto de Cooperación Iberoamericana (Institute for Co-operation with Latin America), a Spanish Foreign Office organization

ILO: United Nations International Labour Organization

IMF: International Monetary Fund

INI: Instituto Nacional de Industria (National Industrial Institute), a National Development Corporation for Spain

MAE: Ministerio de Asuntos Exteriores (Spanish Foreign Office)

MAPAI: Israeli Labour Party

MAS: Military Agency for Standardization (a NATO agency)

MGMC: Military Committee Meteorological Group (a NATO agency)

NADEFCOL: NATO's Defense College

NATO: North Atlantic Treaty Organization

NEWAC: Electronic Warfare Advisory Committee (a NATO agency)

NPT: Non-Proliferation Treaty (limits the development of atomic armaments and experiments)

OECD: Organization for Economic Cooperation and Development

OEEC: Organization for European Economic Cooperation

Palacio de la Moncloa: Official headquarters of the Spanish government

Palacio de Santa Cruz: Spanish Foreign Office

PCE: Partido Comunista de España (Spanish Communist party)

PCF: French Communist party

Plataforma Cívica para la Salida de España de la OTAN: Civic Platform for the Campaign to Leave NATO, Spain

Polisario Front: Saharaui national liberation organization in the Western Sahara

Portavoz: Spokesperson

PSOE: Partido Socialista Obrero Español (Spanish Socialist

Workers party)

Sindicatos Verticales: Vertical trade unions, official trade-union movement controlled by the Franco regime

UCD: Unión de Centro Democrático (Union of the Democratic Centre), a Spanish centrist party during the transition to democracy in the 1970s, whose leader was former Prime Minister Adolfo Suárez

UGT: Unión General de Trabajadores (National Union of Labour), Socialist-controlled trade-union organization

UNESCO: United Nations Educational, Scientific and Cultural Organization

UNICEF: United Nations Children Fund

USSR: Union of Soviet Socialist Republics

23-F: *Coup d'état* attempt in Spain, on 23 February 1981, which included the takeover of the Spanish Parliament by military and national police forces

Acknowledgements

There are so many people in Britain and Spain who have helped us with our research, that to name them all would be virtually impossible. However, we would like to mention a few individuals without whose support and cooperation this book would have not been written.

In Britain, Professors John Fisher and Frederick F. Ridley supported our application for financial support, allowing research visits to Spain to gather data and carry out interviews. Christopher Pycroft and Felix Zamora helped in various ways, and our thanks go to them too. In Spain, Manuel Medina, Juan Antonio Yáñez-Barnuevo, Julián Santamaría, Francisco Aldecoa, Erick Schnake, Angel Viñas, Maria Yrigoyen, Miguel Angel Martínez, Francisco Fernández Ordóñez and Fernando Perpiñán opened doors, gave interviews and facilitated access to sources. Many more in the civil and diplomatic service, and ministries, talked to us on a variety of subjects, on condition that they would remain anonymous. Their information is invaluable and our thanks are due to them.

Special gratitude is due to the Board of Latin American Studies, the Staff Travel Fund and the Visiting Academics Fund of the University of Liverpool, for the financial support provided.

Claudio Pollack encouraged the use of his word processor, succeeding against all odds in making it possible for one of us to profit from the benefits of modern technology. For overcoming a long-standing prejudice and making our task significantly easier, our thanks go to him. Pat Brooksbank and Alice Kershaw typed the final draft of the book with their usual intelligence and efficiency, spotting errors and even improving the text. All responsibility for errors and/or omissions is entirely ours.

B. Pollack
G. Hunter

Liverpool
May 1987

Introduction

In recent years, Spain's political history has been characterized by paradoxes and contradictions. Spain's foreign relations have been one of the major, and perhaps one of the most remarkable, of these paradoxes.

The coming of democracy, after the long years of Franco's dictatorship, has inevitably transformed Spanish society radically. Yet there has been at least a superficial continuity in the area of foreign policy—some would go so far as to say a homogeneity. Firstly, this is indicative of a striking degree of professionalism within the policy-making establishment in Madrid. Secondly, it also points to a commitment, perhaps surprising under Franco, to principles which at times contradicted the regime's ideology and internal politics. Examples of this are not difficult to find: relations with Cuba after the overthrow of the Batista dictatorship; policy towards Chile under the Popular Unity government; and Spanish foreign policy in the Middle East. Some commentators have suggested these as illustrations of attempts at designing and implementing patterns of relationships independent of official United States' foreign policy, and in some cases even antagonistic to it.[1] In other words, according to this analysis the authoritarian/repressive exercise of political and administrative power by the State under Franco did not prevent the development of a highly professional, sophisticated and at times progressive foreign policy, the political goals of which were pragmatic rather than ideological.

As will be demonstrated below, both before and after the establishment of democracy, Spain has systematically supported the claims of the Palestinians to a national home and shown a pro-Arab outlook in the Middle East conflict, maintained diplomatic and commercial relations with Cuba in the face of open United States' pressure, and established equally good relations with the administration of Salvador Allende in Chile at the time of the

American blockade. Under Franco, these decisions were justified as a matter of long-term 'national interest', and were apparently taken without much regard for internal considerations, or indeed for external pressures, most notably from the United States.

Of course the foreign policy paradox is matched by the equally striking internal developments that have affected the Spanish political system since Franco's death in 1975. After about forty years of authoritarian rule, dedicated to the extirpation of all shades of left and liberal opposition, hostile to all forms of popular mobilization, especially independent trade unions and political parties, and rejecting even academic or intellectual challenges to the regime, the repressive apparatus quickly disintegrated. Of the three 'pillars' of the State under Franco (the Church, the army and the Falange), only the army remains as a potential threat to the young democracy, and measures are being taken to democratize it.[2] The Church has gradually but firmly changed sides, no longer the determined ally of authoritarianism and of subversion against the Republic that it was in the 1930s; it now defends pluralism and democratic freedoms; and the Falange party, which had lost all legitimacy and representation under Franco anyway, has all but totally disappeared.

Furthermore, a short and not very successful period of centrist government under Adolfo Suárez and Calvo Sotelo was followed by the inauguration of two Socialist administrations under Felipe González. The transition revealed a remarkable collective demo-cratic will, and a desire to break radically with the repressive past of almost half a century.[3] No less important, the King appointed by Franco himself surprised almost everyone with his strong support for democratic change, and his clear repudiation of any anti-democratic actions. The commitment to democracy by King and people, and indeed by the overwhelming majority of the Spanish elites, in such a young competitive party system—virtually without party politics for half a century—is in itself a paradox that has merited special interest among the academic community and politicians alike.[4]

In this book, we will discuss whether Spanish foreign policy has shown genuine continuity and consistency from the Franco period to the present day, or whether the similarities are more apparent than real. We shall also try to explain the factors— political, economic and ideological—that shape foreign policy, and the relationship that exists between internal politics and foreign policy decisions. Furthermore, we shall examine the main historical goals of Spanish diplomacy, and the degree of success Spain has achieved on some of the most important issues.

Special attention is paid to the period 1976–86, when the democratic transformation and modernization of the hitherto authoritarian and traditional society accelerated, and foreign policy, like other areas of politics, became once again the product of choice and discussion.

Notes

1. Foreign Minister, Fernando Morán, however, considers Franco's foreign policy only seemingly progressive, and more rhetorical than real. See F. Morán, *Una Política Exterior para España*, Planeta, Barcelona, 1980.
2. See *El País* and *Diario 16* (national daily newspapers), and *Cambio 16* (national weekly magazine), from 1981, on the debate about modernization and the reduction of the armed forces, which is still continuing. The Defence Minister, Narcis Serra, is publicly committed to these ends.
3. See B. Pollack, 'Spain: From Corporate State to Parliamentary Democracy', *Parliamentary Affairs*, vol. 31, 1978, pp. 52–66, and 'The 1982 Spanish General Elections and Beyond', *Parliamentary Affairs*, vol. 36, no. 2, 1983, pp. 201–17. Also: J. Story, 'Spanish Political Parties: Before and After the Election', *Government and Opposition*, vol. 12, 1977, pp. 473–93; R. Carr and J.P. Fusi, *Spain: Dictatorship to Democracy*, Allen & Unwin, London, 1979; F.F. Coverdale, *The Political Transformation of Spain under Franco*, Praeger, New York, 1979.
4. See Carr and Fusi, op. cit.; Coverdale, op. cit.; S. Carrillo, *La Ruptura Democrática*, La Gaya Ciencia, Barcelona, 1976; R. Arango, *The Spanish Political System: Franco's Legacy*, Westview Press, Boulder, Colorado, 1978; J. Maravall, *The Transition to Democracy in Spain*, Croom Helm, London, 1982.

1

Foreign policy under Franco: the early years—pragmatism or opportunism?

The Second World War: from neutrality to non-belligerency

'Foreign policy during the Franco regime (1939–75) was virtually defined, inspired or corrected by Franco himself', according to Fernando Morán, career diplomat and former Minister of Foreign Affairs in the government of Felipe González.[1] Ministers, however, it is generally recognized, did play a role, but their influence in shaping foreign policy varied. Clearly it depended as much on their individual styles and personalities and conception of diplomacy and foreign affairs as either ideological, or technocratic and pragmatic, as on their personal relationship with the Head of State.

Spain's policy of neutrality, and at times even open sympathy for the Axis, undoubtedly reveals Franco's personal stamp. His identification with Fascism was well known and has been well documented. After the defeat of the Republicans in the Civil War in 1936, it seemed more than likely that Spain would adopt a corporative structure internally, and tighten its links with Italy and Germany.[2] The assistance that Franco had received from Italy and Germany during the Civil War—troops, armaments and cash—made this seem almost inevitable.[3] In the event, however, at the beginning of the Second World War Spain embarked on a policy of active neutrality, in spite of strong pressures exerted by both Hitler and Mussolini. The participation of Spanish troops fighting alongside the Germans was insignificant, and in no way contributed to military or geopolitical victories. Of course Franco could always claim to have paid well for Italian and German collaboration by offering Spain as a testing ground for Axis material and tactics during the Civil War.[4]

The relationship between Franco's Spain and Nazi Germany was

complex and in fact only lukewarm. Furthermore, Franco's reluctance to tie himself too closely to Hitler was fully reciprocated. It is
more or less clear that the Spanish Civil War took the Germans by
surprise, and their enthusiasm at first was not great. In fact, it
appears that initially they expected Franco to be defeated, and
expressed their support for the British suggestion of non-intervention. A.J.P. Taylor concluded that 'Mussolini was Franco's real
Patron', and that Hitler only became actively involved in the Civil
War to keep Italy estranged from Britain and France. He goes on to
say that 'all along, Franco was quite as concerned to assert his
equality and independence as to do anything to please the Germans',[5] and their relationship began to fall into a cycle of concessions and retreats: there was an element of mutual dependence.
It was as important to Franco to gain international recognition at
the time of war, as a nationalist/Fascist leader, as to distance
himself from the Germans by proclaiming his neutrality and
independence, in case the Germans lost the war.[6]

The Munich agreement, revealing the democracies of Western
Europe to be far from united in their approach to Fascist and Nazi
threats, fuelled the impetus, on both sides, for some form of
partnership.[7] After the Munich agreement was signed, Franco
proclaimed Spain's neutrality, but seemed to move closer to
the Axis powers in the granting of mining concessions to the Germans, for example.

However, documents released by the German Foreign Office
show that Spanish foreign policy during the war years was more
independent that was previously thought. They show that the pre-
war concessions to German firms to look for and exploit Spanish
mineral resources had a very limited scope (leaving the Germans
frustrated and complaining), and that they were subsequently
cancelled shortly after the end of the Civil War; also that all the
cultural treaties signed by the two nations during this period had
little practical effect on either side. It also emerged that
the Germans were unable to understand General Franco's motivations, that they did not consider him a reliable ally, and that they
had to improvise continuously in their policies towards Spain.[8]

During the Second World War, the triumphant Spanish Nationalists had the opportunity to test the major aspects of the
pro-Fascist, corporatist ideology that characterized the Falange
movement. Within this ideology, however, the traditionalist,
diffuse, xenophobic patriotism, based heavily on military and

religious symbols, and on anti-Communism and anti-liberalism, impeded any open identification with, or support for, Nazi Germany or Fascist Italy. Neutrality, albeit with demonstrations of friendship towards both Germany and Italy, was better suited to Spain's strong Catholic tradition and its nationalism, and neutrality was to be at the centre of Spain's foreign policy during the first years of the war.

Franco's foreign policy during the war years had some specific, Nationalist goals. While the Francoists concentrated their energies internally on radical political and economic reform,[9] externally they set about to achieve, under the various guises of neutrality, non-belligerency, and then neutrality again, several policy goals. Amongst these, the need not to alienate the Allies unduly was always present, and possibly at the forefront.

Spain's neutrality was officially proclaimed in September 1939, shortly after a mutual assistance pact with Portugal had been signed. In June 1940, with the German forces very close to Spain on the country's northern border, the Foreign Minister, Juan Beigbeder, revealed a series of imperialist claims to Germany and Italy, which included French Morocco, the Orán sector of Algeria, parts of West and Equatorial Africa, and Gibraltar. Soon afterwards, Franco offered to enter the war as an ally of the Axis, if his territorial demands were met, in addition to the delivery of important war equipment to Spain.[10] At this time, 1939–40, British and French military power was in a state of deep collapse, and the prevailing view was that the Allies had only limited, if indeed any, possibilities of success.

Entering the war would have entailed an official declaration of war from Spain though, and that would have left the country wide open to attack, presumably by the British and Free French troops through Gibraltar. Franco's idea, it is generally thought, was that if and when Spain would enter the war, it would do so during the last minutes of it, so as to be able to profit from victory without having to face the risk of invasion.

Some of Franco's claims were, in fact, old, rather popular goals inside Spain, such as that to Gibraltar, for example. Others, like the claim to French Morocco and Orán were part of the imperialist, neo-colonialist aspirations of the Falangista movement. Finally, Spain needed Equatorial Africa to complete its claims to empire — after all, how could any nation have claims to imperial legitimacy without an African possession?

The concession of these territories to Spain depended, of course, on the Axis winning the war. For two weeks after the fall of France, Franco was 'euphoric about the chances of an impending Axis triumph'.[11] In the frenzy that followed, Spanish troops occupied Tangier (a first step towards the establishment of a Spanish colony covering perhaps the whole of northern Africa), while demands were put on Britain to give up Gibraltar, and to put pressure on France to cede some of its African territories. In this, Franco exploited French distrust of German intentions to try and convince it that it would be preferable for Spain to replace France in Africa, before Germany could set foot there.

Soon afterwards, however, Franco changed the juridical position of Spain from one of neutrality to one of non-belligerency, while proclaiming Spain's 'will to empire'. This could be interpreted as a manoeuvre to pressurize both sides to make concessions, though in fact Mussolini had claimed a similar status for Italy prior to entering the war.[12] In July 1940, Madrid signed a complementary protocol to the mutual assistance treaty with Portugal, drawing the two countries even closer militarily. This can be used to support the theory that Spain was preparing to enter the war on the Axis side. Other interpretations, however, see the protocol as born of Spain's and Portugal's joint desire to stay out of the war, rather than a sign of their wish to participate in it.[13]

Certainly there can be no doubt of Franco's sympathy for the Axis powers. Even before he could claim control of the whole of Spanish territory, Spain's foreign policy was acquiring distinctly anti-liberal and anti-Communist overtones. Just before the end of the Civil War, the Nationalist government based in Burgos had signed a friendship treaty with the German Reich and adhered to the Anti-Comintern Pact.[14] The Nationalists' anti-internationalism also led to the repudiation of the League of Nations, from which it withdrew in May 1939. Equally, the Spanish press and educational system reflected a notorious pro-Axis bias throughout the Second World War, and, in general, the various agencies of socialization were used to instil support for the Axis cause. On the other side, these gestures of solidarity can be interpreted more as a set of internal propaganda measures than anything else, with the aim of mobilizing support among the disaffected Falangista intellectuals.

Furthermore, by August 1940, the British were showing indications of resisting and even counter-attacking, and there were also signs that the United States might be ready to enter the war too.

Non-participation, therefore, seemed the only course open to Spain once again. Some observers think, in fact, that Franco had decided definitely on non-intervention by the end of 1940, with or without Germany's acceptance of Spanish demands.[15]

By the autumn of 1940, Germany still had not responded to Franco's colonial claims. Its own ambitions were in evidence. As a result, Franco sent Ramón Serrano Suñer to Germany to find out Germany's real attitude to Spain. He could hardly have chosen a person more sympathetic to the Nazi cause, nor could the Germans have aspired to a more congenial envoy. A close relative of Franco, Serrano Suñer had been Minister of the Interior and a doctrinaire Fascist, and was a national leader of the Falange. He was reputed to favour a policy of imperialist expansion, and of close cooperation with the Axis.

When Serrano arrived in Germany, Spain was suffering from an economic recession brought on by a drastic decrease in vital British exports; Spain's economic dependence on Britain and the United States was considerable, and this factor could have prevented Franco from closing ranks with the Axis powers. Furthermore, Germany was failing to make up on Spain's economic losses, and the protestations of friendship had not been translated into practical help.

Although little was achieved by Serrano Suñer's visit to Germany, Franco appointed him Foreign Minister shortly after, when Beigbeder's pressures on France and Britain for territorial concessions proved inconclusive.

Serrano Suñer and the ideological period of foreign policy

With Serrano Suñer as Foreign Minister, Spain's foreign policy acquired a distinct ideological tone. Paradoxically, this occurred just when it became patently obvious that Spain would not enter the war. During his term of office, Spain's identification with the Axis reached a peak, and its commitment was gradually toned down throughout 1942 and 1943. Highly emotive speeches were common in this period, in which the existence of an international conspiracy of Masons, liberals, Communists and Jews was used to justify calls for 'national unity', and the doctrine of *Hispanidad* found favour. *Hispanidad* was seen then as the idea of Spain as leader of a pan-Iberian movement of continental proportions, including not only Latin America, but also an as yet non-existent

Spanish Empire to be built with the spoils of war and the generosity of the Axis.[16]

However, the meeting between Hitler and Franco at Hendaya in the autumn of 1940 demonstrated that their respective goals were far apart. Hitler was obsessed with the need to convince Spain to enter the war, while Franco was interested only in presenting a claim for commodities and armaments, without committing himself to actually joining it. He argued that the shortages precipitated by the loss of British and American supplies and the drain on Spain's finances and economy by the Civil War made it impossible for him to provide either troops or weaponry.[17]

German pressures on Spain continued none the less, and Serrano Suñer was invited to Berlin in November 1940 to discuss Spain's preparations for joining the fighting. Serrano Suñer went, but these preparations were clearly non-existent, and it became increasingly obvious, even to Germany, that Franco was in fact playing for time. Spain rejected Hitler's request in December to enter the war before January 1941, repeating the argument that Spain was unable to play a more active role because of its economic problems and shortages of weapons.

So, Spanish commitment to the Axis in the end came to nothing more than a general, broad, sympathetic identification with the goals and ideology of Fascism and Nazism. However, both Franco and Serrano Suñer were aggressive in their verbal expressions of sympathy and defence of the Axis. Serrano Suñer had become the most ardent defender of the Axis inside Spain, and he did not trouble to hide his preferences when representing his country abroad. He boasted of his support for Germany and Italy without restraint, and blamed the spread of liberalism and Communism for all of Spain's problems. He was in fact relatively content with non-belligerency since it represented, at least juridically, a step further than neutrality towards entering the war.

Meanwhile, Franco used the Spanish media and his many public appearances and speeches to the Falange party to show his utter contempt for liberal democracy and Communism, and his sympathies for the Axis. However, he hinted in a subtle manner that he actually preferred the Italians to the Germans, thus reaffirming the impression that the Falange was much more a purely Fascist movement, at least on the surface, than a Nazi one.[18] Furthermore, Serrano Suñer visited Rome in an attempt to 'separate the Italians from the Germans in terms of attitudes towards Spain'.[19]

Foreign policy and Nationalist rhetoric served an important purpose internally, of course, and during Serrano Suñer's term of office, the Falange dominated foreign policy-making. The Nationalists were able to manipulate the Foreign Ministry in part because of the purges carried out after the defeat of the Republicans in 1936, when the entire civil service had been virtually dismantled, to eliminate supposed sympathizers with liberalism, communism, Masonry and/or Jews. Officials that were too bland for the Nationalist's tastes, were summarily dismissed in this period, and diplomats abroad, especially in the Allied countries or countries sympathetic to the Allies, could be dismissed for showing the slightest sympathy for their host governments.

The beginnings of pragmatism: the politics of adaptation

By 1942, the outcome of the war was uncertain. Spain's confidence in an Axis victory had evaporated. Serrano Suñer's identification with, and support for, the Axis was slowly becoming a liability rather than an asset. His dogmatic approach to international issues had now extended to related areas as well. Not even the Guard of the Foreign Ministry was safe from the long reach of the Falange; militiamen replaced the regular army and the police in positions of security, and only those who could pass a strict vetting system were accepted for duty. For the first time in Spain's diplomatic history, Spanish diplomats were forbidden to marry foreigners, causing widespread discontent among the ranks of the Foreign Service.

Serrano Suñer was increasingly seen as the Axis representative in Spain, and paradoxically this ended up by harming his standing internally. Some of Spain's right-wingers, not strongly identified with the Falange though by no means democratic, persuaded Franco that Serrano Suñer's time was now up, and that a replacement was needed if the country was going to adapt to the changed political circumstances. The man appointed to replace him was General Francisco Gómez Jordana.

Although officially the replacement of Serrano Suñer by Gómez Jordana did not entail a change of policies, it was inevitable that the removal of such an orthodox Nationalist, closely identified with the Axis, would bring about some fundamental shift in policy. And as Spain's attitude cooled considerably, German activities in Spain

—espionage, commerce, trade and propaganda—suffered a number of difficulties. Gómez Jordana supposedly gave a more sympathetic hearing to allied diplomats; while, initially in this period, Franco himself seemed to leave foreign policy in the hands of the professionals, in order to concentrate on pressing internal problems,. both political and economic.

By the end of 1942, it was clear that the British and Americans were preparing a military offensive that would take them as far as Africa. Spain did what it could diplomatically to prevent the Allies from taking North Africa, where it still hoped to claim some colonies. French Africa was captured, notwithstanding, however, by the Allies, which caused dismay in Nationalist circles about the course of the war. Spain's imperial dreams seemed to be disintegrating, and the Axis possibilities of winning the war looked remote. Soon after, rumours spread about the possibilities of an Allied invasion of Europe through the Iberian peninsula. Franco tried to counter-balance this psychologically by reinforcing the alliance with Portugal (a natural historical ally of Britain), hoping to dissuade possible invaders from either side and, at the same time, to try and obtain a more sympathetic hearing with Britain. The Portuguese partnership was all the more needed in case the Germans decided they wanted to cross Spain to confront the Allies in Africa.

Gómez Jordana's term of office reflected the changing nature of the war, namely the considerable German and Italian military defeats. His diplomacy showed a marked departure from that of his predecessor, and the verbal, commercial and logistic support to the Axis, which characterized the earlier period, was replaced by a low-key, non-ideological diplomacy. The fall of Mussolini in Italy pushed Spain further in search of a new pragmatism.

The evidence suggests that by the end of 1943 both Franco and Gómez Jordana had all but abandoned hopes of an Axis victory. However, the sense of opportunity that had helped Franco throughout his military and political career did not desert him. His actions, though considerably more muted than when Serrano Suñer was Foreign Minister, began to take the form of trying to consolidate a grand alliance of 'Christian' nations against the rising spectre of Bolshevism and the Soviet Union. If the Allies were to accept his rationale, then he could transform a political defeat, which is what the collapse of the Axis would mean to Spain, into a political victory. In order to gain credence with both sides, Gómez

Jordana called for a negotiated settlement to the war, and reinforced Spain's claim to neutrality, which it had again quietly acquired.

The beginning of 1944 signalled another important 'adaptation' by Spain: close cooperation with the Allies regarding refugees from the Nazis. A few thousand refugees were in fact allowed sanctuary in Spain, thus mitigating the somewhat hitherto staunch support lent to the Fascist and Nazi regimes. Even here, however, when Berlin complained about Spain's new-born pragmatism, Franco replied that the concessions were made under duress; it was the price Spain had to pay to avoid further economic reprisals from Britain and the United States.[20]

Franco's opportune, if not opportunistic, cooling of relations with the Axis was in great evidence at the beginning of 1944. Even the media, which used to be a vehicle for pro-Axis propaganda, reflected the changes of the previous year. The death of Gómez Jordana in August 1944 provided Franco with yet another opportunity to pursue his policy of new realism. The appointment of José F. de Lequerica as Gómez Jordana's successor brought Spain one step further from the Axis, and one nearer to the Allies.

De Lequerica had never been as notoriously pro-Fascist as Gómez Jordana, let alone Serrano Suñer. His function was to try and convince the Allied nations that Spain could play a very useful role in the reconstruction of Europe once the war was over. At the same time, however, he tried to reassure Germany, albeit in a surreptitious fashion, that Spain was still a friendly country, and that it could do a lot to help Germany after the war.

The shift in Spanish foreign policy embraced areas far away from the conflict. The pursuit of *Hispanidad*, which had been discredited by strong suspicions on the part of the United States and Britain, which alleged that it was a mask for Nazi espionage, propaganda and penetration in Latin America, was dropped, and Franco embarked on a diplomatic offensive with many Latin American countries to improve Spain's relations on a bilateral level. This was also designed to establish enough support to protect Spain from the isolation it would almost inevitably suffer after the war.[21]

Resentment towards Spain was widespread within the democratic community in Europe and outside, with countries like Mexico, Australia, New Zealand and the United States adding their weight to a growing feeling that Franco's opportunism should not go unpunished. Trying to cover lost ground, Franco let it be known to Allied diplomats that he was 'very happy' about Allied victories in 1944, and offered to extradite German and other European Nazi collaborators to those countries where they could stand trial, if they entered into Spanish territory.[22] He duly did so when the moment came.[23]

Finally, according to Halstead, in 1944 Franco removed pictures of Mussolini and Hitler from his Pardo Palace office, and replaced them with one of the Pope. The turning was now complete.[24]

The years of isolation: the crusade against Communism

The year 1944 signalled the compulsory abandonment of Spain's pro-Axis foreign policy. This was evident not only in a number of practical attitudes adopted by the Madrid government, but also in a distinct change of language in its references to world problems, in public speeches, articles, and the propaganda leaflets of Spanish politicians and diplomats.[25]

The defeat of the Nazis brought menacing charges for Spain. In France, the new government of General de Gaulle was deeply antagonistic to the Franco regime, and thousands of Republican refugees found a renewed solidarity there. Many of them had in fact fought alongside the French Resistance against the German occupation, or with the Free French troops in Africa. In Mexico, the Republican government in exile had secured official recognition as the legitimate government of Spain, while other Latin American countries, which had also received thousands of Republican exiles, looked with frustration and resentment towards Spain. The doctrine of *Hispanidad* reached rock-bottom. Only Argentina, under the populist regime of General Juan Perón—the most pro-Axis country of Latin America during the war—could be said to show any sympathy and solidarity with Spain.

Liberated Europe was not very sympathetic either. Not only the Soviet Union and the United States, but all the new Western European democracies deeply resented Franco's collaboration and opportunism, and were prepared to exact some sort of punishment.

Franco, meanwhile, aware of the creation of the United Nations, eagerly cooperated with the Allies on a number of issues. Firstly, he made it abundantly clear that he was available for an international crusade against Communism, should it now follow the defeat of Fascism and Nazism. Secondly, the regime publicized the help that it gave to Jewish refugees during the war, and claimed that Spain should be at the forefront of any new world organization that might emerge after the war.[26]

Internally, Franco tried to improve his image by enacting the first declaration of civil rights since he took over. He also replaced pro-Nazi members of his Cabinet with more moderate personalities, especially Monarchists, who were considered sympathetic to Britain, France and the United States. This public relations exercise was completed by the appointment of a new Foreign Minister, Alberto Martín Artajo, a Catholic intellectual who, it was felt, would be able to attract support from the newly democratic Italy, France, Latin America and, most important, sectors of the United States. The Catholic North American political elites responded positively to his appointment, and this fact helped considerably to heal the wounds and eventually end Spanish isolation.

The policy of give-and-take that Franco had pursued during the war, however, was to continue. The civil rights charter enacted shortly after the war was no more than cosmetic, a luxury for international consumption; the repressive nature of the regime remained untouched: political parties forcibly stayed outside the law, press censorship continued, and independent trade unions were forbidden. Suggestions by sympathetic right-wing circles in Western Europe and the United States that he should dismantle the Falange and the vertical state-controlled trade unions, were met with a curt rejection.

The most notable aspect of Spain's isolation after the war was its rejection by the international community as a founder member of the United Nations. Mexico had asked for and obtained Spain's exclusion from membership of the new organization in San Francisco. In fact, the Mexican government had begun a campaign against Spanish membership at the Inter-American Conference of War and Peace in Chapultepec, Mexico, in February–March 1945, and the idea had gathered momentum at the San Francisco meeting.[27] The reaction of the international community was generally favourable to Mexico's position, and the Potsdam agreement of July–August 1945 helped make the idea more tenable. The French even went so far as to suggest, shortly afterwards, an allied invasion of Spain, a suggestion that was rejected by both the United States and Britain. Undeterred, however, the French gave enthusiastic help to Spanish exiles organizing raids into Spanish territory.

It was decided, then, that Spain should not be admitted into the United Nations. Internal repression in Spain hardened international opinion still further, as in February 1946, for example, when the civil guard captured a number of infiltrators and, after summary trials, executed them. In March 1946, the Allies declared that Spain could not participate in the United Nations 'as long as General Franco continued in control'.[28] Up until 1948, when the necessities of the Cold War made the United States keener to end Spain's isolation, the Franco regime suffered humiliations and attacks from the United Nations, which continually approved resolutions against Franco, and even supported an economic blockade.

In this hostile world, the Spanish economy suffered badly, as very few countries were prepared to continue normal trade relations with it. Of the major exporters of commodities, only Argentina remained faithful to the Franco regime, loyal to the friendship between Franco and Perón, and provided much-needed wheat and other produce now scarce in Spain as a consequence of the United Nations' supported economic blockade.[29] The years 1946 and 1947 were probably the worst for Spain. The wounds of the war had still not healed, and a vast number of countries refused to forgive Franco his neutrality, which was at best seen as opportunistic and at worst pro-Axis.

Franco was unable to ignore the hostility of the international community, and in response he played the anti-Communist card, pursuing authoritarian policies internally, and reiterating his availability to the Western powers for a crusade of international proportions. When the onset of the Cold War disturbed the postwar *modus vivendi*, Franco's Spain was the first to benefit. His campaign for an anti-Communist crusade (alas, for Franco, not an anti-Jewish or an anti-Mason one since anti-Semitism had been discredited by the horrors of the Nazi regime, and President Truman was a Mason) began to find a willing audience.

But before the Western powers finally gave respectability to Franco's Spain, there were two years of strenuous confrontation in the United Nations. Although by 1948 the United States was proving more friendly, other countries continued to isolate Spain. Franco had to wait until December 1955 to be allowed in, and then only because of a package deal secured by Dimitri Molotov, the

Soviet Foreign Minister, and John Foster Dulles, the US Secretary of State, which ensured admission for several Eastern European countries as well. However, little had changed within Spain to encourage the United Nations to grant recognition to the Franco regime in its own right: it remained as intolerant of opposition and as repressive as ever.[30]

Notes

1. Fernando Morán, 'Foreword' to J.M. Armero, *La Política Exterior de Franco*, Planeta, Barcelona, 1978, p. 13.
2. For data on Franco's pro-Fascist views, see: Paul Preston (ed.), *Spain in Crisis: The Evolution and Decline of the Franco Regime*, Harvester, Brighton, 1976; J. Linz, 'An Authoritarian Regime: Spain', in E. Allardt and Y. Littunen (eds), *Cleavages, Ideologies and Party Systems*, Helsinki, Transactions of The Westermaak Society, 1964; and from the same author, 'From Falange to Movimiento Organización: The Spanish Single Party and the Franco Regime, 1936–1968', in S.P. Huntington and C.H. Moore (eds), *Authoritarian One Party Systems*, Basic Books, New York, 1970. Also useful are: A. de Miguel, 'La Herencia del Franquismo', *Cambio 16*, Madrid, 1977, and J.M. Armero, *La Política exterior de Franco*, op. cit.
3. See H. Thomas, *The Spanish Civil War*, op. cit.
4. H. Holborn, *A History of Modern Germany*, Eyre and Spottiswoode, London, 1969, p. 77.
5. A.J.P. Taylor, *Europe: Grandeur and Decline*, Penguin, Harmondsworth, 1967, p. 226.
6. On Spain's reluctance to enter the war, see, C.R. Halstead, 'Spanish Foreign Policy, 1936–1978' in J.W. Cortada (ed.), *Spain in the Twentieth Century: Essays on Spanish Diplomacy, 1898–1978*, Aldwych Press, London, 1980, pp. 41–94. Also, S. González, *España Neutral*, Gráficas Espejo, Madrid, 1947.
7. A.J.P. Taylor, *Europe: Grandeur and Decline*, op. cit.
8. *Documents on German Foreign Policy, 1918–1945*, Series D, vol. III, *The Spanish Civil War*.
9. For internal politics, see Carr and Fusi, *Spain: Dictatorship to Democracy*, op. cit.; J. Linz, 'Opposition under an Authoritarian Regime: The Case of Spain', in R.A. Dahl (ed.) *Regimes and Oppositions*, Yale University Press, New Haven, Connecticut, 1974; G. Germani, 'Political Socialization in Fascist Regimes: Italy and Spain', in S.P. Huntington and C.H. Moore (eds), *Authoritarian One Party Systems*, op. cit.; V. Alba, *Transition in Spain: From Franco to Democracy*,

Transaction Books, New Brunswick, New Jersey, 1978. On trade unions and other pressure/interest groups, see J. Amsden, *Collective Bargaining and Class Struggle in Spain*, Weidenfeld & Nicholson, London, 1972, and J.M. Maravall, *Dictatorship and Political Dissent: Workers and Students in Franco's Spain*, Tavistock Publications, London, 1978.

10. For details, see United States Department of State, *Documents*, vol. 9, *The War Years*, 1940, Washington, D.C., 1956.

11. C.R. Halstead, 'Spanish Foreign Policy, 1936–1978', in J.W. Cortada (ed.), *Spain in the Twentieth Century*, op. cit. p. 63.

12. It is difficult to guess Franco's real intentions: if anything, these ambiguities furthered his case for neutrality.

13. Spain played the Portuguese card on several occasions, whenever Franco's feeling of isolation reached crisis point.

14. United States Department of State, *Documents*, op. cit. pp. 884–6.

15. C.R. Halstead, op. cit. p. 64.

16. J.M. Armero covers this issue well, op. cit. See also Ministerio de Asuntos Exteriores, *Archivos Generales*, 1940–2. Franco's obsession with the existence of an international conspiracy of liberals, Jews, Masons and Communists did not end with the defeat of the Axis; the need for political accommodation more than anything else led to a change in the language he used.

17. See *Unpublished Documents on British Foreign Policy*, Public Records Office, London (2299/75/41). Also, *Unpublished Documents on U.S. Foreign Policy*, quoted in Halstead, op. cit. Also useful, Ramón Serrano Suñer, *Memorias*, Planeta, Barcelona, 1977; and S. Hoare, *Embajador ante Franco en Misión Especial*, Sedaway, Madrid, 1977.

18. There are several good works on this subject. See all of J. Linz's writing on Spanish authoritarianism which have already been cited. Also, G. Brennan, *The Spanish Labyrinth*, Cambridge University Press, Cambridge, 1950; E. Díaz, *Pensamiento Español*, Cuadernos para el Diálogo, Madrid, 1974; W. Lacquer, *Fascism*, University of California Press, Berkeley, 1976; and N. Poulantzas, *The Crisis of the Dictatorships: Portugal, Spain and Greece*, New Left Books, London, 1976.

19. C.R. Halstead, op. cit.

20. United States Department of State, *The Spanish Government and the Axis*, Washington, D.C., 1946.

21. Ministerio de Asuntos Exteriores de España (MAE), *Archivos Generales*, 1943, 1944, 1945.

22. C.R. Halstead, p. 73.

23. Pierre Laval, the pro-Axis French Prime Minister, was one of the unfortunate former allies of Franco who was handed over to stand trial. He was convicted of high treason in de Gaulle's France and executed. Laval had helped Franco throughout 1936–9, and when the end of the war was near he escaped to Spain.

24. C.R. Halstead, p. 73.
25. See Armero, op. cit., Cortada, op. cit., and Morán, op. cit.
26. It is generally accepted that Spain did in fact allow refugees temporary shelter in Spain, and this is certainly the case of a few hundred European Jews (including Sephardi Greek and Balkan Jews) who were given Spanish passports to enable them to be able to leave their countries when the Germans arrived. Armero, op. cit., however, claims that this was as a result of bribery rather than solidarity.
27. C.R. Halstead, 'The United States and the Spanish Question', unpublished Master's thesis, University of Virginia, 1953.
28. *New York Times*, 5–6 March 1946.
29. See A.J. Lleonart, *España y ONU* I (1945–6) and II (1947), Estudio Introductivo y Corpus Documental, Consejo Superior de Investigaciónes Científicas, Madrid, 1983.
30. See W. Minter, P. Schmitter and S. Payne, *A History of Spain and Portugal*, University of Wisconsin Press, Madison, 1973. Also useful is S.G. Payne, *Politics and Society in Twentieth Century Spain*, op. cit. An overall political, sociological, and historical view is provided by Paul Preston (ed.), op. cit. For the 1930s, a vital period to understand future developments in Spain, see R. Robinson, *The Origins of Franco's Spain: The Right, the Republic and Revolution, 1931–1936*, University of Pittsburgh Press, Plymouth, 1970; and H. Thomas, op. cit. In Spanish, see J. Vicens Vives, *Aproximación a la Historia de España*, Editorial Vicens Vives, Barcelona, 1978, and S. Vilar, *La Naturaleza del Franquismo*, Ediciones Península, Barcelona, 1977.

2

The struggle for respectability: the United Nations versus Spain

The admission of Spain to the United Nations in 1955 did not substantially alter the patterns of its foreign policy as they had been taking shape ever since the defeat of the Axis powers in the Second World War. The isolation of Spain by the international community was perhaps one of the most important factors in determining those patterns, but the fact that they remained virtually unchanged after 1955, and for a number of years to follow, is indicative of the complexity behind the Franco regime's international behaviour.

The remarkable continuity of Spanish foreign policy under Franco began to be interrupted only along the way to democracy once the dictator had significantly loosened his personal control of the instruments of power, while delegating increasingly important political affairs to his ministers and advisers. It is patently clear that, quite apart from the factual results of Spain's pariah status created by the victor anti-Fascist nations, remnants of the pro-Fascist, authoritarian leanings of the Francoist apparatus proved systematically resistant to the challenges of the pro-democratic forces inside Spain. Whether as a result of both this impermeability and the international pariah status imposed on Spain or not, the so-called 'autarquía' (autarky) which characterized economic policies up to the end of the 1950s served only to enhance the core of Francoist foreign policy. Autarky was a complement, or perhaps the internal dimension, of foreign policy after the war and up to the beginning of the 1960s, and can be defined as a set of economic policies aimed at strengthening Spain's economic infrastructure, with the theoretical aim of enabling a certain degree of independence and self-sufficiency. Angel Viñas calls this period *el primer franquismo* (the first Francoism), and confines it to the period between 1939 and 1951.[1] Though economic autarky did indeed begin to operate during the war (partly because of sheer need and partly because of ideological dogma), and continued with only minor cosmetic alterations up to the late 1950s and even early 1960s, foreign policy, however, did have to suffer a process of adaptation, due to the fact that Spain's unspoken (after 1945) friends had been defeated in the war.[2] There is a distinct change of emphasis, from the highly verbose defiance of what are seen as machinations of both international Communism and capitalism (including at the centre of it all the Masons and the Jews) to a more cautious approach aimed at, especially around 1951, obtaining legitimacy as a 'respectable' European nation. Results of this relative de-ideologization process are the gradual admission of Spain to a variety of technical United Nations' bodies, beginning in 1951, until full political integration in 1955. These include the improvement (albeit to an insignificant degree) of relations with some European countries; the Concordat with the Vatican; the admission (in 1957) into the Bretton Woods system and the International Monetary Fund; and, above all, the military pacts with the United States, whose first protocols were signed in 1953.[3]

Viñas distinguishes three periods within *el primer franquismo*. The first is characterized by the identification of Spain with the Axis powers, though, as is generally recognized (including by Viñas), this association was somewhat plagued with contradictions and not a few frictions. Some of these have been grossly exaggerated, as is shown in Chapter 1 of this book. The available evidence does indeed support the view of a Spanish foreign policy almost systematically pro-German and pro-Italian between 1939 and the end of the war in 1945. This did not preclude Franco, however, from proclaiming Spain's neutrality when it became reasonably clear that Germany, and especially Italy, would lose the war, nor did it impede him from adopting a certain degree of equidistance and even equanimity at some juncture. Franco's satisfaction was made clear to the Allies when they began consolidating their victories in 1944, after he had rejected the signature of pacts with Germany which he considered harmful to Spanish sovereignty. He also pursued a discreet policy of helping German and French Jewish refugees to find temporary asylum in Spain and, later, to resettle Moroccan and other Northern African Jews in Spain. Furthermore, especially after the overthrow of Mussolini, espionage and other anti-Allied activities which took place openly in Madrid, Barcelona and Malaga (the latter because of the proximity of Gibraltar and Northern Africa) were severely curtailed.[4]

The origins of autarky, which were to be imprinted on the Spanish economy until the early 1960s, can be traced back to the needs of the Second World War, but also as important then, and even more after the defeat of the Axis powers, was the ideological affinity of Francoism to Fascism and Spain's sympathies for Nazi Germany, though this is not to sustain the view that they were synonymous, for they were not. The description of a nationalist, corporatist, syndicalist, Catholic intergralist movement, permeated by a set of traditional authoritarian values, would perhaps be fairer. Furthermore, there were important elements in both Fascism and Nazism which were not present in Francoism: the active racism of Nazism and the more reluctant racism of Italian Fascism, the patterns of permanent mass mobilization, the reluctance or distance from the Christian Churches were not present in virtually any of the stages of Francoism.[5] But what cannot be denied is its close association with both Germany and Italy during the war, and the adoption of styles and even to a certain extent contents very much reminiscent of Fascism and Nazism. Among these were: the militarization of society at all levels; the loss of legitimacy of a 'civilian dimension of power'; the absolute personal control of government by Franco; the public stigma attached by the controlled (and only possible) media to any dissension; the abhorrence of all 'internationalisms' (Judaism, Communism, liberalism, trade unionism, the Masonry) and their bizarre dumping together as orchestrators of a conspiracy against 'Christian Spain', stand as irrefutable proof of the true nature of Francoism and where its sympathies lay, even after the defeat of Germany and Italy. Public evidence of this is abundant, not only in newspapers and other periodicals published during the war and even in the 1950s, but it is also substantiated by close examination of available documents in the Spanish Ministry for Foreign Affairs' official archives, and some US Department of State's documents.[6] It is not surprising, therefore, that the end of the war initiated a long period of isolation for Spain only to be ameliorated, but not totally eradicated, with its admission to the United Nations in December 1955.

The adoption of Fascist styles and, in certain areas, of Fascist contents as well, constituted the stumbling-block to any legitimization of Spain by the international community after the war. The official expression of this community, the United Nations, exhibited a consistent resistance to grant this legitimacy, by repeatedly avoiding granting Spain membership. Individual countries, especially Britain, the Soviet Union, The Netherlands, France and the United States among those that took part in the war, and Mexico, Chile, Brazil, Uruguay and Colombia in Latin America, plus a host of Third World nations, came to compose an unstructured but active anti-Franco lobby for many years. Though diplomatic relations did exist with a few of these countries throughout the war, or were gradually re-established after its end, they tended to be more formal than anything else, and very little ever emerged from Spain's bilateral relations.

The second period analysed by Viñas begins with the rather undignified attempts by Franco to convince the Allies of his new democratic credentials, once the defeat of the Axis nations was absolutely certain, and ends with the accord with the Vatican and the military bases' pact with the United States in 1953. These are the first signs of acceptability received by the regime, and the change of mind experienced by President Harry S. Truman regarding Franco and Francoism is thought to have been an important element in the process of gradual legitimization and integration of Spain.[7] Truman accepted Franco not so much because he had a change of heart towards him and his associates, for which there were no objective reasons, but because the State Department's intelligence was busy trying to build up a new strategic alliance against what it saw as the growing threat of international Communism. Indeed, with the Cold War tensions mounting (of which the Korean war would be but one of its 'hot' explosions), and a galloping anti-Soviet paranoia developing in Europe, the democratic–capitalist side of the anti-Nazi/Fascist alliance felt it could no longer afford the democratic niceties of opposing and isolating Franco's Spain. Though the increasing courting of Spain by the United States provoked initial reluctance and even rejection among some of its European allies (especially France, The Netherlands and, to a lesser extent, Britain), each and all of them finally succumbed. The culmination was the admission of Spain as a full member to the United Nations in December 1955.

The signature of the Concordat with the Vatican and the pacts with the United States signalled the beginning of what Viñas considers as the third, and last, of the periods within autarky in Spain. These two developments were accompanied by a number of parallel, and no less important if less known, advancements of Spanish diplomacy, such as a marked improvement of relationships with some Latin American countries which had hitherto shown varying degrees of antagonism towards the Francoist regime, especially Chile, Uruguay, Colombia, Brazil and Costa Rica. Mexico remained until after the death of Franco the sole sovereign power to grant official diplomatic recognition to the Spanish Republican government in exile, which had its head-quarters in Mexico City for many years. Furthermore, the early 1950s are the starting-point of increased efforts to cement the historical links of Spain with the Arab world, efforts that were to become especially successful later on. This task would be facilitated by the hostility between the new State of Israel and Spain, a phenomenon that prevented mutual diplomatic recognition until 1986, when the Socialist administration of Prime Minister Felipe González put an end to this anomaly, but only after several unsuccessful attempts towards mutual recognition by Israeli leaders after the death of Franco. The non-recognition syndrome between Spain and Israel has complex, somewhat inextricable reasons, and the various available interpretations are analysed later in this book.

The admission of Spain to the United Nations offers an interest-ing example of how political expedience can overwhelm the most salutary of reasons. As recently as the General Assembly of 1954, as at most previous ones, had the organization heard impassionate pleas from many quarters condemning Spain's record during the anti-Fascist war and subsequently on human rights. All was forgotten in 1955, but not all was forgiven, as shown by the opposition of the Soviet Union and other countries.[8]

The study of Spanish foreign policy under Franco, however, both before and after its admission to the United Nations, always stopped at the doors of the Spanish Foreign Office; certain archives there were rarely open to researchers, and the position was in fact worst with archives in virtually all the relevant state institutions.

Angel Viñas makes this vital problem clear when he refers to the 'inaccessibility of the State archives'. Furthermore, he complained in 1982, several years after the death of Franco and with the democratic government already installed in the Moncloa Palace, that it was still difficult to gain access to certain files on foreign policy during the Franco regime. In 1977, it is true, some archives in the Ministerio de Asuntos Exteriores were made public, includ-ing the 1945–77 period, but still those covering 'sensitive' areas were excluded. Important data which could be provided by the various ministries, and by a number of key administrative institutions of the State, were still unavailable as late as 1985.[9]

One of the paradoxes of Spanish foreign policy under Francoism is that Franco reserved, as has been said before in this book, important areas of design and execution of policies for himself. Research into foreign policy had to concentrate on the highly personal style practised by the Head of State, especially his secret or open dealings with successive envoys sent to him by the Western governments—most notably the United States and Great Britain —anxious to 'legitimize' Spain as an 'acceptable' partner. The admission to the United Nations was the culmination of a complicated process of pressures prompted by Cold War necessities, and an exercise in subterfuge and even intrigue in which the United States, and to a lesser extent the United Kingdom, played a variety of games aimed at getting Spain accepted as a legitimate ally in the post-war confrontation with Communism and the Soviet Union. The cultivation of General Franco's sympathy was crucial to this strategy, and there was no better inducement for him than the anti-Communist crusade undertaken by the United States after the defeat of Nazism and Fascism on the battlefields. That Franco's regime had been pro-Axis, and that he had instituted a particularly repressive regime inside Spain, did not matter. The years between 1945 and 1955 would see several attempts to end Spain's isolation, headed by the United States, and amidst resistance by countries such as The Netherlands, France, Mexico and Scandinavia. The admission of Spain into the United Nations in 1955 was achieved only after: (1) the United States had unsuccessfully tried to incorporate Spain into the NATO alliance in 1950; (2) Spain had made overtures towards Arab countries, attempting to give shape to a form of 'neutralism' which would become an important feature of Spanish foreign policy in the future; (3) the new State of Israel had made it clear (in 1948–9) that it would not recognize the Franco regime; and (4) the United States had achieved partial satisfaction by obtaining military, naval and air facilities in Spanish territory in 1953, while Spain had in turn abrogated part of its sovereignty by signing these pacts and the Concordat with the Vatican.

The American interest in Spain's membership of NATO can be traced back to the early 1950s. Just five years after the end of the war, and when the Franco regime was at its most repressive, the

Pentagon was already putting pressure on the State Department to emphasize the desirability of making Spain a full member of the NATO alliance. Documents published recently, and studied by Ramón Orozco and Arjun Makhijani, make it clear that few scruples were in evidence as a result of Spain's recent anti-Allied behaviour. The overall struggle against Communism appeared to be much more relevant.

The integration of Spain into NATO seemed to be, in fact, an obsession of policy-makers and intelligence officers in the United States. A 'top secret' document issued by the National Security Council in 1950 is the first indication of American anxiety over Spain's isolation, and documents dated 5 October 1960 still repeat the same theme; the need to integrate Spain into NATO had not disappeared from the core of the political agenda for the Americans. The United States' role acquired further significance during the Spanish socialists' term of office, when the country's integration into NATO approved by the Calvo Sotelo government, was confirmed in a referendum. It is more or less clear that the Reagan administration considered the referendum to be a vital progression in the strategy to incorporate Spain firmly into the Western alliance, and no doubt made this view known to Spanish politicians, especially to Prime Minister Felipe González and high-ranking foreign policy officials.

The attempts by the United States to make Spain a full member of NATO surprised Franco himself. According to the documents studied by Orozco and Makhijani, the American Ambassador, Stanton Griffiths, was told by Franco in March 1951 that he (Franco) doubted that all the United States' allies would welcome the invitation. There is evidence to suggest that there was widespread opposition from at least some of America's allies, even to official talks with Franco. France, The Netherlands, Scandinavia, and the United Kingdom especially, opposed any contacts with Franco which would be seen as efforts to 'legitimize' his regime. The problem of overcoming European misgivings prompted Ambassador Griffiths to propose the establishment of military bases in Spanish territory instead. On 14 March 1951, Franco told the American Ambassador that he approved of this plan, and a scheme to build up to ten military bases in Spain began to be implemented. The speed with which Francisco Franco accepted the American plan showed the considerable degree of control exercised by him over foreign policy decisions, thus confirming the highly centralized nature of the Spanish State, and the General's unchallenged hold on the country at large.

The documents studied by Orozco and Makhijani make it clear that European opposition to Spain's 'legitimization' provided almost insurmountable difficulties on the way towards full NATO membership. The alternative plan, military bases, was put forward as soon as it was evident that most, if not all, of the other members of NATO would object to sharing the strategic defence of Europe with the Franco regime. The main objective of these bases for the Americans were: (1) to defend American global interests; (2) to push the 'defensive borders' in case of war as far from the United States as possible; (3) to provide 'incentives' for the Soviet Union to divert aggression forces and armaments towards areas other than the United States; (4) to implement the Atlantic section of a global defence plan which would also include the Pacific and the Arctic; and (5) to consolidate Spain's anti-Communist commitments.[10]

The highly personal nature of Franco's handling of the negotiations which led to the establishment of the American bases is further demonstrated by the extreme dearth of available information on these matters. Though Angel Viñas' lucid account of the 'secret pacts' between Franco and the United States relied heavily on Spanish documents made public by the Spanish Foreign Office, there are some gaps which could not be filled. This is not Viñas' fault, but the Ministry's, and its failure to provide the much-needed detailed accounts of Spain's, and more specifically of Franco's, role in the whole affair. The candidness of the American documents is, however, quite illuminating.

The use of Spain as a major base for the then powerful B-47 airplanes, capable of carrying nuclear bombs, is categorically stated by the newly revealed documents, which make illustrative reading in a number of other areas as well. In a document categorized as 'top secret' on 30 November 1956, one year after Spain had been admitted to the United Nations, the National Security Council of the United States declares its intention to use the bases in Spain to attack the Soviet Union, if necessary.

The establishment of the bases in Spain was not without problems. The Spanish government complained that two of the bases were too near Madrid and Zaragoza, major urban centres which could be exposed to total destruction in the case of war. Spanish dissatisfaction on this point did not move the United States to correct the situation, though promises were made that remained mostly unfulfilled.[11]

The, by now, traditional policy of friendship towards the Arab world was also the personal responsibility of Franco. After all, Moslem (and Jewish, for that matter) influence on Spanish culture had been considerable for several hundred years, the product of the occupation of most of the Spanish territory. The process of unification of Spain undertaken by the Catholic kingdoms had put an end to those centuries of Moslem domination, but had left a distinct imprint on Spanish society. Franco had made ample use of the Moorish troops from Spanish Morocco during the anti-Republican insurrection, and they had played an important role in the defeat of the loyalist armies. The diplomatic efforts to incorporate Spain into the United Nations could always rely on the enthusiastic support of most Arab member states. An examination of the voting record of successive general assemblies of the United Nations show that Spain could generally count on the support of most of the Arab countries in the international organization, plus a few Latin American countries. Most of Europe, both Western and Eastern, systematically opposed these attempts, but the signature of the military pacts with the United States in the early 1950s seemed to signal a significant shift, from open or overt hostility to Spanish membership on the part of some Latin American and Western European countries, to gradual acceptability.[12] During the process of Spain's 'legitimization', the Arab group of countries offered the most systematic support to the membership bids, higher in fact than the support of any other regional group. At the same time, the Franco regime began to strengthen its links with these countries in a number of areas. Spain also gave support to the decolonization process taking place after the war, further antagonizing France and Great Britain.

The close relationship that was to characterize Spanish–Arab diplomatic history after the war would include, amongst others, cultural interchanges, military training and educational treaties. Furthermore, it would also include mutual support on contentious issues not directly affecting Spanish and/or Arab interests.[13]

The somewhat 'neutralist' foreign policy which Spain would pursue under Francoism constituted perhaps the most paradoxical general pattern in policy-making after the war. Franco himself, again, influenced these policies personally, as he did in his dealings with the Americans leading to the military pacts of 1953, and on policies towards the Arab world. The new, decolonized, independent Moslem nations, and former British and French colonies, found in Spain and General Franco an enthusiastic supporter, though in many instances this support remained at verbal level, without materializing into significant concrete measures. The Arab countries and Franco's Spain shared a common mistrust of the West, a kind of 'Third World-ism' with nationalist overtones, a general anti-British and anti-French attitude which, for different motivations, created a sense of common purpose and mutual understanding. In some cases, the pro-Axis, and therefore anti-colonial, behaviour of Spain during the war had contributed to strengthen the impression in the Arab world of Spain as a potential ally in any conflicts that could develop in the post-war era between the former colonies and the metropolitan powers.[14]

Another important factor in Spanish foreign policy before its admission to the United Nations in 1955 was the partition of Palestine and the consequent creation of the State of Israel in 1948. Though Britain had been the mandatory power in Palestine since the defeat of Turkey—the occupying power before the First World War—by a decision of the League of Nations, Spain under Franco did not exhibit a consistent anti-colonialist pattern in this case. Its strong pro-Arab policies deterred it from showing any support for the Zionist ideal of a national home for the Jewish people, in spite of the support given to Jewish national aspirations by both the United States and the Soviet Union. This pattern of behaviour would continue unaltered later on, and attempts to establish mutual recognition between Spain and the new Jewish state would fail in 1948 and 1949, after the first Israeli Prime Minister, David Ben Gurion, would disavow such *rapprochement* out of hand. According to parliamentary records and other sources, the generalized assumption that the failure to agree on mutual recognition had been the sole responsibility of Franco was not correct. Ben Gurion's strong dislike of the pro-Axis record of the Falangista movement and important government officers, moved him to block any attempts aimed at normalizing relations. Not even the 'normalization' of relations between Spain and the Western democracies would change this antagonism. Only the democratization of Spain in the 1970s would give some impetus to mutual efforts at establishing diplomatic relations. These would inevitably fail, again and again, showing the extent of Spanish commitments to the Arab outlook of the Middle East conflict. The entry of Spain to the European Economic Community and NATO, under the Socialist administration of Felipe González, would finally allow mutual recognition between Israel and Spain to take place.[15]

It is still not absolutely clear where the responsibility for non-recognition lay in the two or three years after the State of Israel was created in 1948. Franco had showed a compassionate attitude towards the Jews escaping Nazi persecution during the war. Being officially 'neutral', Spain offered sanctuary to them, though almost invariably on a temporary basis, until they could find countries prepared to receive them. The racist aspects of Nazism were never important in the Falange ideology, though it frequently made populist use of an anti-Semitic language which was part of a broader anti-liberal, anti-Communist, anti-capitalist, anti-trade-union tradition with roots in Spanish right-wing nationalism. Franco's doctrinaire commitments generally stopped when the need for pragmatism was evident to him, and this indeed showed clearly during the last years of the war, when the defeat of Germany and Italy became a distinct possibility. He did not hesitate then in shifting from outright identification with the Axis powers (though 'technically' neutral) towards increasing and verbose support for the forthcoming crusade against 'international Communism'.[16] By 1948 and 1949, the scenario is one of deep mutual distrust between the Jewish people, fresh from the horrors of the Holocaust, and Francoist Spain, a country which had been sympathetic to the German cause. Any overtures by Franco to recognize Israel then would have been none other than a piece of characteristic opportunism, while a similar pragmatic attitude by the young Jewish State would have been even more difficult at the time. It will suffice to say that the non-recognition pattern between the two countries strengthened even further Spanish–Arab understanding, consolidating the support of Arab votes in favour of Spain's admission to the United Nations in 1955, but also alienated liberal, left-wing and Jewish opinion within the United States, which exercised significant pressure to stop the American administration from advocating Spain's candidature. At the end of the day, however, the global strategic interests of the United States, particularly those prompted by the needs arising out of an increasingly 'hot' Cold War, pushed it actively to endorse Spain's application for membership. Part of the price to pay by Spain would be the American military bases and an ever increasing role for the United States in the Spanish economy.[17]

The treaties which granted military bases in Spain to the United States, and the Concordat with the Vatican, are contradictory aspects of a policy that pursued both neutrality and pragmatism. As will be seen later in this book, the general paradox of Spanish foreign policy was that while, on the one hand, the country was striving to achieve a degree of independence from the big powers' conflicts—trying to remain detached from the East–West confrontation—on the other, it was embarking on measures which would result in more, not less, dependence upon the West, especially the United States. Already in the late 1950s, Spain had begun to abandon 'autarky' in economic policies, a model which had been dictated by both doctrinaire requirements and the country's isolation after the war. The gradual acceptance of Spain by the international community was matched by an opening-up of the formerly closed Spanish economy to foreign investment.[18] This enabled the United States to develop a policy of both public and private capitalist and financial investment, accompanied by efforts to influence Spain's educational, cultural, and technological structures. The American presence in Spain began with the military accord of 1953, followed in the late 1950s by significant increases in investment and loans which by the late 1960s had already become significant in such sectors as food manufacturing, metals, agricultural products, building, banking, cinema and information technology, wholesale commerce, electronics and electricity, pharmaceuticals, finance, car manufacturing, textiles, engineering, shipping, marketing and public relations, paper, oil, petrochemicals, insurance, transport and communications and several other, but minor, categories.[19] In the cultural and educational fields, American influence was no less important, and took the form of several bilateral agreements which would significantly increase Spain's cultural, educational, and technological vulnerability.[20]

The military agreement within the United States in 1953 was the first development in a long process by which General Franco kept his 'neutralist' option open, while at the same time opening Spain up to increasing American penetration of its economy, and influence in its education and culture. It also marked the beginning of Spanish military dependence on the United States.[21]

But before the American bases were finally established, and after their existence had been accepted as a *fait accompli* by the Spanish people, a vigorous, sometimes bitter polemic took place at all levels of Spanish society. Perhaps the best chronology describing the inexorable march of events leading and up to the final signing of the main treaty is offered by Manuel Vásquez Montalbán, quoting Ignacio Fernandez de Castro's *De las Cortes de Cádiz al Plan de Desarollo.*[22] Beginning in 1945, this crescendum develops as follows:

1945: Don Juan de Borbón 'invites' Franco to abandon power and to re-establish the monarchical regime.
The new, and illegal, Alianza Nacional de Fuerzas Democráticas (National Alliance of Democratic Forces) recognizes the second Republican government in exile, under Giral, as the legitimate government of Spain.

1946: The Confederación de Fuerzas Monárquicas (Confederation of Monarchical Forces) is formed integrated by CEDA, *Liga and Renovación Española* (Spanish Renewal), a generally democratic coalition of right-wing forces. They search for an agreement with the National Alliance in order to ensure a democratic transition under a monarchical system. There are rumours of imminent Allied intervention against the Madrid government, as pressures from many quarters in Britain, France, The Netherlands, Scandinavia, the United States, Mexico, and others, mount. Sanctions are being called for by important sections of international public opinion.[23]
In December 1946, the General Assembly of the United Nations condemns the Spanish regime and recommends the withdrawal of ambassadors by all member states;
The talks between the Republicans of the National Alliance and the Monarchists of the Confederation fail, after the Monarchists decide that they would be the winners in any future restructuring of the Spanish state, undertaken by Franco;

1948: Spain is excluded from the Marshall Plan, whose main aim is to restore devastated Europe to some kind of economic, social and political stability, bearing in mind the increasing Soviet control over the Eastern areas liberated by the Red Army;
British Labour Cabinet member, Ernest Bevin, encourages and succeeds in providing political talks between the Spanish democratic left and right; Spanish leaders Indalecio Prieto and Gil Robles engage in these talks;
The Republican government in exile denounces the passivity of the Western democracies in relation to the Franco Regime;

In November, a pact betwen the Socialists and Monarchists (known as the *Pacto de San Juan de Luz*) is announced. The core of this pact is to fight for the restoration of a democratic regime in Spain;

There are sporadic but relatively significant guerrilla actions against the regime in several regions of Spain;

1950: The American Congress votes a US$62,500,000 credit to Spain;

The French government outlaws the Spanish Communist party in exile, and closes all its offices in France;

The General Assembly of the United Nations withdraws the previous condemnation of Spain;

Spain is admitted by FAO, the specialized United Nations' agency;

Admiral Sherman visits Spain as official envoy of the United States.[24]

Already in 1950, the anti-Communist preoccupations of some of the European nations were in evidence. It is true that for important sections of public opinion Franco was still and would continue to be an international pariah. This was certainly the case of the trade-union movements, the European left (including Socialist, Social-Democratic, and Communist parties), and of the political centre (Liberal and Social-Christian, or Christian-Democratic, parties). The right was divided between those who would stick to traditional nationalist, reactionary anti-Communism, and who had temporarily abrogated their long-standing positions to support the anti-Nazi and anti-Fascist war effort, and those who had acquired a new political ethos in which the anti-democratic nature of Hitler's Germany, Mussolini's Italy, and Franco's Spain was of paramount importance.[25]

Other sectors which opposed the normalization of relations with Franco's Spain included the American Jewish community, the Eastern European countries, Yugoslavia, a variety of organizations of intellectuals and academics in Europe and the United States, and some Latin American countries, especially Mexico, which recognized the Republican government in exile (with headquarters in Mexico City) as the only legitimate representative of the Spanish State.[26]

But the inexorable progress of strategic considerations in the planning tables of the Western nations' chancelleries was to prove unstoppable. Churchill and Franco had corresponded as early as October 1944, and there is little doubt that those letters shared a common fear, real or imaginary, genuine or opportunist, of the threat posed by the Soviet Union. The Spanish Foreign Office would efficiently play the anti-Communist card from then onwards, under the overall guidance and personal leadership of Francisco Franco, who always kept close control over both internal and external policy planning and decisions.

The desire to legitimize Spain had probably been discussed by policy-makers in the United States as early as 1946. Vasquez Montalbán mentions accounts by important diplomatic and political actors at the time of that year's United Nations' General Assembly in New York, when the Republican government in exile and a few sympathetic member states were pressing the international organization to approve and implement sanctions against the Franco regime, based on article 51 of the United Nations Charter. This article authorized a variety of measures against countries which constituted a 'threat to peace'. After much debate, with the active participation of Spanish Republican envoys José Giral (head of the government in exile), his Foreign Secretary, Alvaro de Albornoz, his Ambassador to Washington, Jaune Miravitlles, and other Republican leaders just arrived from France and Mexico, the argument to justify the United Nations' condemnation of Spain was found: a number of military barracks established by the Franco government near the French border should be seen as an attempt to invade the south of France, where important contingents of Republican exiles lived. Furthermore, the building of a major ship for the Spanish navy, by Spanish government-controlled shipbuilders, should be accepted by the international community as proof of Franco's aggressive intentions.[27]

The installation of fortifications, heavily manned, on the French border, and the construction of the 30,000-ton military ship would have been seen as dangerous enough as to pose a 'threat to peace' in different circumstances, but policy-makers in Washington were already trying to avoid the further isolation of Spain, and, moreover, were also busy creating the conditions to make Franco a legitimate ally in the anti-Communist drive prompted by the Cold War. The harsh internal repression taking place in Spain at the time did not seem to matter much. A few days after the arrival of the Republican delegation to the United States, and almost without reasonable time to study their agruments for sanctions, the head of the

Spanish Desk in the State Department invited Miravitlles for talks. He told him that the Spanish barracks on the French border were not 'offensive'; quite the opposite, the American government thought they were in fact 'defensive' installations, as the Spanish government was fearful of a Republican invasion from the south of France. He added that the 30,000-ton ship which, according to Republican sources, was being built could not be produced by Spain, and this conviction had been corroborated by American intelligence agencies. Therefore, any hopes of applying article 51 to Spain had disintegrated, and this was made explicit to Miravitlles.

The insistence of the Republican government, however, moved the United States to work out a compromise resolution, which still called on member states to withdraw their ambassadors from Madrid.

The American position was not without contradictions. Though the general impression in Republican quarters was that the United States was about to turn its back completely on them in order to recognize openly the Franco regime, they were to be proved wrong as early as February 1947. A variety of sources confirms this, especially the Pentagon papers on United States' relations in the 1940s.[28]

El Diario de Barcelona made an exhaustive study of the documents published by the Pentagon in a series of Sunday editions in 1972, and it is remarkable that these very interesting revelations have not merited further research yet. To sum up, what they show is a degree of disagreement within the American government in relation to the Franco regime. It is clear that influential advisers in the State Department wanted to 'replace' Franco and, by implication, his regime. Vásquez Montalbán thinks that the instigators of such attitudes were Monarchist and Republican sectors in Spain and in exile, and that the leader of such an, unnamed, coalition inside Spain was none other than General Beigbeder, a former military officer in Spanish Morocco who had been Foreign Secretary under Franco in 1940.[29]

The American counterparts in this plot were the United States' representatives in Madrid, Bonsal and Culbertson. Memoranda of meetings between Bonsal, who was chargé d'affaires in Madrid in 1947, and Spanish representatives show a considerable degree of United States' involvement in a 'rupturist' solution of the Spanish crisis precipitated by the Civil War. Under American protection, talks took place in Bonsal's home, with the participation of General

Beigbeder, Tomás Peyro's moderate Republicans and Maffit, a political attaché in the American Embassy, and presumably also an intelligence officer.

The important factor to notice here is that Peyro's Republicans kept extremely good relations and contacts with the Spanish Socialist Workers party (PSOE), and this could not have been unknown to the American Embassy. Through the Republicans, the United States was trying to have Franco removed while at the same time creating the conditions for a new regime in which at least part of the Spanish left would have a role to play. The provisional government to be formed, however, would include seven Monarchists, seven Republicans and three or four members of the armed forces. Though no Socialists would be invited to join the Cabinet, their acquiescence would be required if this new and odd coalition of Monarchists and Republicans was to have any chance of succeeding. After all, Socialists (and Communists) could still put into operation their not inconsiderable historical control over two of the most powerful trade-union organizations. There is no doubt, however, that this was an American attempt to get a moderate united opposition to Franco to act, and that the main aim was to be the dismantling of the Franco regime.

The report by Bonsal to the Secretary of State, dated 7 February 1947, strongly supports the view that it was in the interest of the United States that a 'moderate' government was formed in Spain as soon as possible. The American rationale was not substantially different from the set of motivations that have apparently determined American foreign policy choices since. The consolidation of dictatorial regimes in areas under the United States' sphere of influence, which could be seen as generally favourable to American global strategic interests, often ends up creating such polarization in the affected societies that the way is left open for right and left 'extremism' to exercise an abnormally strong influence. The change of heart by the American State Department, for example, over the dictatorships of Trujillo in the Dominican Republic, Somoza in Nicaragua, Marcos in the Philippines, and Pinochet in Chile, are continuations of this pattern of behaviour. The suggestion could be made that in most of these cases the Americans have become fearful that the systematic repression of all shades of opposition by repressive regimes blocks the development of alternative and, more appropriately, 'moderate' opposition forces which could ultimately become governments, while at the same time feeding the conditions under which a mass movement on the left, controlled by a Communist or an anti-American, nationalist, Third Worldist kind of party, could seize power.

Bonsal recommended the encouragement of the opposition activities of the anti-Franco military and, especially, the middle classes, and he suggested that this could be done by hinting to them that such a transitional government as was being organized would be speedily recognized by the United States and Britain, and Francoism would be as speedily delegitimized.

American involvement in the search for a democratic solution for Spain is further proved by a memorandum written by the head of the State Department's European Desk, D. Hickerson on 10 March 1947, and, in addition, by Dean Acheson (then acting Secretary of State) when writing to the British Embassy in Washington on 7 April, 1947 (a document that was categorized as 'top secret' at the time).

Hickerson was a high-ranking official at the State Department, and the mere fact that a meeting between him (as chairman), American diplomat Paul T. Culbertson and Spanish politician and renowned intellectual Salvador de Madariaga, was held indicated American willingness, at least in principle, actively to explore the options open to them in terms of a regime change in Madrid. The meeting showed a shrewd though, some might add, opportunistic vein in de Madariaga's arguments: the lack of action on the part of the Western powers, most notably Britain and the United States, against Franco, could and very likely would be construed as a new form of appeasement of a Fascist regime. Furthermore, the Soviet Union would exploit this to its maximum advantage. The last thing the Soviet Union wanted, he added, was a moderate government in Madrid. It was only in the Soviet Union's interest, and in its interest alone, that the Franco regime continued unchallenged.

Acheson's letter to the British government confirmed, if there were still doubts, that the message being put forward by the Spanish political centre and the moderate right was getting through to the United States' foreign policy decision-makers. Acheson stated clearly that: (1) the continued permanence of Franco in office, or even of a successor appointed by him, would not allow Spain to escape the economic stagnation in which it found itself, as the United States and Britain could not be seen to help such an internationally unpopular regime; (2) this inability to help left Spain open to increasing pauperization and, therefore, social and political conflict and, ultimately, a breakdown of legitimacy and the rise of Communism; (3) the ever increasing anti-Franco activities of opposition groups within Spain and in exile were worth considering, especially since many of these groups were not Communist; (4) the establishment of a government including such non-Communist forces could open the way for a quick, and vigorous, programme of economic aid to Spain, and certainly for a number of other measures to demonstrate British and American sympathy. This initiative would be shortly followed by other United Nations' member states; (5) elections should follow after a reasonable period of transition, and relations between Spain, Britain and the United States should enter a new phase in which active political and economic support would be forthcoming; and (6) these changed circumstances would then allow Spain's admission to the United Nations.

As will be seen next, American priorities seemed to shift rather quickly. The somehow liberal, clearly non-sympathetic approach towards the Franco regime, which had been no doubt influential in the immediate aftermath of the war within the State Department, would give way to a pragmatism in foreign policy which would be characteristic of the years to follow. No longer would the reminiscences of Nazi and Fascist atrocities be a major foreign policy issue, nor would the pleas of moderate opposition forces within totalitarian, and/or authoritarian regimes be a factor as powerful as it used to be in 1947, or even 1948. The pressures of a rabidly anti-Communist administration in Madrid, the development of the Cold War, a Concordat with the Vatican conceding important areas of state sovereignty to the Catholic Church, and the signature of the military pacts with the United States, would inexorably give shape to an American 'understanding' and tolerance of the Franco regime. Not even the most ferocious repression against every form of opposition would, after the pro-Franco course had been firmly chosen, alter the United States' new approach.

The international hostility towards Franco's regime had not diminished two years after the end of the war. On the contrary, the feelings in favour of Spain's isolation by the international community ran as strongly as in the immediate aftermath of the war, when calls against any accommodation with Francoism included the imposition of collective non-recognition (implemented by the United Nations), economic sanctions, and even military intervention.

The increasing and ever more comprehensive attempts by exile groups in Europe, Latin America and the United States to have the regime at best isolated and treated as an international pariah, and at worst overthrown, prompted a quick reaction from Madrid. The open hostility of the Soviet bloc countries further increased the urgency for Franco's diplomacy to act speedily and efficiently. The diplomatic efforts by the Republican government in exile were well known to the Francoist envoys, who kept the Spanish Foreign Office abreast of events.[30]

A confidential report by the United States chargé d'affaires in Madrid, Paul T. Culbertson, written in July 1947, shows the extent to which the Palacio de Santa Cruz (Spanish Foreign Office) was concerned about the prospects for Spain's relations with the rest of the world.

Culbertson described the content of two meetings he had had with the Spanish Foreign Secretary, Martin Artajo, and the Director of the Instituto de Cultura Hispánica, Joaquin Ruíz Jiménez.[31] Artajo's main aim was clear, according to the content of this document: to convince the United States that Spain's heart and mind were with the Western democracies, and that the need to contain the spread of Communism should be the main priority after the war. Artajo reminded his American interlocutors that Spain had been neutral during the war, in spite of German pressures to incorporate the Spanish armies into the Axis war effort. Spain, he added, had suffered considerably for its resistance and, rather than succumb to German pressures, had stoically accepted the risks involved in its position. He showed surprise at the fact that the United States would so willingly maintain cordial diplomatic and economic relations with 'totalitarian' countries such as the Soviet Union and Yugoslavia, while at the same time expressing a degree of reluctance towards Spain, whose government was only 'authoritarian' and was clearly evolving towards a form of democracy adjusted to Spanish realities.

Culbertson's answer was unsympathetic, and rather short, basically stating the American view that, whatever changes were taking place in Spain, these were not helping the cause of a democratic Spain. Though a detailed account of these conversations is not available, it is only reasonable to wonder whether the American diplomat did question Artajo's pretension, very fashionable for several years among Francoist politicians and diplomats after the war, to a claim of real neutrality during the conflict.

As has been shown in the first chapter, Spanish 'neutrality' was technically designed to help relieve Franco of the military responsibilities which participation alongside Italy and Germany would have created for his regime. But all the available evidence points out to an active Spanish collaboration with the Axis war effort. And if the mere fact of the so-called División Azul (Blue Division) of the Spanish armed forces fighting alongside the Germans is not considered enough, there are ample historical data to substantiate the assertion that Spanish neutrality during the Second World War was none other than a practical expedient to save the country from more bloodshed, at a time when the wounds of the civil war were still wide open. A benign view of this behaviour could and did see a regime deeply worried about the possibility of shedding more Spanish blood and, therefore, could credit it with a sense of responsibility. Culbertson seemed to have been taken by Franco's personality and in a memorandum dated 27 July 1947 there is a distinct change of emphasis, from the previous diplomatic and public face of what could be seen as 'moderate hostility', towards a language that, for the first time, attempts to make the Caudillo's case to the full.[32] This 'secret' memorandum is a detailed account of Culbertson's meeting with Franco, and shows a desperate attempt by him to convince the United States that it should abandon its sometimes lukewarm, and at times hostile, attitude towards the Franco regime. Franco virtually blackmailed the United States by claiming the existence of promises by Churchill which included the allocation of former French colonies to Spain, especially in North Africa. He suggested he had documents to prove this, but would not use them, so that French–British relations would not suffer. The Germans, Franco added, had promised him territorial adjustments in favour of Spain after the war, which would include Andorra. He had rejected these offers. This behaviour proved that his regime was conscious of international tensions and felt a sense of responsibility towards international cooperation. This is why, in spite of the pressures that were brought to bear on Spain for it to enter the war, it had invariably maintained neutrality. In view of all this, why should Spain suffer ostracism now?

The criticisms to the systematic repression unleashed by the regime against the opposition, and even against moderate critics of human rights abuses by the security services, were clearly in the forefront of Franco's effort to neutralize and ultimately bring the

Americans to the pro-Francoist fold. These criticisms were as strong as ever in the United States, Europe and Latin America, where reputable newspapers and politicians made frequent denunciations of the poor human rights record of the Spanish government.[33] Franco was eager to demonstrate that his regime was gradually evolving towards some form of democracy, and told Culbertson that the exiled community could come back without fear, if they wanted, and gave a few examples of individuals who had done so already. By using this type of argument, Franco was hoping to defuse the core of the prevailing anti-Franco propaganda: that his regime was totalitarian and anti-democratic and, therefore, unworthy of support by the Western democracies. Not surprisingly, the apparent contradiction of maintaining relations with the Soviet Union and other countries under the Soviet sphere of influence, while trying to deny the legitimacy of the Franco regime, was exploited by Franco in a systematic way. And though for sometime this argument did not carry enough weight, it was now evident, from Culbertson's memorandum, that a major change of heart towards Spain was a distinct possibility.

Franco explained in minute detail to Culbertson what he described as a social and political plan to improve the educational standards of the population, and to lessen the impact of poverty, all of which impressed the American representative positively. He concluded that Franco was a 'sincere and honest man' and that he was genuine in his convinction that his actions were in the best interests of Spain.

The rest of Culbertson's memorandum is little less than a plea to the United States' government to listen to Franco's case, while developing the rationale in favour of his definitive legitimization. This document is particularly important because it marks a turning-point in United States–Spanish relations. From then onwards, the American position would clearly aim at incorporating Franco's regime to the Western family of nations, a process which would acquire even more significance with the admission of Spain to the United Nations in 1955, just two years after the first protocols granting the United States military bases on Spanish territory were signed.

The most poignant document stating the case for Franco, however, was written by Culbertson on 30 December 1947. The arguments advanced by the American diplomat, in a highly controversial letter to the Secretary of State, were as follows.

(1) The State Department listened to both sides of the Spanish problem without prejudice;
(2) however, 'hopes' of the Spanish opposition, *vis-à-vis* United States' attitudes towards the regime's isolation and ultimate overthrow, were ill founded;
(3) opposition to the regime from exile Republican groups strengthened internal opposition and this, in turn, pushed the regime to become even more repressive;
(4) the Catholic Church would be in favour of the regime being supported and consolidated.

In view of all this, Culbertson ended his letter by asking for American 'official and direct assistance' to Franco.[34]

The recommendation to normalize United States—Spanish relations found fertile ground in both the State Department and sections of public opinion both inside and outside the United States. Firstly, the Catholic Church was actively engaged in an international campaign to gain sympathy for the Franco regime; secondly the political climate was distinctly changing, from the cooperation that had existed between the left and the democratic, anti-Nazi and anti-Fascist right and liberals everywhere in 1945, to distrust and antagonism in 1947. By 1950 the effects of the Marshall Plan to help the reconstruction of a devastated Europe began to be felt, and socialists and Communists were in retreat in most Western European countries. Furthermore, the anti-colonialist explosion in Africa and Asia fed the suspicion by the West of Stalin's involvement in several national liberation movements in these areas, without there being given due consideration to the profoundly complex issues at stake for most of these colonies, whose metropolitan powers were in fact invariably the nations of Western Europe.

The development of the concept of the Cold War no doubt helped Franco significantly. Further help came from the fact that the United States had assumed, after the war, the leadership of the Western world. Its desire to 'normalize' Spain's international status was not a mechanical consequence of American anxiety to enlarge the anti-Communist alliance, but it reflected the prevailing preoccupation and even paranoia permeating important sections of the American political and economic elites. This pattern would have its climax in the McCarthyist phenomenon inside the United States, but it would have few similar consequences elsewhere in Europe, though virtually all European countries would finally conform and accept the legitimization of the Franco regime.

The next step was the visit to Spain in 1950 of three American negotiators, in charge of trade and commerce, Admiral Sherman, General Spry and Sydney Suffrin. The Korean war was already creating problems for President Truman, now under increasing pressure from powerful congressmen like Senator Taft and important political allies in both branches of Congress to force a pro-Franco definition by the United States. The delay in reaching any concrete agreements is thought to have had more to do with Truman's personal hostility to the Franco regime, than with a well-thought-out diplomatic strategy by the State Department. These talks cemented the United States–Spanish understanding which would later pave the way for the establishment of US military bases in Spain, and mutual diplomatic recognition.

The chronology of events could not be more indicative. In 1950, the *de facto* relationship between Washington and Madrid was elevated to official diplomatic recognition, and the Spanish representative in the United States, José Félix de Lequerica, was given ambassadorial status. The first Ambassador of the United States in Spain was also appointed. In 1953, the military pact with the United States was signed, giving the US Pentagon considerable autonomy to establish and control a number of bases in Spanish territory, in Rota (Cádiz, navy), Torrejón de Ardoz (Madrid, air force), Morón de la Frontera (Seville, air force), and Zaragoza (army). Other centres were established to perform logistic functions (administration, services, stocks, transport, radar systems of support, intelligence gathering), and were located in El Ferrol, Cartagena, Rota, El Arahal (near Morón), Ecija, Ciudad Real, Alcalá de Henares, and Adamuz, to the north of Córdoba.

The United States was the first major power to shift position on the issue, and it was followed by Britain, France, Belgium, The Netherlands, Canada and others. Important groups within these countries kept constant pressure applied against recognition, but the wave in favour proved unstoppable. In Britain, for example, the Attlee Labour government showed distaste and antagonism towards the Franco regime, an attitude which continued well after the arrival of a Conservative government. Successive British governments, however, both Conservative and Labour, conceded to the new 'realism' in international politics, and granted it continued diplomatic recognition.

In the United States, the fight for recognition was headed by the leaders of important multinational corporations, such as the Coca Cola company executive, James Farley; the former Chairperson of the Chamber of Commerce, Eric Johnson; influential politicians such as Rewey Short, Chairperson of the Armed Forces Committee of the House of Representatives, and Sam Freley, ex-Democratic party President; and conservative diplomats headed by Myron Taylor, whose links with the Vatican, where he had represented the United States, were well known.

At the end of 1949, Spain made it known that it would make overtures towards Eastern Europe, if and when the West was not more forthcoming with economic and military aid. This threat gave Dean Acheson the excuse needed to open up several lines of credit to the Franco regime, including loans by the Export–Import Bank and the National City Bank of New York.[35]

Also in 1953, in fact only one month before the agreement, the Spanish government signed the Concordat with the Vatican, which recognized the identification between Church and State, established Catholicism as the 'official' religion of Spain, and gave the Church overall control of important areas of state responsibility, mainly in education and the media, where virtually unlimited censorship was exercised. It is no wonder, therefore, that the hitherto open sympathy of the Vatican towards the Franco regime turned to outright support and was taken as further evidence by the United States government of a significant degree of international acceptance of Spain.

The culmination of this long and sometimes contradictory process of incorporation of the Franco regime into the community of nations would be its admission to the United Nations in 1955. Its candidature was put forward, and supported, by the United States and some of its allies.

No longer would the Franco regime be an international pariah. But if a new era of United States–Spanish understanding had begun, this would not preclude the design and execution of a somehow independent foreign policy by the Palacio de Santa Cruz right through the Franco regime's term of office, and into both the transitional period and the parliamentary monarchy.

Notes

1. Angel Viñas, *Historia*, 16, Extra, XXIV, p. 80.
2. The *legajos* (Sections) of the *Archivos Generales* of the Ministerio de Asuntos Exteriores de España (MAE), covering the period between 1945 and 1959, show that the language used and the content of the text, in diplomatic correspondence, memoranda and reports at the end of the war, was indicative of a more 'adaptable', less 'ideological' approach to international relations by the Franco regime. Specially indicative are, among others, the following *legajos*: MAE, R-3599, R-3188, R-232, R-2830, R-2832, R-3599, R-2633, R-8694, R-2028 (EI), R-7741.
3. Details of the military pacts with the United States can be found in MAE, *Archivos Generales*, 1953, 1954, 1955, 1956, 1957 and 1958. For specially informative and relevant data, see Angel Viñas, *Los Pactos Secretos de Franco con Estados Unidos: Bases, Ayuda Económica, Recortes de Soberania*, Grijalbo, Barcelona, 1981. This is a brilliant account of the various aspects of the negotiations.
4. See Chapter 1 for details.
5. For a lucid analysis of the nature of Francoism, see Juan J. Linz, 'Opposition in and under an Authoritarian Regime: Spain', in R. Dahl (ed.), *Regimes and Oppositions*, Yale University Press, New Haven, 1974. Also, by the same author, 'An Authoritarian Regime: Spain', in E. Allardt and Y. Littunen (eds), *Cleavages, Ideologies and Party Systems*, op. cit. A discussion of the various aspects involved can be read in B. Pollack and J. Taylor, 'The Transition to Democracy in Portugal and Spain', *British Journal of Political Science*, vol. 13, 209–42. A list of relevant writers is presented by the authors at the end of the article.
6. See US Department of State, *Foreign Relations of the United States*, 1939–1957. Also, MAE–*Legajos* 1939, 1940, 1941, 1942, 1943, 1946, 1947 and 1948.
7. For an assessment of the factors which influenced the change of position by the United States, see Charles R. Halstead, 'Spanish Foreign Policy, 1936–1978', in J.W. Cortada (ed.), *Spain in the Twentieth Century: Essays on Spanish Diplomacy, 1898–1978*, op. cit.
8. See United Nations, *General Assemby: Debates*, New York (1945–55).
9. A. Viñas, *Los Pactos Secretos de Franco*, op. cit.
10. See *Cambio 16*, 'Los Estados Unidos negocian con el General Franco la entrada en la OTAN', Madrid, 17 March 1986, pp. 30–1.
11. *Cambio 16*, op. cit., p. 31.
12. See United Nations voting records, New York, for 1946–55.
13. See MAE, *Legajos* from 1947 onwards. They are illustrative of the 'special relationship' between Spain and several Arab countries. See also United States Department of State, diplomatic correspondence and other documents for the 1947–55 period.

14. See *Arriba*, Falangist newspaper, Madrid, especially selected issues in 1947, 1948 and 1949. In addition, interviews with several Spanish Foreign Office officials undertaken in 1984 and 1986 confirm that this was the generalized view in the 1950s. Documents made available by both the US State Department and the British Foreign Office (Public Records Office) show preoccupation by Britain and the United States with the good standing of Spanish–Arab relations.

15. The official debates of the Cortes Españolas are of great help to understand the issue.

16. See works by J. Linz, already quoted.

17. For Jewish opposition to Spanish membership of the United Nations, see the *New York Times* and the *Washington Post*, 1948, 1949, 1950, 1954 and 1955. Also the *Jewish Chronicle*, London, especially during 1948, 1950, 1951 and 1952.

18. See Javier F. Paniagua, *La Ordenación del Capitalismo Avanzado en España, 1957–1963*, Anagrama, Barcelona, 1977. Also M. Vásquez Montalbán, *La Penetración Americana en España*, Cuadernos para el Diálogo, Madrid, 1974.

19. M. Vásquez Montalbán, op. cit., pp. 253–350.

20. For an extensive bibliography, see B. Pollack and J. Taylor, 'The Transition to Democracy in Portugal and Spain', op. cit.

21. See A. Viñas, *Los Pactos Secretos* . . ., op. cit. Also M. Vásquez Montalbán, *La Penetración Americana* . . ., op. cit.

22. M. Vásquez Montalbán, ibid., pp. 93–4.

23. See the *New York Times*, the *Washington Post*, the *Manchester Guardian*, *Excelsior* (Mexico City), among others, November and December 1945, and selected issues in 1946.

24. This chronology was included in M. Vásquez Montalbán, *La Penetración Americana* . . ., op. cit., pp. 93–4. Translation and expanded version belong to the authors.

25. The debates in the House of Commons and the French Parliament between 1946 and 1950 are illustrative of these contradictions.

26. The *Jewish Chronicle* of London, some Jewish provincial newspapers in Britain, and several Jewish periodicals in Latin America (especially Buenos Aires, Santiago and Rio de Janeiro) and the United States published condemnations of the haste exhibited by some European countries and the United States in taking steps towards the Franco regime's legitimization.

27. Quoted by Vásquez Montalbán, *La Penetración Americana* . . ., op. cit., pp. 95–6. This version was corroborated to B. Pollack by two former members of the Spanish Republican government-in-exile's administrative headquarters in Mexico City. They asked to remain anonymous.

28. Sources for the analysis of United States' attempts to depose Franco in 1947 are: (1) Pentagon documents made public in the early 1970s on

US foreign relations in the 1940s, and extensively quoted by *Diario de Barcelona* in successive Sunday editions in 1972; (2) conversations with three Spanish Republican politicians close to the Republican government in exile, who want to remain anonymous; and (3) M. Vásquez Montalbán's *La Penetración Americana . . .*, op. cit.

29. See M. Vásquez Montalbán, ibid., p. 96.
30. Information gathered from exile group sources.
31. Joaquin Ruiz Jiménez would later become one of the leaders of the Democratic opposition to Franco, playing an important role in the process of democratic transition. He was appointed Defensor del Pueblo (Ombudsman) by the Socialist government of Felipe González.
32. Memorandum from P. Culbertson to the Secretary of State, Madrid, 27 July 1947 (Secret), quoted by *Diario de Barcelona*, op. cit.
33. See *Ercilla* (Santiago, Chile), 1946–7. Also Cámara de Diputados de la República de Chile, *Debates parlamentarios*, 1946 and 1947; US House of Representatives debates in 1946 and 1947; British House of Commons debates in 1946 and 1947; and French Parliament debates in 1946 and 1947.
34. Culbertson Memorandum, op. cit.
35. See also the *Washington Post* and the *New York Times*, selected issues in 1946 and 1947.

3

Challenges to US foreign policy: neutrality or rhetoric?

The incorporation of Spain into the United Nations in 1955 signalled an end to the international isolation of the Franco regime. Gradually, countries which had been hitherto reluctant to grant Spain recognition did so. United Nations membership provided most countries with the legal excuse needed to cease hostilities and, with the notable exception of Mexico, which did not recognize the Madrid government while Franco was still in office, most other United Nations member states established diplomatic and other relations with it. The Republican government in exile continued to be recognized as the legitimate Spanish government by Mexico until the Francoist state showed clear signs of disintegration in the 1970s. The election of the first democratic Spanish government after the demise of Francoism eliminated the most important reason for Mexico's non-recognition, and also caused the self-dissolution of the Republican government in exile.

Has there been continuity in Spanish foreign policy? There is almost permanent debate on this question, and opinions can be put into two major categories: (a) there are those who consider Spanish foreign policy as reasonably consistent in terms of content, though this consistency only began to develop once the regime had settled as an internationally accepted entity in the mid-1950s; and (b) some current of opinion does not accept that there has been any consistency in Spanish foreign policy, identifying the main features of it as mere opportunism aimed at increasing Spanish influence abroad. Basically, in this case, Spain is seen as part of the United States' sphere of influence.

Roberto Mesa Garrido and Francisco Aldecoa Luzarraga hold the first view, stating that there has been a continuity which can be traced back at least to 1957, when Fernando Castiella initiated a foreign policy which they describe as 'nationalist, open and democratic in its objectives and also, partly, in its results'.[1]

Castiella begins to consolidate a process by which Spain is gradually reincorporated into the accepted family of nations, but his policy was, according to Mesa and Aldecoa, in contradiction with the internal nature of the Francoist regime. This contradiction would in fact constitute a threat to the regime itself, as a 'progressive foreign policy' would reflect the aspirations of important sections of the Spanish people, but not necessarily those sections on which the regime relied for social and political support.

The analysis by Mesa and Aldecoa links the evolution of the internal political structures and actors to the design and execution of foreign policy, and shows the striking dichotomy between a foreign policy with distinctly independent patterns of behaviour and rather conservative, even repressive, internal policies.

The design and execution of a nationalist, open and democratic foreign policy initiated by Castiella in 1957, would influence many aspects of future foreign policy actions by successive Spanish governments. The 'principles of Spanish foreign policy' analysed by former Foreign Secretary Fernando Morán, in fact, are not significantly different from those put forward by Castiella in 1957, and followed by virtually all foreign secretaries since, including those during the transitional period between the authoritarian and the democratic regime, and to some extent even those under the parliamentary monarchy and the Socialists.[2]

Castiella's term of office between 1957 and 1969 allowed Spanish diplomacy to create a rather independent foreign policy which included, among other aspects: a hardening of the relations with the United States with regard to the American bases in Spanish territory; overtures to Third World countries, especially the Arab world; systematic opposition to Israeli policies in the Middle East; active support for the decolonization process; close, friendly relations with Cuba even after the United States-led economic and political blockade of the early 1960s; and claims to Spanish sovereignty over Gibraltar. This period also saw mutual interest by the Soviet Union and Spain to normalize their relations.

Castiella's foreign policy disturbed the United States continually, and displeasure was shown more than once. Particularly difficult to digest was Spanish policy towards Cuba after the revolution took over from Fulgenicio Batista, and Spain's Middle Eastern policy, where Spain systematically identified with Palestinian national rights and against Israel. For many, these policies were short of incomprehensible and prejudicial to Spain as a Mediterranean country with claims to influence the outcome of the Middle East conflict.

The anti-Americanism which was evident in some aspects of Castiella's foreign policy contributed to his downfall, as did the increasing separation between internal and external politics. Gregorio López Bravo replaced him in 1969, in an attempt by the more conservative sections of the governing political elite to reverse the seemingly inexorable 'neutralist' foreign policy under Castiella. For Mesa and Aldecoa, the installation of López Bravo in the Santa Cruz Palace was aimed at adjusting internal politics to foreign policy. Obviously, the opening-up of the Spanish economy to American-, European- and Japanese-controlled multinational corporations required a more flexible, less 'nationalist' foreign policy. The slow process of permitted, carefully guided political liberalization of the regime also put constraints on a foreign policy designed to satisfy a different internal political and sociological configuration.

Fernando Morán describes Castiellas's foreign policy as 'statist, nationalist and semi-independent',[3] recognizing the progressive contents and style adopted by foreign policy-makers under his direction. His successor, López Bravo, became far more aware of the changes in both the internal sociological and economic geography of Spain and the external alignments of international and economic policies. López Bravo's policies, according to Morán, could be categorized as neo-liberal, technocratic and modernizing. The increasing incorporation of Spain into a new and complex economic world where the development of multinational corporations seemed to be the most important factor had brought about an anti-corporatist drive by the Spanish political elites. The order of the day had been the injection of massive investment into Spanish industry (tourism by no means being the only one). Consequently, the design and execution of foreign policy experienced a series of 'adaptations'. These were the beginnings of modernizing efforts by the more 'liberal' elements within Francoism or, to put it another way, by the less nationalist, corporatist, neo-Fascist, and traditionalist sectors.[4]

López Bravo's foreign policy did not depart significantly, though, from the basic foundations given to it by Castiella. There was a change of emphasis which affected several areas, but the basic policies remained. These were: (a) the consolidation of a decidedly pro-Arab policy; (b) continued reluctance to recognize the State of Israel; (c) systematic support to Palestinian rights to self-determination and national identity; (d) close relations with all Latin American countries, independent of political regime or ideological persuasion, an attitude that prompted both Castiella and López to keep close links with Fidel Castro's Cuba even at the peak of the United States-led economic and political blockade. López Bravo did also extend a friendly hand to the Popular Unity government in Chile, between 1970 and 1973, though American pressures in this sphere dictated a more subdued behaviour by the Spanish Foreign Office; (e) a continuation of Spanish claims to sovereignty over Gibraltar; (f) continued support for decolonization in Africa and Asia; (g) attempts at improving relationships with the Soviet Union and the Eastern bloc both in diplomatic and economic terms; (h) efforts aimed at the development of an 'Iberian pole' which would include Portugal.

There were, however, changes of emphasis which showed the extent to which the old Francoist guard was giving way to a new breed of modernizer technocrats. Relations with the United States became more open and comfortable, whilst at the same time American investment in Spain increased significantly.[5] The Spanish government became extremely interested in putting forward an image as a liberal, tolerant, political regime, eager to open up the system to alternative ideas, to modernize the economy, and to become a loyal member of the Western alliance. These developments, however, did not go so far as to advocate NATO membership, nor did any member country feel tempted to invite Spain to join.

But perhaps the areas where the relative independence of Spanish foreign policy could be better seen during both Castiella's and López Bravo's tenures as Foreign Secretary were the Middle East, Cuba, Eastern Europe and Chile, without disregarding the general support for national liberation struggles in Asia and Africa, categoric claims to sovereignty over Gibraltar, and reluctance and/or antagonism towards the United States over the Vietnam war.

In this chapter, we shall concentrate on two generally related issues, though not necessarily in every aspect: relations with the Soviet Union and other Eastern European states, and with Cuba after the overthrow of the Batista dictatorship. Both cases are illustrative of a degree of independence and even autonomy by

Spanish foreign policy designers and executors, at times when the anti-Communist behaviour of the Spanish government at home and the development of the Cold War abroad had all but diminished. We shall discuss other issues, especially the Middle East and Latin America, in the next chapter.

Though Spain and the Soviet Union re-established diplomatic relations (after breaking them off when the Republic was overthrown by Franco) in February 1977, *de facto* relationships had in fact existed for many years. Moreover, official diplomatic relationships had already been established with other Eastern European states. The ideological connotations involved in Spanish–Soviet links pre-empted a more comfortable course for both sides to normalize rationally links between both states. The pro-Axis sympathies of the regime during the Second World War, the existence of an outlawed, persecuted Communist party in Spain, the role (for the Francoists) of the Soviet Union during the Civil War, were some of the factors interfering with what both nations considered their national interest. As J. Schneidman has put it, 'Spain and the Soviet Union are not just states. In the minds of many they are symbols. The ideological aura of each state created a problem in reaching formal diplomatic relations'.[6] The complex system of relationships between Spain and the Soviet Union was also influenced by the love–hate relationship between the Spanish Communist party and the Soviet Union. Lastly, but no less important, the Soviet connection was exploited by Franco to counter-balance the retrograde aspects of his government's internal policies, and also to blackmail the United States into becoming more 'understanding' of the regime in Madrid, and as an indirect means to become accepted as a legitimate and respectable ally.

Schneidman divides the history of Spanish–Soviet relationships into four periods:

1. 1940–7, when Franco was viewed as a Hitlerite;
2. 1948–59, when contacts between the two states grew and the Spanish Communist party (PCE) was considered by most Spaniards as a Muscovite creation and therefore distrusted;
3. 1960–76, when the increased contacts between the states blossomed into Spanish diplomatic relations with all Warsaw Pact states except the Soviet Union, and the PCE evolved into a legitimate Spanish political party independent of Moscow;

4.. 1977– , when Spanish–Soviet relations were established, and the Communist party of the Soviet Union attacked the ideology of the PCE.[7]

But the most striking aspect in Spanish–Soviet relations is that, but for the 1940–7 period, contacts developed rather quickly after the war, reflecting the pre-eminence of nationalist, rather than ideological, considerations for both sides. Self-interest seem to be at the core of both nations' considerations almost as soon as the war ended. It is true that at Potsdam, between 17 July and 2 August 1945, Stalin, Attlee and Truman decided to exclude Spain from the new United Nations, while shortly afterwards (December) France called, with Soviet support, for an invasion of Spain by the Allies. United States' and British opposition frustrated this attempt, and the Soviet Union did nothing to enhance it either. The aftermath of the war was rich with bellicose verbal statements of condemnation for the Franco regime by both the Western Allies and the Soviet Union. In terms of policies, they came practically to nothing. Economic measures to isolate Spain did not have the desired effects, as countries, such as Argentina under Perón, came to Spain's help with wheat and other vital foodstuffs, under the very noses of both the Soviet Union and the Western democracies.[8]

It is in the second period when the Spanish–Soviet contacts began to take shape, even when the internal repression in Spain against Communist party members and sympathizers, and other opposition groups, was at its worst. By 1948, some non-Communist states previously antagonistic to Franco began to recognize Spain, the Cold War was developing at an accelerated pace, and France had removed the French Communist party from Cabinet responsibilities and even deported a number of Spanish exiles. Resolutions condemning Spain in the United Nations continued, but gradually support for them decreased and became confined to the Soviet Union and other Eastern European members (Ukraine, Belorrussia, Poland and Yugoslavia), plus Mexico, the only country to recognize the Republican government in exile, based in Mexico City. Even before 1953, at the time of Stalin's death, the Soviet Union had felt it was becoming isolated with regard to Spain, and overtures were being made towards some form of unofficial link. Reliable sources in both the Spanish and the Soviet foreign services attribute significant importance among Soviet motivations to its desire to limit the potential damage to its security as a result of the American bases which were being discussed at the time between the United States and the Franco government.[9]

The contradictions of Spanish–Soviet links in the early 1950s can be better appreciated by the secret agreements between the two countries in the commercial area. While Franco was, in July 1954, calling for a boycott of Soviet goods (yet another contribution to the anti-Communist crusade so dear to him), the *New York Times* was revealing a secret deal to exchange 300,000 tons of Spanish iron for 179,000 tons of Polish coal. The British House of Commons was being informed, more or less at the same time, of a number of suspicious trade accords between Spain and several countries of the Eastern bloc. While these agreements were being signed and actual commercial intercourse between the two sides took place, on the surface there was open antagonism and verbal attacks did not decrease. The controversy over the Spanish gold reserves rented to Moscow during the Civil War (and estimated to have had a market price of around US$70 million, in bullion and coins), which erupted in 1955, gave the opportunity for Franco to accuse the Soviets of using the money to pay that country's considerable foreign debt, contracted during the war. Moscow responded by accusing the Spanish government of owing the Soviet Union US$50 million. The incident, however, did not interrupt the now clear course of events in favour of even more contacts. The Soviets adopted a low profile in relation to the Franco regime, amidst increasing anxiety over the issue of American military bases in Spain. The deal between Molotov, then Soviet Minister for Foreign Affairs, and the United States' Secretary of State, Foster Dulles, which admitted Spain as a United Nations member in 1955, was a concrete example of increasing Soviet anxiety over Spain, and its desire to normalize relationships with the Franco regime.[10]

While these developments were taking place, the PCE was experiencing systematic repression by the Franco regime, and had become atomized into conflicting factions and, therefore, ineffectual. Schneidman summarizes this second period of Spanish–Soviet relations as follows: '1.—Many verbal accusations were made; 2.—commercial and cultural contacts, however, developed, though not in a very significant form; and 3.—the PCE became ineffective'.[11]

The third stage of Spanish–Soviet relations began in 1960 and lasted about seventeen years. During this period, Spain opened diplomatic representations in all Communist states, with the exception of the Soviet Union and Albania. The PCE became increasingly independent of Moscow, assuming with the Italian Communist party the articulation of Eurocommunism, criticisms of the policies and tactics of the Soviet Communist Party and its pretensions to exercise forms of control over the international Communist movement. In Spain, the PCE also became generally accepted as a legitimate member of the opposition against Franco.

The efforts made by the Soviet Union and Spain to normalize their relations were made difficult by the still highly emotional memories of the Civil War, the existence of a considerable number of Spanish refugees in the Soviet Union and other Eastern European states, and the continued repression of dissension by Franco, especially against the PCE. In January 1960, the PCE re-elected Santiago Carrillo and Dolores Ibarruri—'La Pasionaria'—as leaders, and re-enacted traditional, rather orthodox views on class struggle, world revolution, and the anti-Franco effort. In a way, the PCE meeting, held in Paris, was seen by the Francoists as a confirmation of that party's allegiance to Moscow, and provided an excuse to increase repression. On 4 May 1960, and after the Soviet ship Krym had brought 557 Republican, Socialist and Communist exiles living in the Soviet Union back to Spain, Franco's deportation of several of them back to the Soviet Union caused an international furore.[12]

Paradoxically, international press reports confirmed more or less simultaneously that the Spanish government had authorized the visit to the Soviet Union by all those Spanish citizens wanting to attend a USSR–Spain soccer match, while the East German boat, Schwennou, was bringing 150 tractors manufactured in the Soviet Union to Bilbao in the Basque country, one of the areas where the opposition to Franco had been, and still was, more consistent.

In 1962, a climate of political and social unrest developed in Spain, strikes became a regular feature, and the Spanish government continued to accuse the Communists of being the force behind them. Most observers, however, did recognize that the process of industrialization and urbanization taking place at the time was giving shape to a new proletariat, whose political outlook was more modernizing and militant than that exhibited by the previously humiliated, persecuted, and, therefore, frightened working-class organizations. The protest movements of the 1960s were not Communist-inspired, though the PCE undoubtedly was part of them, but a more objective assessment would recognize the presence of other forces as well—Socialists, liberals, Social-Christians, anarchists. Even die-hard Falangistas participated in these broad-spectrum mobilizations, frustrated as they were by the increasing influence within the government of the new technocrats of the Opus Dei.[13]

The founding of Workers' Commissions (Comisiones Obreras), a broad opposition front to Franco, by the PCE in 1963 gave further impetus to the consolidation of an anti-Franco opposition with Communist participation. Moreover, the PCE shifted, for the first time, from its orthodox standings on a variety of political issues, to rather generally progressive, reformist appeals for a wider democratic front against the Franco dictatorship, including even 'progressive bourgeois' sectors. The call, made by a meeting of the 'Congress of the European Union' in Munich, and attended by a Spanish delegation, was endorsed by the PCE. The Spanish delegates were arrested as 'traitors' by the government on their return.

While the government continued to claim that each and every one of these developments were the work of the PCE and the 'international Communist movement', Spanish officials were busy visiting various Eastern European countries (and Cuba) in attempts to sign a variety of cultural and trade agreements. While the Cuban dimension will be discussed in the next chapter, it is interesting to register a number of developments in the 1960s which point in the direction of increasingly open deals between Moscow and Madrid, even when internal repression in Spain was rampant.

During 1963 and 1964, Spanish missions went to Poland, Rumania, the Soviet Union and China. These countries reciprocated with similar, and extensive, visits to Spain. In 1964, important sections of the Spanish media were calling for a 'normalization' of relations between the Soviet Union and Spain.[14]

Frequent meetings took place in several European capitals in 1963, 1964 and 1965 between Spanish and Soviet diplomats, and both attended diplomatic parties offered by their respective embassies, in spite of the absence of formal links. One such meeting, in Paris, between Spanish Ambassador José Maria de Areílza and Soviet Ambassador Sergei Vinogradov, moved Areílza to declare that 'may this year [1964] see the establishment of diplomatic relationships'.[15] It was claimed at the time that the Cuban Ambassador to Moscow was playing an active role in bringing both sides together.[16]

The climate of suspicion surrounding Soviet–Spanish relations, and the crusader language used personally by Franco to refer to what he considered the permanent, and perverse, international Communist conspiracy against Christian Spain, gradually began to give way to more subtle forms of antagonism.[17]

In mid-June 1964, Franco went on record in a speech in Bilbao, praising the Soviet Union, a drastic departure from his previous, obsessive behaviour. This was followed by a remarkable series of cultural agreements with several Eastern European countries, which included reciprocal visits by dance and music groups, opera companies, educationists, scientists and intellectuals.

The trend towards more cooperation was gaining momentum. In 1965, new missions from Poland, Yugoslavia, the Soviet Union, Bulgaria, Hungary and China arrived in Spain, and on 22 January 1965 the Spanish Cabinet formally approved the implementation of a policy of closer contacts with Eastern Europe. That same year, Soviet tourists began taking their holidays in Spain, joining the millions from other European countries who were already doing so.

The award to Communist poet Rafael Alberti of the Lenin Peace Prize by the Soviets in 1965 did not provoke more than a raising of eyebrows in Madrid, and in 1966 and 1967 cultural and trade exchanges increased. Visits by journalists of both countries opened up a new vein in the current state of improved relationships: the new policies were now put to the public by way of thorough analyses of Soviet society in the Spanish media, and Spanish society in the Soviet media. The language was one of moderation and even understanding. Long gone were the days of crude anti-Communism of the die-hard Falangists, and also gone were the days of Soviet abhorrence of Francoism.[18]

While the Soviet–Spanish 'Spring' was taking place, the PCE was plagued by internal divisions and factionalism. The Sino-Soviet split had deeply affected the party's internal cohesion, prompting the development of pro-Chinese and pro-Soviet factions at all levels of the PCE's bureaucratic apparatus, and also affecting party members and sympathizers at the grass-roots. They were united, though, in their opposition to Franco, particularly the Maoist faction, which also disliked the process of normalization of relations between Moscow and Madrid.

The opposition to Franco in the mid 1960s received significant support from sectors within the Catholic Church. The Church had hitherto been sympathetic to the regime, or at the very least reluctant to lend any institutional encouragement to anti-regime groups. Particularly relevant at this time were student and other groups identified with the Jesuit religious order. Some of these groups came under the influence of the more radicalized sectors of the Latin American Catholic Church, the progressive social thought inherited from Jacques Maritain's philosophical school of advanced Christianism, and the Catholic anti-establishment, anti-capitalist insurrectionary movements in Latin America.

By 1967, a formidable coalition of social and political forces was putting the Franco regime under increasing pressure to liberalize. Accustomed to mobilization from traditional opposition groups—such as the organized, yet illegal, trade unions, the left-wing parties, and traditional anti-Franco organizations (intellectuals, students)—the collaboration of radical Church sectors added a new dimension to the opposition. Even within the government, the more liberal factions of Opus Dei were overtly, but significantly, arguing for more, not less, liberalization, the opening-up of the system to some form of opposition, and the 'tolerance' of intellectual dissension. These attitudes were not infrequent in newspaper articles and other documents, in spite of the prevailing system of press censorship.[19]

The wave of mobilization unleashed in 1966 and 1967 reflected the now definitive sociological changes that began taking shape in the late 1950s and early 1960s. The modernization of Spanish society was a fact, and the urbanization which generally goes with it brought about the consolidation of a new, more complex class system, in which both a national, European, modernizing bourgeoisie and a similar proletariat would play increasing roles, ultimately facilitating the transition to democracy later on. The reaction of the Spanish State was drastic: the police invaded factories, monasteries, universities, even convents and churches, and embarked on massive arrests. At the height of the turmoil, PCE's Secretary General Santiago Carrillo rejected any form of terrorism and called for all those in favour of a transformation of the Franco regime to join forces in peaceful, but organized protests. The Catalan wing of the party rejected Carrillo's call, but their position was to become increasingly isolated.

The deterioration of the internal political situation in Madrid, however, did not impede the continuation of the new Spanish–Soviet understanding. Goods were bought and sold between Spain and several Eastern European countries, with a value estimated at about 4 or 5 billion pesetas each way.[20]

Schneidman's account of the by now accelerated pace of Soviet–Spanish reconciliation is both illustrative and poignant. He says that Spanish–East European trade flourished in 1966, 1967 and 1968, despite the turmoil. Spain sold 4.6 billion pesetas in goods and purchased 4 billion. One hundred and seventy Pegaso trucks were sold to Poland; three ships were built for Yugoslavia. Shoes and nylon shirts were sent to Russia in exchange for oil, newsprint, and asbestos. Spain and Rumania established consular relations on 5 January 1968; Spain and the Soviet Union established a regular shipping service on 17 February of the same year, and Boris Smislov arrived in Barcelona to purchase land for a mission. While students and workers rioted in the streets of Madrid, Yevgeni Yevtushenko gave a May Day concert in the Spanish capital.[21]

Two things were already clear in relation to the improvement of Soviet bloc–Spanish relations in 1968: (1) these improvements were taking place while the Franco regime was embarked on an exacerbation of its repressive practices, alarmed as it was by the broadly based nature of the protest movement in the big industrial conurbations in Madrid, Bilbao and Barcelona; and (2) while the Soviet–Spanish new *détente* flourished, the PCE drifted away from its historical supporters, the Soviet Communist party (CPSU). In fact, the closer Spain and the Soviet Union became, the farther the Spanish Communists felt from their Soviet counterparts.

The invasion of Czechoslovakia by the Warsaw Pact countries in 1968 further alienated the PCE from the Soviet Union, but did nothing to deter the inexorable course towards mutual Spanish–Soviet recognition. At the meeting of Communist parties at the Kremlin in June 1969, the PCE kept a low profile and ended up refusing to sign the final statement approving the invasion. Shortly afterwards, the PCE's Central Committee would openly condemn the invasion, in a historical vote which marks the rupture of the long partnership between Spanish and Soviet Communists.

While the Spanish Communists drifted away from orthodoxy and towards Eurocommunism and the Spanish government continued its unmitigated policy of internal repression, moves towards diplomatic recognition continued. New trade accords were signed by Spain and Poland and the Soviet Union in 1968 and 1969; and on 14 July 1969 Poland and Spain established consular offices. In the same year, a high-ranking diplomatic and commercial mission arrived in Madrid from Moscow, the result of which was, among others, the granting of fishing facilities to the Soviet fleet in the Canary Islands. Spanish Foreign Secretary Gregorio López Rodó paid a supposedly 'secret visit to Moscow during the last week of 1969, but his presence was not unknown to diplomatic circles in Washington, Moscow, London and Madrid'.[22]

By 1970 the PCE was suffering an uncontrollable upsurge of factionalism, but the mainstream group continued to enjoy the official recognition of the Soviet Union, in spite of the fact that it had become openly anti-Soviet. From then onwards, the PCE would be a natural participant within the various Eurocommunist meetings taking place in Europe, most of which aimed at breaking up the monolithic hold exercised by the Soviet Communist party over the international Communist movement.[23]

The disenchantment of the PCE with Soviet and other Eastern European nations' behaviour towards the Franco regime was made public by Carrillo on a number of occasions. Early in 1971, Carrillo publicly emphasized the 'international character' of the Communist movement, and bitterly criticized attempts by the Soviet communist party and the government of the Soviet Union to impose ideological patterns and organizational structures on other Communist parties. For the first time, he also declared his condemnation of the improved Spanish–Eastern bloc links.[24]

Other developments in the now bitter disagreements between the Soviet party and the PCE included open warnings to Moscow not to mount Slansky-type Stalinist purges and trials against Alexander Dubcek's Czech Communists, appeals to the Soviets and other Warsaw Pact countries not to interfere with the national right of all peoples to their own sovereign expression, nor with the right of countries to choose their own road to socialism.[25]

The scism within the international Communist movement, which was made evident by the Sino-Soviet conflict, acquired new impetus with the launch of Eurocommunism, openly embraced by the Italian and Spanish Communist parties and supported by a number of other Western European Communist parties and one of the factions of the Japanese Communist party. The repudiation by the PCE of the Warsaw Pact intervention in Czechoslovakia, which included virulent verbal attacks, assumed a different connotation when it decided not to participate in the 14th Congress of the Czech Communist party in May 1971. For the Spanish Communists, the authority and legitimacy of the Soviet-imposed leadership, after the unbrotherly overthrow of Dubcek, was at the very least under serious doubt. Not content with this, the PCE sent high-level delegations to convince the Communist parties of several European countries, including those of the Netherlands, Sweden, France, Rumania, Denmark, Italy and Britain, that the PCE position was correct, and that the Soviet Union should be told so in no uncertain terms. Support for the Spanish standing was provided in most cases with a varying degree of enthusiasm, and in no case did any of the contacted parties effectively defend the Soviet stand. The PCE also managed to get significant support from the Chinese Communist party, eager as it was to isolate the Soviet Union in any way it could. Obviously, the radical course of the cultural revolution in China had important implications for the complex issue of Communist strategies and tactics. In this context, the Eurocommunist phenomenon could not be, nor was it, seen by the Communist leadership in China as a desirable development *per se*. But the mere fact that the existence of Eurocommunism would weaken the strategic and political hold of Communism by the Soviets made it attractive to the Chinese.[26]

By 1970–1, the PCE–Soviet split was all but complete. Enrique Lister and other high-ranking officials of the Spanish Communist hierarchy were expelled because of what was seen as recalcitrant pro-Soviet views. Shortly afterwards, the Soviet Communist party attempted to destabilize the PCE by sending a delegation of the influential pro-Soviet World Federation of Trade Unions to try and influence the behaviour of Workers' Commissions—the PCE-dominated trade-union movement in Spain. Furthermore, at the Budapest World Peace Assembly in May 1971, the Soviets attempted to grant recognition to the expelled Lister group, without actually denying legitimacy to the official PCE delegation. A deeply embarrassed PCE delegation had to suffer the humiliation of seeing the Spanish seat empty, rather than sharing it with the pro-Soviet Lister sector.[27]

The open and increasingly bitter PCE–CPSU controversy did nothing to help those opposing the Franco government's overtures towards mutual Soviet–Spanish diplomatic recognition. Indeed, it did very little to strengthen the few individuals who, for one reason or another, were still opposing those links from the Soviet side. The state of affairs by 1970 and 1971 showed, on the one hand, Spain's anxiety at the continued rejection of its desire to become a member of the EEC, and Soviet eagerness to exploit this in

Spain's favour, on the other. The Soviet Union's main strategic considerations at the time were twofold: (1) to do all it could to stop Spain becoming a member of the EEC and NATO; and (2) to open up new commercial areas for Soviet products.[28]

In order to push developments towards achieving those goals, the Soviets increased their efforts significantly during 1970 and 1971. Following a pattern in Eastern bloc international relations, delegations from several Eastern European countries visited Madrid and signed various trade, cultural, and other agreements, and Poland and Bulgaria interchanged consular offices with Spain, while Prague and Madrid re-established diplomatic relations at the ambassadorial level. The consular links with Bulgaria and Poland, and the higher ranking diplomatic relationship established with Czechoslovakia, were indisputable signs that relations between Moscow and Madrid were now unstoppable.

Another significant event was the establishment of an air link between Madrid and Moscow by both the national Spanish airline company, Iberia, and its Russian counterpart, Aeroflot. In 1972, commercial interchange increased and the Spanish government came out publicly in support of the old Soviet aspiration for 'an all-European Conference on Security and Cooperation', and reiterated Spanish claims to sovereignty over Gibraltar.[29]

In 1973, East Germany and Spain established diplomatic relations, shortly followed by the opening of Chinese–Spanish diplomatic links at ambassadorial level. Objections by sections of the ultra-right in Spain were greeted with the repressive zeal normally reserved for liberal and/or left-wing opposition dissenters, and included the closing-down of the neo-Fascist newspaper, *Fuerza Nueva*.

During the crescendo towards full diplomatic recognition between the Soviet Union and Spain, the Soviets never hid their rejection of further United States–Spanish military cooperation. The military bases already on Spanish territory, granted to the United States by a number of treaties, revisions and protocols from the mid-1950s onwards, were seen by the Soviets as direct attempts by the United States to encircle the Soviet Union and its allies with as many military enclaves as possible. Though the neutralization of Spain seems to have been a distant, but not that remote, dream of Soviet foreign policy-makers in the 1960s and 1970s, when mutual recognition took place in February 1977, the Soviets had all but abandoned that aspiration. It was then clear that despite what could be

construed as challenges to American policy by the Franco regime
(on such issues as a Soviet–Spanish *rapprochement*, the Middle
East, Gibraltar, Cuba, decolonization, and others), Spain would
not go so far as to cancel the military treaties with the United
States, even less to advocate active neutrality, in the Swiss
or Austrian mould. The signature of the treaties, and the subsequent addenda throughout the years, were and still are one of the
more controversial issues in contemporary Spanish politics, and
one which cannot be understood without assessing the broader
strategic issues of the military and political needs of the Atlantic
alliance and, more specifically, the problem of NATO membership.
Though these are discussed later, it is necessary at this stage
to evaluate the motivations behind the Soviet and Spanish set
of attitudes.

For the Soviet Union, Spain's geographical position placed it as
an extremely desirable ally or, failing that, a neutral country.
Situated at the doors of Africa, next to the British naval base of
Gibraltar, Spain had also developed a good rapport with many
Third World countries, especially in the Middle East and Latin
America. Spain's historical links with the Arab world and Latin
America constituted elements which the Soviets appreciated
highly as potential factors in any future exacerbation of East–West
relations and, certainly, in any military confrontation with the
United States and/or the NATO alliance. The overall Soviet desire
at least to neutralize Spain was not free from contradictions, for
one of the best ways to ensure a certain degree of independence in
foreign policy was for Spain to become 'European', and that would
mean becoming a member of the EEC and NATO. Membership in
these two cases would bring, from the Soviet point of view, a much
desired 'Europeanization' and therefore would help to ameliorate
Spain's collaboration with the United States in military matters.
NATO and/or EEC membership for Spain, however, was not
something that the Soviets relished, as in their view the two
institutions could be easily manipulated by the Americans and
their allies in Western Europe. Where the opportunity for Soviet
manipulation arose, however, was some recognition of anti-
Americanism within certain EEC and NATO quarters, i.e. nationalist, right-wing governments and/or socialist or social-democratic
governments. Such sentiments could offer a certain flexibility to
Soviet interests, an anti-Atlantic attitude which, for different
motivations, could help to create a semi-neutral, mildly anti-

American political phenomenon in Western Europe. The existence of a strongly European Spain, with either a nationalist, right-wing government or a socialist administration, would both fit into the general Soviet view of the 'ideal' Spanish government.[30]

Coincidence in certain areas of foreign policy between the Soviet Union and Spain helped to create hopes in foreign policy-making circles in Moscow that some form of Spanish 'neutrality' was after all possible. This included: remarkably similar approaches to the Arab–Israeli conflict where, if anything, the Spanish historical position was even more anti-Israeli than the Soviet one; Cuba; decolonization in Africa and Asia; and, in the early 1970s, support for the Popular Unity government of Salvador Allende in Chile, and the right of countries to elect whatever system of government they chose. The Soviet Union and Spain also coincided, generally and sometimes specifically, on the issue of national liberation wars against the metropolitan, colonial European nations, the dangers to peace posed by the two military alliances, and the need for disarmament. Long-standing international Soviet goals appeared to be also the preoccupation of Spain's foreign policy, even when the internal policies of the Franco regime were at its most repressive.

In February 1977, Spain and the Soviet Union finally established diplomatic relations. Before this, the PCE had been recognized *de facto* as a legitimate political party, and Santiago Carrillo had all but totally broken with the CPSU by publishing *Eurocommunism and the State*, where his known views on Soviet interference with other Communist parties were elaborated in detail. The Soviet reaction was to counter-attack in a number of articles in the Soviet media.

The re-establishment of diplomatic relations between Spain and the Soviet Union (they had of course been particularly close during the Republican years) reflected Moscow's long-standing aspirations, eager to do all it could to stop what it saw as the inexorable course of a hitherto independent Spanish foreign policy towards the United States' sphere of influence. The signature of the military pacts with the United States in the 1950s, the attempts by successive American administrations to get Spain into NATO, the increased level of multinational and especially American investment in Spain, and the obvious anxiety within the Spanish political elites to become 'European' (including EEC membership), had created the impression within the Soviet foreign policy apparatus that measures were needed to keep Spain as a reasonably 'neutral' country, albeit in a rather limited sense. Other aspects of Spanish foreign policy at the time had basically shown a remarkable continuity, especially with regard to the Middle East, decolonization, and Latin America (including the complex Cuban issue). Thus the base element from which to build up a more solid Spanish 'neutrality' was already there.

Schneidman considers the official inauguration (or reinauguration) of relationships in 1977 as the beginning of the latest phase in Spanish–Soviet relations.[31] In an otherwise excellent piece, he concludes that the Soviet Union only reluctantly recognized Spain, though the evidence to substantiate that claim is not conclusive. All the available data (including confidential memoranda in the Spanish Foreign Office, interviews with senior diplomats, parliamentarians and advisers—both Soviet and Spanish—at various times in the 1966–77 period, and several relevant articles in the Spanish and Soviet media) suggest otherwise.[32]

In addition to that evidence, there is the conclusive fact of the tendency towards relations, which included previous diplomatic interchanges with virtually all the other Eastern European states, China, and Cuba. Only Albania was conspicuously absent from these efforts. Commercial, cultural, educational, technological and tourist agreements proliferated right through the 1960s and 1970s between Spain and most countries in Eastern Europe. The signature of consular agreements with Communist countries other than the Soviet Union had generally been the sign of more to come, and usually meant that the Soviet Union was about to enter into similar arrangements itself. The pattern with Spain was indeed repeated with several Third World countries, especially in Latin America, as in the case of Colombia, Chile, Venezuela and Peru. These ended up establishing relations with the Soviet Union after fulfilling similar stages.

Schneidman recognizes, however, the importance given to Spain by Soviet policy-makers when he writes that

since the days of Peter the Great, the Soviet Union has desired to be a Mediterranean power. As long as the United States maintains its position within Spain, the Soviets cannot achieve that end. Spain, therefore, has become important to the latter, and it will use its diplomatic post in Madrid to wean Spain away from United States influence.[33]

We suggest that it is not so much that Spain has become important in the last few years, but it has been important for the last two or three decades, or even longer. The issue of relations with the Soviets, on the other hand, has been exploited to its advantage by successive Spanish governments, with general success. What has been done is none other than to exploit American anxiety over relations first, a pattern which in their eyes would unbalance the political equilibrium in the Mediteranean; at the same time, Soviet expectations have been played intelligently by Madrid's foreign policy-makers by showing a distinct independence on issues dear to Moscow (the Middle East, Israeli–Palestinian conflict, Cuba, decolonization). In this way, the Palacio de Santa Cruz has achieved not an inconsiderable image as an independent and imaginative foreign policy-maker, capable of putting forward policies that are free from the conservative and/or reactionary internal constraints that characterized most of the pre-democratic period during Franco's term of office.

Several developments after the establishment of relations between Spain and the Soviet Union only confirmed the high priority which the Soviets accord Spain in their foreign policy plans. According to data provided by Spanish Customs, and quoted by the Madrid daily *El País*, the Soviet market had, by 1983, become, the most dynamic of all foreign markets for Spanish products. Exports had increased by 98.3 per cent since 1982.[34] Spanish imports from the Soviet Union in 1983 amounted to $492.9 million, an increase of 1.4 per cent on the 1982 total of $487.2 million. Spanish exports to the Soviet Union totalled $344.5 million in 1984. Official statistics show a steady increase in commercial interchange between Spain and the Soviet Union, ever since the first significant trade agreement was signed in 1972. This is put as high as 1,200 per cent between 1972 and 1983 by reliable sources in the Spanish Foreign Office. It is also important to analyse the nature of trade between the two countries. While Spanish exports have traditionally been in the heavy industrial sector (steel and iron), fruits and agricultural produce, the main Soviet export to Spain has been oil, a commodity which Spain does not possess, thus making Spain highly vulnerable to political pressures from its selling partner. Spain's consistently friendly relationships with the Arab world would, at least theoretically, put it in a safe position as far as oil needs are concerned. It is indicative, however, of Spain's vulnerability in terms of oil dependency, that it sought to diversify its import market towards the Soviet Union, rather than depend totally on Arab crude. The frequently frustrated attempts at establishing diplomatic relations with Israel in the 1970s and 1980s were not totally irrelevant in prompting Spain to look for Soviet crude. In all fairness (and at least in public), the official line is one of strictly commercial considerations: Soviet oil is relatively cheaper, not just in terms of net price per barrel, but also its transport to Spanish ports is considerably cheaper than the cost of importing from Venezuela, Mexico and/or Ecuador, or alternatively from the Arab states. The net result has been a marked diversification in Spain's oil policies: oil is now supplied by several Arab countries, the Soviet Union, and some Latin American countries. This diversification is not totally unintentional, as many sources have confirmed, but responds to the need to ensure absolute independence from the oil factor for foreign policy-designers and makers.[35]

The Soviets did all they could to facilitate a shift in the pattern of Spanish oil dependency, including advantageous (for Spain) transport contracts, competitive prices, technological assistance to improve Spain's administrative controls over stocking, distribution and refinement, just to mention a few aspects. Furthermore, a bilateral commercial agreement signed in Madrid between the two countries in February 1984 opened what the liberal/progressive daily *El País* called 'a new framework for relations, and one which offers a number of avenues for cooperation in a number of areas for the next 10 years'.[36] To the traditional areas of Soviet–Spanish cooperation—such as the steel and iron industries—were added new and strategically important economic sectors such as petro-chemicals and naval engineering. The political implications of these developments are clear: increased influence for the Soviet Union. The prevailing mood in Madrid is one generally in favour of keeping the Soviet link, though there are signs of uneasiness at the prospect of more imports of Soviet crude, a development which would be seen by some foreign policy experts as undesirable, as it would increase Spain's dependency on the Soviet Union in energy matters.

The integration of Spain into NATO after the referendum of 1986 obviously did not please the Soviets. Significant pressures were brought to bear on the Spanish government, at various levels, to show this displeasure. Though the process which ended up with NATO membership for Spain is analysed later in this book, it will suffice to mention now the fact that these pressures did not alter the course chosen by Felipe González's government several months, and perhaps years, before the referendum took place. As early as mid-1984, reliable sources in the Moncloa Palace confided that there would be, in their opinion, no alternative to membership of NATO for Spain. The only problems at that moment were logistical: when to hold the referendum and how to present a wording which would allow the government the flexibility necessary to negotiate integration.[37]

The pressures exerted on Spain by the Soviet Union to keep a low military profile in the context of the Cold War were perhaps at their highest during Konstantin Chernenko's term of office. On the occasion of the historical visit to the Soviet Union by King Juan Carlos, in May 1984, Chernenko praised Spain's determination not to allow nuclear armaments on to its territory, and added that the Soviet Union would never use nuclear arms against countries which had renounced their stockpiling and/or development. He also emphasized the role that Spain could play in helping to reduce tensions in areas of continued conflict, such as Central America and the Middle East.[38] It would be naïve not to see that special Soviet interest in a possible Spanish contribution to ease tensions in some areas of international conflict was centered around certain issues, i.e. those where Spain and the Soviet Union would be more likely to coincide, rather than those where they would differ.

The visit by King Juan Carlos to the Soviet Union could be construed as further proof, if any more were needed, of the remarkable changes that had been taking place since Franco's death. The visit provided ample opportunity for both countries to show the extent to which the old scores had been settled, giving way to a new, close relationship which would have been unthinkable only a few years before. The visit marked a turning-point in Spanish–Soviet relations, and Spanish commentators even referred to a 'Soviet fascination for Spain', typified by the publication of numerous books, articles and even dictionaries in the Soviet Union, with the aim of popularizing Spanish culture and language.[39] This 'fascination' would be shattered, however, with Spain's decision to enter NATO, which would be seen by the Soviets as a step in the wrong direction.

The process which brought about the re-establishment of relations between Spain and the Soviet Union was closely observed by the United States. According to confidential materials in the Palacio de Santa Cruz, interviews with officials involved in various consular and diplomatic talks, and information provided by diplomatic sources elsewhere, the United States never doubted that diplomatic relations would be re-established. But American diplomats were more concerned with a damage-limitation exercise than with actually stopping the reopening of representations between Madrid and Moscow.

The nationalist/progressive foreign policy pursued by Castiella, altered in style but not significantly in content by López, could not avoid having as one of its fundamental aspects mutual recognition with the Eastern European world. The design of a foreign policy which would put Spain into the twentieth century could not possibly ignore the existence of the Communist world, nor would Spain's aspirations to act as a link between Europe and the Third World be realized without Soviet acceptance. For the United States, the main challenges of these policies could be construed as: (a) destabilizing American hegemony in the Mediterranean, including the British enclave in Gibraltar; (b) facilitating Soviet influence in Europe and the Third World with the potential use of a 'neutral' or sympathetic Spain by the Soviets; (c) weakening the military standing of the United States by questioning the legitimacy of the American bases in Spain and even asking for their removal; and (d) weakening the standing of the NATO alliance, as the United States has always considered its Spanish bases as part of the defensive (and even offensive) capability of NATO. This latter assumption has been systematically rejected by Madrid, which does not want to be seen, not yet at least, as part of the military structure of NATO.

Another, but by no means the only other, controversial issue in which there has been a radical departure from American policies, has been Cuba. The complex and never-ending conflict in Central America centered around Cuba and Nicaragua and the Contadora peace efforts have provided Spain with another opportunity to test the possibilities of an independent foreign policy.

Ever since Fidel Castro overthrew the Fulgencio Batista dictatorship in 1959, Spanish–Cuban relations have been characterized by a high degree of understanding, and even friendship. Though there have been hiccups (expropriation of Spanish-owned properties by the Cuban revolutionary government, expulsion of Spanish priests at the beginning of the revolutionary period, for example), these have been the exception rather than the rule. On the whole, both Fidel Castro's and Franco's foreign policies in relation to their countries have been pragmatic. The transition to democracy in

Spain under Prime Ministers Arias Navarro, Suárez, and Calvo Sotelo, and the democratic period under Felipe González, have helped maintain the core of Spanish policy towards Cuba. This could be summarized as follows:

1. Spain has a historical obligation towards Latin America and does not discriminate between the various political regimes there. There is, therefore, and there always will be, a 'special relationship' with the Latin American countries;
2. Spain's national interest in relation to the Third World, especially Latin America, does not necessarily coincide with the United States'. Spain sees its role as one of a link between Europe and the Third World and, in the case of Latin America, as representative of its culture and traditions;
3. Spain should be seen by Latin America as the 'perennial' friend that can be trusted, irrespective of political regime. Spain should play a role helping to integrate Latin America into the modern world, encouraging that continent's development and (especially for Felipe González' government) supporting the replacement of authoritarian/totalitarian right-wing governments by democratic governments.[40]

Quite naturally, Spain has been reluctant to 'ideologize' its relations with Latin America. This pattern, which has been maintained with remarkable continuity by all of Franco's foreign ministers and successive governments, has brought about benefits to most involved parties, and it has most certainly helped Cuba to beat the United States' orchestrated political and economic blockade which began in the early 1960s and has remained basically unaltered ever since. Once the Nicaraguan dimension was added after the overthrow of the Somoza dictatorship, Spain's role has continued to be one of support for a peaceful solution to the problems of the area, and one which embraces recognition of the legitimacy of the Sandinista government in Nicaragua and the renunciation of the use of force by all the participants in the dispute, including the United States and United States-supported forces. Spanish policy towards Nicaragua has been one of low-key, but categoric support for the mediating efforts of the Contadora group of countries, Mexico, Venezuela, Colombia and Panama. It is apparent that Spain has not sought to antagonize unnecessarily the United States on this issue, while at the same time putting forward vigorous but restrained views to ensure that the conflict does not escalate into a regional, Vietnam-type war with the risk of an American–Soviet conflict.[41]

At the peak of United States' antagonism towards Cuba, in the early and mid-1960s, Spain maintained a firm rejection of pressure to become part of the international blockade against the Castro government. This policy included:

1. The signature of numerous cultural and commercial treaties between the two countries. Worth mentioning are the creation of a fishing fleet for Cuba by the Spanish State's shipyards, including freighters, trawlers and refrigerator ships,[42] and a five-year trade agreement valued at about US$100 million per year. Furthermore, open signs of the fruitful Spanish–Cuban relations under Franco and Castro took the form of cultural accords which materialized in visits to Spain and Cuba by ballet, symphonic, theatre and university groups, and frequent symposia on the culture of both countries, attended by academics and intellectuals.[43]

2. The rejection of United States' pressure to isolate Cuba completely after the take-over by the revolutionary movement '26th of July'. Spain, alone among Western European countries, kept transport services going to and from Cuba, including those provided by the Spanish State-owned airline, Iberia. At one time, Iberia, together with Aeroflot (the Soviet airline) and Cubana de Aviación (the Cuban State airline) were the only air companies servicing Cuba.

3. The establishment in Madrid of a major Trade Office by Cuba, which would act as headquarters for Cuban exports and imports. The tobacco industry's trade with Europe and other commodities important to Cuba, are managed there.

4. The repudiation of American efforts to subvert the Cuban regime, including the Bay of Pigs invasion and diplomatic efforts in the United Nations and other organizations to get Cuba isolated and sanctioned. The Spanish government has consistently opposed anti-Cuban resolutions in the General Assembly, and has stated its opposition to any form of sanctions in bilateral relations as well.[44]

The inauguration of the parliamentary monarchy and a democratic regime in Spain did not fundamentally alter the main patterns of Spanish–Cuban relations. Fidel Castro welcomed the election of a Socialist government in Madrid, and when Felipe

González visited Havana in 1986, he was given an extremely friendly welcome. The communique issued at the end of the González–Castro talks reiterated the long-standing goals of Spanish–Cuban relations, i.e. respect for the sovereignty and territorial integrity of all the states in Central America and the Caribbean area, non-interference by the super powers in the Nicaraguan problem, support for the Contadora group, and repudiation of the military activities of the 'Contras'. Felipe González' visit received ample coverage in Havana and Madrid, and confirmed the excellent state of relations between the two countries.[45]

The historical closeness of Spanish–Cuban relations has helped the development of expectations *vis-à-vis* a possible Spanish role in the Nicaraguan conflict. The smaller Latin American nations, especially in Central America, have from time to time expressed their hopes of a potential role for Spain as a counter-balance to American influence in searching for peace and social justice. These hopes have increased with the installation of a Socialist government in Madrid, and have more likely than not been exaggerated. As has been said, Spanish foreign policy towards Central America has been consistently more low-key than its foreign policy towards Cuba. This has been perhaps a consequence of the shift from a nationalist, Third Worldist foreign policy under Franco towards a more Atlantic, European foreign policy under the Socialists.

Though the fundamental commitments of foreign policy remain, however, this shift of emphasis has brought about an attitude which shows clear-cut, verbal support for development and democracy in Latin America and the process of pacification in Central America. However, at the same time this foreign policy shows a lack of tangible efforts to provide the means to make them possible.

There is perhaps a divorce between Spanish intentions and actions in the Latin American case generally, and Central America especially. This dichotomy is recognized privately by advisers, politicians and diplomats involved in the discussion, design and execution of Spanish–Latin American and Central American policy. The lack of concrete measures to contribute to a strengthening of democracy in the area, advance social and economic development and social justice, and create the conditions for these to flourish, especially in Nicaragua, has not been helped by cynicism and indifference. There have been a number of initiatives to reverse this course, especially after the election of the two

Socialist governments. Some of these initiatives were coordinated by the Instituto de Cooperación Iberoamericana (ICI) and the Secretaría de Estado para la Cooperación Internacional con el Tercer Mundo. In 1984, a significant impulse was given to a number of programmes with many Latin American countries, including Cuba and Nicaragua. These included projects in the scientific, technological, agricultural, educational, transport, health, shipping and engineering areas.[46] At the same time, ICI officials were trying to give shape to a scheme whose main aim would be to establish the basis for a systematic plan of cooperation with Central America. This plan was presented by the Spanish government as a 'new philosophy of aid', an 'alternative' to the traditional policy of aid with strings attached. In a major article in *El País*, Antonio Fernández Poyato, then Coordinator for the Plan of Total Cooperation with Central America in ICI and member of ICI's Board, stated that 'peace in the region requires the eradication of the various problems which affect their peoples'. He added that it is difficult, if not impossible, 'to achieve a true peace in Central America while 70% of its population suffers from serious malnutrition, and has to struggle to survive with a per capita income below $100 per year'. The analysis goes on to add that 'of each 100 newborn children, 20 die before reaching the first year; of each 100 inhabitants, 60 are illiterate. According to reports by the United Nations' Economic Commission for Latin America (ECLA), more than 8 million people in Central America live under extreme poverty . . .'.[47]

The plan calls for major investment schemes in a number of areas in Central America, mainly along the general lines of the ICI's *Resumen de Programas* (Programming Brief) for 1984.[48] The plan's philosophy is defined as:

1. The practical expression of the Spanish government's determination to cooperate with 'the spirit of Contadora', promoting peace and development in the area.
2. The need to readapt the policy of aid (from the traditional ways lacking planning and coordination and practised for years by the Spanish administrations) to an 'alternative' model which would integrate the various organizations, mainly in the public sector, dealing with aid issues.
3. The plan would be initiated with countries in the Central American area which are deemed to be most in need. Not

unrelatedly, the chosen countries were Nicaragua, Honduras and Costa Rica, the most politically sensitive and those most at risk from the threat of social and political instability and/or upheaval.

The new plan of cooperation with Central America recognized the financial constraints affecting it, as the Socialist government was already embarked on a public austerity policy aimed at reducing the public deficit and controlling inflation. This has been criticized by the PCE, and even Socialist sectors and the trade-union movement.[49] According to unofficial sources, the plan was a reaction—not necessarily well thought-out or coordinated—to pressure from several Latin American countries, especially those affected by the Nicaraguan conflict, for Spain to play a more active role in the area. When President Luis Alberto Monge of Costa Rica visited Madrid in June 1984, he appealed to Spain to strengthen this role, and stated that 'we need the help of Spain to bring peace to Central America'.[50] During his four-day visit, President Monge did not hide his anxiety at what he saw as a stalemate in the confrontation between Nicaragua and the Reagan administration. For a country without an army, as is the case for Costa Rica, the continued escalation of the conflict poses ominous risks. Spain's policy towards the area includes a recognition of Costa Rica as a stabilizing force, being one of the longest-lasting democracies in Latin America, and Prime Minister González reaffirmed to President Monge Spain's commitment to a democratic and independent Costa Rica. In the complex chess-board of the Central American subcontinent, Costa Rica is a vital piece for Spanish foreign policy. This is why it is the largest recipient of bilateral aid in the area and is likely to remain so in the next decade.[51]

The success of the Contadora effort and the integrity and security of Costa Rica are two of the pillars of Spain's policy towards Central America. But the exercising of influence requires relations with all the states in the area. Diplomatic recognition of Guatemala had ceased in January 1980, after the Guatemalan government had sent troops to the Spanish Embassy, apparently to take some refugees out and arrest them. This action, in clear violation of articles 22 and 29 of the Vienna Convention on diplomatic relations, caused the death of thirty-nine people, both Spanish and Guatemalan, and prompted Spain to withdraw recognition of the Guatemalan State. In September 1984, however, and after a mediation by President Belisario Betancurt of Colombia, diplomatic relations were re-established, thus removing the last impediment to full and open participation by Spain in the process of a peace search in Central America.

The support of Spain for Contadora has been total, but not active. Already by 1984, the Palacio de Santa Cruz had made it clear to the United States that it saw in Contadora the only way for a conflict as protracted as that in Central America to be resolved, and that it did not approve of American interference in the area. This categoric denunciation of American behaviour was not made public at the time, but there was general consensus in Spain that the United States was not being helpful. Far from it, American actions were considered ill-founded and American intentions, to say the least, ethically dubious.[52]

In 1986, the Contadora group of nations had been trying to revitalize their mediating effort to bring peace and stability to the area. Tension, already heightened by increased attacks by US-backed Contra forces against Nicaragua, had been further increased by the Salvadorean and Honduran internal war fronts, the deteriorating social and economic situation in Costa Rica, and the internal repression in Guatemala. Within this context of mounting conflict—aggravated by the complex scandal of Iranian money used to boost the Contra's activities—a possible Spanish role acquires more relevance and urgency, particularly now that the United States' standing seems to be weakening. Foreign Minister Fernández Ordóñez travelled to the area and offered Spain's 'mediation' in the Nicaraguan internal confrontation between the Sandinistas and the opposition. Fernández Ordóñez' strategy seems to be based on the following assumptions:

1. The United States is losing legitimacy as 'broker' in the area, if indeed it ever had it.
2. The loss of face by the United States is creating a dangerous vacuum of power and influence.
3. A new broker is needed who could be trusted by all parties, a prerequisite that the United States has never been able to show as possessing.
4. For Spain to play this new role it would be necessary first to 'legitimize' the Nicaraguan opposition, making it acceptable to the Sandinista government, and then make the opposition accept the legitimacy of the Sandinistas.

5. Any interference by countries or groupings of any other organizations outside the immediate sectors concerned is counter-productive and should be resisted. This includes attempts at interference by the United States and/or United States-supported groups.
6. The commitment to democracy in the area by Spain—which has in the past concentrated on strengthening Contadora and the stability of Costa Rica—should now extend also to strengthening the Nicaraguan government.[53]

Spain has since embarked on an active, though subdued, programme of encouragement of Contadora.[54]

The configuration of a Central American policy by Spain, which includes important points of disagreement with American foreign policy in the area, has however been affected by the difficulties between Spain and the United States in renegotiating the status and number of American bases in Spain. A policy which promised to be a departure from the more traditional, low-key approach adopted before has now effectively become entangled with other issues—equally vital to American perceptions of where its interests lie—especially the Middle East and Latin America; and the protracted issue of the military bases in Spanish territory and the potential Atlantic/Mediterranean military role of Spain seems to have become increasingly important both politically and strategically.

Notes

1. Roberto Mesa Garrido and Francisco Aldecoa Luzarraga, *Apuntes del curso sobre Politica Exterior Española*, Facultad de Ciencias Políticas y Sociología, Departamento de Relaciones Internacionales, Facultad Complutense, Madrid.
2. Interviews with several Foreign Ministry officials, 1984 and 1986.
3. F. Morán, *Una Política Exterior para España*, op. cit., p. 16.
4. See F. Morán, ibid., and M. Vásquez Montalbán, *La Penetración Americana . . .*, op. cit.
5. M. Vásquez Montalbán, ibid.
6. J. Lee Schneidman in J.W. Cortada (ed.), *Spain in the Twentieth Century . . .*, op. cit., p. 155. His article on Spanish–Eastern European relations is both rich in data and illuminating.
7. Schneidman, ibid., p. 159.

8. The Argentine media at the time was full of praise for Franco.
9. Interviews with five senior Spanish and Soviet diplomats in 1972 (at the United Nations in New York), 1984 and 1986, confirmed this. Informal conversations with several advisers and diplomats indirectly linked to policy decisions and discussions in this area generally tended to show agreement.
10. The deal was not generally well received, as shown by the almost universal rejection of the Mexican media, and such influential newspapers as the *New York Times* and the *Washington Post*. In Britain, the Labour party was dismayed, and similar reactions were registered by most Socialist parties in Western Europe. Most of the Arab countries and a number of Latin American countries approved, though.
11. Schneidman in Cortada (ed.), *Spain in the Twentieth Century . . .,* op. cit., p. 164.
12. The issue was extensively reported by the quality international press, especially the *New York Times, The Times, Los Angeles Times, Manchester Guardian, Excelsior,* and several national Latin American newspapers (notably *Ercilla* of Santiago, Chile, and Argentinian and Brazilian newspapers). The Soviet media covered it too.
13. See *Le Monde*, March and April 1960; paradoxically, and according to senior Spanish diplomats, talks between the Soviet Union and Spain were taking place almost at the same time as the Spanish opposition was organizing massive protests against the Franco regime.
14. The Falangist newspapers *Arriba* and *Pueblo*, and the Catholic Church's *Ya* are particularly illustrative. According to Foreign Office sources, the move was favoured by Franco himself but was blocked by the more Atlantic, pro-American factions of Francoism. The Opus Dei technocrats would have also played a role.
15. Schneidman in Cortada (ed.), *Spain in the Twentieth Century . . .,* op. cit., p. 166.
16. This was confirmed to one of the authors by a Cuban diplomat serving in the Cuban Embassy in Chile from 1970 to 1973.
17. For an examination of Franco's style, see *Arriba* and *Pueblo*. Also useful were a number of documents made available to the authors, covering a variety of issues in 1963, 1964 and 1965, and produced by the Falange (memoranda, internal reports, letters, specially commissioned studies). They confirm Franco's deep-rooted distrust of everything remotely associated with 'Communism' and the Soviet Union. Pragmatism would, however, replace that extremely ideological stand later on.
18. Frequent articles in *Ya, Arriba* and *Pueblo* are illustrative; also in *ABC*, though to a lesser extent. In the Soviet press, *Izveztia* and *Trud* showed great concern and interest.
19. See *Pueblo, Ya, ABC*.
20. Schneidman in Cortada (ed.), *Spain in the Twentieth Century . . .,* op.

cit., p. 168. If tourism is added to other invisible earnings, that amount is considered rather conservative by experts in the Palacio de Santa Cruz.

21. Schneidman, ibid., p. 168. In addition, talks with several Spanish Communists who had lived in exile for a number of years showed deep frustration and disenchantment at the Soviet Union's behaviour. There was a general feeling of 'betrayal' of the cause of 'internationalism'.

22. Confidential (restricted use) memoranda seen by one of the authors in the Chilean Foreign Office, and informal talks with American and British diplomats in 1972 confirm this.

23. See José M. Maravall, 'Political Cleavages in Spain and the 1979 General Election', *Government and Opposition*, vol. 14 (1979), 299–317. Also, by the same author, 'Spain, Eurocommunism and Socialism', *Political Studies*, vol. 27 (1979), 218–35. Also useful is J. Story, 'Spanish Political Parties: Before and After the Election', *Government and Opposition*, vol. 12 (1977), 474–93. Coverages of the four general elections are given by B. Pollack, and B. Pollack and G. Hunter in a series of articles in *Parliamentary Affairs*, published by Oxford University Press for the Hansard Society for Parliamentary Government.

24. See *Mundo Obrero*, 8 January 1970 and 19 February 1971.

25. See *Mundo Obrero*, especially selected issues in 1970 and 1971; several issues in February, March and April are also relevant. A few in November and December are also useful. See also *L'Unitá* (official Italian Communist party daily newspaper) and *L'Humanité* (French Communist party newspaper). The years 1970 and 1971 register a peak in Eurocommunist disenchantment with orthodox Soviet policies.

26. This was the view of senior Chinese academics visiting Liverpool University, in October 1986, as part of a delegation of the Chinese Institute for International Relations, Beijing. In talks with members of staff from the Department of Political Theory and Institutions of the University of Liverpool, they showed distrust for Soviet intentions and a desire to strengthen relations with Western Europe, especially Britain. They also saw better relations with the United States as important. In both cases, the 'expansionism' of the Soviet Union would thus be checked.

27. Accounts by Schneidman, op. cit., were confirmed to B. Pollack by two PCE delegates to the Budapest Congress of 1971. There is little doubt that the Soviet Communist party tried to isolate the Spanish Communists, attempting to give official recognition to the splinter Lister group.

28. United Nations, New York, General Assembly, 1971. Assessments by Soviet diplomats and Spanish advisers coincide.

29. See coverage by most of the Spanish media in 1972. The most blatant

nationalist rhetoric was used and abused.

30. Extensive talks with several Spanish MPs, diplomats and foreign policy advisers, as well as documents on foreign policy made available to B. Pollack, have provided the core of the information for this analysis.

31. Schneidman, op. cit., p. 174.

32. Soviet anxiety over the issue of relations with Spain was revealed by the diplomatic correspondence of the period. The Soviets seem to have begun an offensive to re-establish diplomatic links in the mid-1960s, but the repressive nature of the Franco regime, and particularly its anti-Communist policies, prevented Soviet diplomacy from pursuing their case further. On the Spanish side, both Castiella and López Bravo would have welcomed closer Spanish–Soviet links when they were foreign secretaries, if only to emphasize Spanish independence from the United States, especially with regard to the bases problem. It is clear that the re-establishment of diplomatic relations was as important for Spain as for the Soviet Union, and generally seen as a 'useful' and necessary step by both sides as early as 1966. The internal repression in which the Spanish regime was engaged in the mid-1960s, and Communist opposition to it, soon became irrelevant.

33. Schneidman, op. cit., p. 177.

34. *El País*, 14 May 1984.

35. Spanish preoccupation with ensuring a constant supply of crude played a role in prompting efforts to diversify Spain's sources. Dependency on Arab oil was seen as undesirable, in view of the possibilities of pressures arising out of the establishment of Spanish–Israeli diplomatic relations. This view was confirmed to the authors by well-informed sources within the PSOE's International Department. The main aim of Spanish planners was to ensure a diversified supply of oil so as to guarantee a relative freedom from political and other pressures.

36. *El País*, 14 May 1984.

37. In talks with B. Pollack, a senior foreign policy adviser to Prime Minister González recognized in 1984 that there was no question of the government recommending adhesion to NATO in a clear-cut way. The impression was given, however, that the Socialist government was already committed to NATO membership, but it was well aware of the political risks that position would entail.

38. See *Diario 16*, Madrid, 11 May 1984; also *El País*, Madrid, 14 May 1984.

39. See Pilar Bonet, 'La fascinación soviética por España', *El País*, 16 May 1984.

40. See F. Morán, op. cit.; also, by the same author, 'Cuatro Años cumplidos: España a Punto, 1982–1986: Balance de una Gestión', PSOE, 1986; and 'Politica Exterior Española', *Leviatan*, Summer 1984, II Epoca, No. 16, pp. 7–20, 1984.

41. Spanish Foreign Secretary, Manuel Fernandez Ordonez, confirmed to B. Pollack that Spain was historically committed to the preservation of the sovereignty and territorial integrity of all Latin American republics. He also repeated his country's support for the Contadora peace effort for Central America, and repudiated any attempts by European countries, or the United States, to interfere. (Interview, June 1986).

42. Schneidman, op. cit., p. 167, refers to a total of 42 ships, based on information given by the *Washington Post* and *The Daily Telegraph*. Other sources in Spain and the Cuban Foreign Trade Ministry put the total at between 60 and 65 ships. Between 1964 and 1970, at least 100 ships of various kinds were, according to these sources, supplied to Cuba by Spain.

43. For an assessment of the level of Spanish–Cuban relations in the 1960's, see *Gramma*, official periodical of the Cuban Communist party, especially issues in 1963, 1964, 1965 and 1966. In Spain, *Ya*, *Arriba*, *ABC*, and *Pueblo* are illustrative of the extent to which the Spanish political class close to France was committed to the preservation of Cuba's independence and integrity.

44. See United Nations' records, 1962–75, especially the General Assembly's voting record.

45. See *Gramma*, Havana, Cuba, issues in November 1986. Spanish coverage was considerable too, both in the written media and in radio and television.

46. See Instituto de Cooperación Iberoamericana (ICI), *Resumen de Programas previstos para 1984* (internal document).

47. See *El País*, 9 July 1984.

48. See ICI, *Resumen*, op. cit.

49. Criticisms by the Socialist-controlled UGT and the Communist-controlled Workers' Commissions (*Comisiones Obreras*) have been particularly severe.

50. *Diario 16*, 12 June 1984.

51. See ICI, *Resumen*, op. cit; also *Programas* (Plans) for 1984, 1985 and 1986 (internal documents).

52. This feeling was conveyed to B. Pollack by Miguel Angel Martínez, then Deputy Chairman and currently Chairman of the *Cámara de los Diputados* (Lower House of the Cortes (Parliament)) Foreign Affairs Committee, in 1984. It was shared by Manuel Medina, Chairman at that time of the Lower House's Defence Committee (currently one of the Spanish EEC Commissioners). Support for Contadora, and repudiation of any American attempts at disrupting or frustrating its efforts, was expressed by Juan Antonio Yáñez, Foreign Affairs Adviser to Prime Minister González, and Ángel Viñas, then Executive Adviser to Foreign Secretary F. Morán (interviews, 1984).

53. Some of these issues are discussed in *El País*, 20 January 1986. Others

were put to B. Pollack by Foreign Secretary Fernández Ordóñez in an interview in June 1986.

54. For a coverage of Spanish efforts, see *El País*, 13 January 1986, 20 January 1986, 30 April 1986. Further treatment is given in issues of *El País*, *Diario 16* and *Cambio 16* in March, April, June, August, November and December, 1986.

4

Special relationships: Latin America and the Middle East

Latin America and the Middle East are two areas where Spanish foreign policy has been at its most consistent. This continuity can be traced right back to the first decade of the Franco regime and throughout his full time in office. Furthermore, it can be safely stated that Spanish foreign policy after Franco's death, during the transition to democracy and under the democratic regime, has not been substantially different from Franco's foreign policy towards both areas.

Spanish Latin American policies have of course been influenced by what could be called the post-colonial syndrome. Spain owes a special allegiance to the former colonies, and vice versa. Their common culture, religion and shared historical development for several centuries make it natural for a 'special relationship' to exist, irrespective of particular junctures at any given times, such as changing political circumstances, diverse development levels, or relative importance as national states.

The most remarkable areas where the consistency of Spanish policies towards Latin America has been demonstrated are Cuba and Central America (already discussed in the previous chapter), and the generally neutral attitude exhibited by successive governments towards the rather unstable patterns of political behaviour of most Latin American countries. It has already been shown that Spanish policies towards Cuba and the Central American, almost permanent, crisis arising out of the Nicaraguan problem have provided opportunities for supporting the sovereignty and territorial integrity of all the states in the area, including a firm defence of the rights of the Sandinista government and close relations with the Cuban government headed by Fidel Castro. Spanish South American foreign policy has consistently, and historically, followed the same independent pattern, without generally succumbing to pressures to take sides in favour of or against specific political regimes in that area. Perhaps the most notable exception to this trend of 'subdued neutrality' was in the relationship with the government of General Juan Perón in Argentina. Here the closest of relationships developed right from the very early stages of the Franco regime, perhaps symbolizing the mutual admiration of the two regimes for aspects of the corporatist/neo-Fascist tradition. Spanish pro-Peronism under Franco and Peronist pro-Francoism under Perón complemented each other. Both were, after all, pariah regimes immediately after the war because of their pro-Axis sympathies. Both were headed by charismatic, personalist caudillos with a Catholic–integralist vision of society where the Church and the armed forces cemented the pillars of the State. Both restructured their societies in an authoritarian style, and permeated them with an authoritarian value-system where participation and the democratic generation of political mandates were either non-existent or directed from above.

In addition to the structural similarities between Peronism and Francoism (and in spite of their differences—differing attitudes towards participation, varying degrees of Church identification with the political regime, contrasting ideological internationalization and identification of the armed forces, among others), there was the issue of the personal friendship between Franco and Perón. This not altogether unimportant factor would duly take Perón to Madrid to live in exile after his overthrow by a military triumvirate in 1955.[1]

The close Franco–Perón relationship, both personal and structural, was behind the only instance where a certain 'ideologism' seemed to determine Spanish foreign policy patterns. In most, if not all, other cases of Spanish–Latin American relationships, pragmatism was and has been the order of the day, be it in providing trade outlets for the Cuban revolutionary government and political asylum to the ousted dictator Fulgencio Batista; or supporting the Nicaraguan government politically and financially, while trying to legitimize the Nicaraguan opposition; or giving encouragement to the Contadora initiative for Central America, while keeping a low profile in case it collapses. Even in such internationally contentious issues as the Popular Unity government headed by Dr Salvador Allende in Chile, Spanish foreign policy showed remarkable continuity and maturity, never succumbing to American pressure to isolate Dr Allende's government, or to influence it.

The 'neutrality' of Spain with regard to the prevailing political regimes in the Latin American area, however, is prompted as much by historical considerations as by self-interest. It would be extremely naïve to attribute only emotional and/or altruistic motivations to any foreign policy. National or nationalistic considerations, self-interest and the pursuit of certain goals have been, and are, at the core of all nations' foreign policy. The pursuance of Spain's neutrality in Latin America is a *sine qua non* condition of its foreign policy, for there are so many regional conflicts with deep roots in its history and geography that no country with any aspiration to influence could afford to take sides. On the other hand, too committed a neutrality could denote, rightly or wrongly, a degree of indifference that could not, again, be afforded without risks. Some of the conflicts which can be mentioned and which constantly have called for definitions by the European countries, especially Spain, could be categorized into the following groups:

1. *Disputes between a Latin American country and Great Britain or an associated country in the area.* Cases to mention, for example, are the Venezuelan–Guyanan border disagreements where Venezuela accuses the United Kingdom of having enlarged, during the colonial stage, Guyana's territory at the expense of Venezuela's. United States' pressures at the end of the 19th Century prompted the United Kingdom to accept an international tribunal's findings determining the Venezuelan–Guyanan borders, but Venezuela alleges that it was not part of the tribunal, which included North American, British and Russian judges.[2]

Spain's attitude on this conflict has been rather ambiguous, but eminently low-profile, encouraging a peaceful resolution of the problem by direct talks between Venezuela and Guyana, opposing at the same time any internationalization of the dispute.

Spanish caution here is, according to Foreign Ministry sources, provoked not so much by lack of conviction on the Venezuelan cause as by the presumption of British support for the Guyanan position and the understandable desire not to create yet another contentious issue (in addition to Gibraltar) with the United Kingdom.[3]

Another border conflict inherited from British colonial demarcations is the Guatemala–Belize dispute over land situated on the

Atlantic Central American coastline, south of the Yucatan peninsula and next to Guatemala. During the Spanish colonial period,
Great Britain managed to obtain Madrid's recognition of a kind of
autonomous status for this area, which came to be known as
British Honduras, now Belize. In the last century, Great Britain
enlarged its control, reaching up to the Costa Rican border, but
Unites States' pressures partly removed British occupation and
administration, which at one time included extensive areas in
Honduras and Nicaragua, a fact which is scarcely known and has
received surprisingly little attention.[4] Guatemala has never recognized the validity of the border with Belize and still claims
sovereignty over it. The incorporation of Belize into the United
Nations has weakened the legitimacy of the Guatemalan case, and
Spain, as with the Venezuelan–Guyanan dispute, has preferred to
keep away, seeing it as a potentially risky issue in terms of
aggravating its relationship with the United Kingdom. In both
cases, the importance for Spain of the Gibraltar issue has precluded
any formulation of a policy of solidarity or support for its former
colonies.

A third contentious issue which affects directly or indirectly the
United Kingdom, and therefore hinders potential Spanish participation, is the persistent and seemingly unsolvable Antarctic problem. The lack of any conclusive legal documents giving a particular
country clear rights over the Antarctic, or parts of it, makes a
resolution of this old international dispute very difficult.[5] A number of countries systematically claim Antarctic rights (including
Great Britain, the United States, the Soviet Union, Canada, Australia, New Zealand, Argentina and Chile), but the most contentious aspect, from a Hispanic–Latin American perspective, is the
Chilean and Argentine claims to sections which are also claimed by
Great Britain.[6] As in the previous cases, the British connection here
has very probably deterred Spain from showing its pro-Latin
American standing, though it has done so in a low-key way on a
number of occasions.

There is, however, a notable exception to this trend of Spanish
neutrality or, at best, moral support for Latin American border
disputes with a British connection. This is on the issue of the
Falklands/Malvinas.

The Falklands/Malvinas confrontation between Argentina and
the United Kingdom has prompted a major departure from the
described behaviour, and Spain has in fact come out strongly in

support of the Argentine claim of sovereignty over the South Atlantic islands. The Spanish government has supported all United Nations resolutions in the last few years, declaring the Malvinas a colonial issue, and asking for a resolution of the conflict which clearly considers Argentina's sovereignty as an issue of paramount importance. During the visit to Spain of President Raúl Alfonsín and by Prime Minister Felipe González to Argentina, bilateral statements were issued where Spanish commitment to an Argentine Malvinas was unequivocal.

The departure by Spain from a position of timidity on other contentious issues with Latin American–British connotations to one of categorical support for Argentina against the United Kingdom could be attributed to several causes.

First, it reflects the weight of the Argentine nation-state in Latin America and its standing in the world. Argentina, for Spanish foreign policy-makers, is a 'first rate' country, both in geo-political and economic terms. With Brazil, Argentina is the most urbanized, industrialized and modernized country in the Latin American area and, in political terms, one of the most influential. Spain can ill afford to ignore one of the most powerful Latin American countries.

Secondly, there are also 'ideological' considerations. Argentina's claims to sovereignty over the Falklands/Malvinas touch a sensitive nerve within the International Department of the Spanish Socialist Workers' party. With decolonization a consistent preoccupation of successive Spanish governments during and after Franco, the British continued political and, moreover, military presence in the South Atlantic is seen as an anachronism which cannot be tolerated, a factor far worse than any of the other contentious issues still pending, like those affecting Venezuela and Guatemala. Furthermore, in sharp contrast to these two cases, there is no legal decision or treaty legitimizing British control over the islands which, in the eyes of the Spanish Foreign Office, the British virtually appropriated in 1830 without recourse to legal instances.

Thirdly, support for the Argentine position commits the Spanish government, especially under the PSOE, to reinforce the development of democracy and democratic routines in that country, a goal to which they accord the utmost importance for the future of the continent. It is in the strengthening of democracy in Latin America where the PSOE government sees its most important political role.

2.   *Disputes between a Latin American country and the United States.*
As Sepúlveda makes clear, these are conflicts provoked by what he
calls 'revisionist' attitudes by the Latin American countries, when
they try to alter contractual agreements agreed upon, with or
without varying degrees of intimidation and/or pressure by the
United States. The two main issues in this category are the
Cuban–United States differences over the American naval base in
Guantánamo, and the Panama Canal problem.

The first problem poses a dilemma for Spanish foreign policy:
the juridical foundation of the United States' continued control
over Guantánamo is based on the peace treaty of 1898, which
ended the Spanish–United States war and prompted Cuban
independence from Spain.[7] The defeat of Spain by the United
States gave the latter control of Cuba, Puerto Rico and the
Philippines, though very shortly afterwards Cuba was given
independent status by the United States which, however, kept the
Guantánamo bay for military purposes. It has retained it ever since
and not even the Revolutionary government under Castro has
tried with any conviction to regain it for Cuba, though it has stated
from time to time that this 'anomaly' should be resolved as it
constitutes a 'colonial enclave' in Cuban territory. Spain has
traditionally abstained from putting forward any forceful opinions
on the subject. After all, both Cuban independence and the status
of Guantánamo are the direct consequence of its military defeat
by the United States and the peace treaty signed by both of them at
the end of the war. This issue touches a rough nerve and has not
merited special attention by the Palacio de Santa Cruz. Unoffi-
cially, however, there is no sympathy for America's continued
presence in Cuba. As with the British in the Falklands/Malvinas
case, it is seen by Spain as an anachronism, a disturbing perpetua-
tion of Europe's 'colonialism' and, more explicity, of Anglo-Saxon
culture and domination on the Hispanic-American soil. Sooner or
later, it should be resolved in a 'non-colonial' way.[8]

The Panamanian–North American differences provide a focal
point for the airing of nationalist grievances for many Latin
American and Third World countries, and here Spain has been a
good deal more sympathetic than in the Guantánamo issue. When
Panama gained independence from Colombia at the beginning of
the 20th Century (and in a move that for many revealed the United
States' strong arm in the region), it subsequently signed a treaty
with the United States allowing the construction of the Panama

Canal, to connect the Pacific with the Atlantic. The treaty gave the United States 'perpetual lease' of the required land, for which the latter would pay some rent. These rather onerous terms made the treaty highly unpopular with various sections of Panama's population. In the 1960s, after violent rioting by students and workers, negotiations were entered into by the Carter administration and the Torrijos government. The negotiations produced a revision of the treaty, giving Panama sovereign control of the Canal at the end of the century.[9]

Panama managed to get significant support for its negotiations with the United States from many Latin American countries, and also countries in Africa and Asia. In Europe, Spain, under Foreign Ministers Castiella and López Bravo, was singularly supportive of Panama's position, strengthening the Third Worldist orientation of foreign policy at the time, especially under Castiella. Other European countries, though, kept completely out of the issue, an attitude which in practice implied support for the United States. Spanish support for the Panama Canal negotiations and the revision of the Panama Canal treaty was not articulated in an aggressive manner, and special care was taken to avoid annoying the United States. As in other, previously mentioned cases, Spanish foreign policy searched for an equilibrium, a balance between advocating nationalist, Ibero-American goals and the realism dictated by a European Spain. The sensitive issue of the American bases in Spanish territory and the no less important issue of Gibraltar often limited the scope of Spanish foreign policy *vis-á-vis* the great Atlantic powers, the United States and Great Britain. This did not prevent it from systematically supporting the decolonization process in Africa and Asia in the United Nations and in bilateral agreements, nor from condemning neo-colonial adventures by Britain and France (Suez), the United States (Guatemala, Dominican Republic, Granada), or Belgium (Congo). Low-key, subdued Spanish diplomacy in the aftermath of the Second World War—but for a short period of isolation—was nevertheless generally progressive, nationalist and independent from big-power manipulation, especially in cases where Latin American interests were at stake. On balance, the Falklands/ Malvinas and Panama are prototypes of these policies, but this continuity is better shown by the support given to the processes of independence in Africa and Asia in the 1950s and 1960s.

3.   Border disputes in Latin America. A third category of conflicts in Latin America is configured by border disputes of a purely regional character, i.e. the Bolivian–Chilean confrontation over access to the sea for Bolivia, the Amazonian conflict between Ecuador and Peru, and the San Andrés islands disputes between Nicaragua and Colombia, to mention just a few. In most of these disputes Spain has just not taken sides, sustaining the need for a peaceful resolution of all differences.[10]

The general trend which emerges, at least during the Francoist period, the transition towards democracy, and then parliamentary monarchy, is one of Spanish neutrality on border conflicts between Latin American countries, when they are of a regional nature; cautious support, when Britain and/or the United States are involved; and solidarity and varying forms of support to Panama and Argentina in their respective disputes with the United States and the United Kingdom.

However, 'invariably, a love–hate relationship colours attitudes of one-time colonials toward the former metropolis'.[11] The loss of almost all of its colonies by Spain in the Latin-American decolonization process of the nineteenth century, and the emergence of new metropolitan powers (Britain, the United States, France), however, significantly reduced the chemistry of distrust which is almost naturally inherited between the former colony and the former colonizer after independence. Furthermore, Spain developed the concept of Hispanism very early on in this century, though its most definite shape would take place only under Franco's term of office. Hispanism was no other than the Spanish response to the idea of a Commonwealth, as espoused by Great Britain, with two main aims: (a) to maintain and extend Spanish influence in Latin America, and (b) through it, to give Spain the opportunity to play some role in the area.[12] The violent confrontations of the civil war weakened the Hispanist crusade, when there were fundamental differences between Spaniards themselves on what Hispanism, and the Latin American–Spanish Commonwealth, would mean. For the nationalist/traditionalist right, the monarchists and the various neo-Fascists groups (including Francoism), the concept of race closely associated with religion was of the utmost importance, the common culture between the Spanish and the Latin American world being a symbol of both. For the republicans, the left and the modernizers, the only possible common denominator was one emerging from secularization, separation of Church from State, and modernization. The 1930s, therefore, saw a drastic decrease in the system of formal and informal links between Spain and Latin America which had been slowly but surely developing since the turn of the century.

Spanish influence in Latin America decreased during the Civil War, not only because of the self-destructive endeavours to which the Spaniards were dedicated and the subsequent self-centrism which affected their behaviour, but also because interest moved towards the United States, with its attractive Rooseveltian policies of the New Deal creating new hopes of progress, social justice and modernization. The radical departure by the United States from previous imperialist policies of interference and intervention in Latin America and the shift from isolationism towards enlightened international cooperation, both achieved under Franklin D. Roosevelt, opened the doors for an era of North American presence and influence that pushed Spain away. The triumph of Franco only exacerbated this trend, which came to be reversed only when the Franco regime was 'legitimized' by the United States through the military pacts of 1953 and Spain's admission to the United Nations in 1955. The emergence of the United States as one of the two largest and most powerful superpowers after the war, though, would never allow for the development of a meaningful Spanish–Latin American Commonwealth. At no time have the various attempts to forge closer links between them been remotely near the concept and reality of the British Commonwealth.

The idea of the common Hispanic heritage—race, religion, culture—imbued in Hispanism never effectively took off the ground in practical terms. As Pike so accurately puts it, 'regardless of how it is viewed abroad, Hispanism in the post-Franco age will likely serve Spaniards as a rhetorical exercise in image building, its benefits confined to the realm of intangibles, though not necessarily insignificant because of that'.[13] It would be only fair to add, however, that Hispanism as a philosophy or a fundamental ethos to justify a Hispanic Commonwealth of nations has been all but totally abandoned by foreign policy-makers in the new Socialist government of Felipe González. What now counts is not so much the 'common heritage'—of which there has been little evidence during the last and present centuries, nor indeed can this heritage be readily identified in Latin America in terms of culture (being a collection of Catholic, secular, liberal European, positivist and North American influences)—as the prospects for democratic growth and consolidation, to which the new Spanish democracy has given support and encouragement. It is in the strengthening of democracy in Latin America, and support for the internal forces which struggle for the replacement of authoritarian/military regimes there, where the present Spanish political class sees a relevant role to play. Hispanism is too closely associated with the most conservative and even reactionary sectors of Spanish society, and certainly with Francoism.

The creation of a kind of Hispanic Commonwealth—with due consideration given to the diverse circumstances of the countries involved—based on Spanish–Latin American cooperation and solidarity around democratic consolidation is not one to be dismissed lightly. Cynicism still takes over when this issue is discussed, and the whole idea is frequently discarded as a piece of empty rhetoric or wishful thinking. This is the general approach adopted by Marcos Roitman in his otherwise challenging book on the policies of the governing PSOE in Latin America.[14] Roitman's views espouse a more or less common assessment of the PSOE government held in certain intellectual and political quarters on the European and Latin American radical left. This opinion does not recognize the relativism of social and political development and class struggle in contemporary Europe, nor does it consider the importance of such factors as modernization, the East–West balance, and big-power politics in present-day international relations.

The indisputable fact is that Spain is just emerging from a long, dark period of authoritarian, and at times totalitarian, rule. The first priority for the Socialist policy-makers has been the creation and strengthening of a system of democratic routines which can only be successful through the establishment of democratic institutions and norms. In turn, the dismantling of the pillars of the Francoist state has been achieved with a reasonably high degree of success. The programme of 'democratization' of the police and the armed forces, though still in operation, has reached a stage from which it is unlikely to be reversed.

For important sections of the modernizing Spanish political elites the consolidation of democracy in Spain will in turn help consolidate democracy in Latin America, and is *per se* a condition for the re-enactment of any new system of Spanish–Latin American cooperation. The PSOE government, however, has seen its commitment to a new Commonwealth based on mutual support for democratic development complicated by the increasing conflict between 'pro-Europeans' and 'Third Worldists', both within and outside the party. This controversy, which is linked to the issues of the Atlantic role of Spain in the NATO alliance, EEC membership, and Spain's historical connections with the Third World, is at the core of the PSOE's foreign policy.

The PSOE's Latin American policies have been sharply criticized by Marcos Roitman, who considers them as ideologically bankrupt and eminently rhetorical.[15] His criticisms, however, do not correspond with the more objective assessment of other experts, who generally accept genuine progressive commitments by the Socialist government *vis-à-vis* Latin America. Of these, Emilio A. Rodríguez' analysis of foreign policy patterns under Franco and after, including the PSOE government, shows the extent to which motivations have changed with democracy, and the real break in the mould of relationships between Spain and Latin America which it brought about.[16]

These motivations are no longer based on the ill-founded Hispanist pretension but on new, modern issues which can effectively provide a basis for a long-lasting Spanish–Latin American entente cemented on realism and solidarity. Yáñez defines a democratic policy towards Latin America in the following terms:

1. support by Spain to the re-democratization process in Latin America;
2. promotion on a systematic basis for scientific and technical cooperation;
3. increase of all types of cultural and educational links and initiatives;
4. development of closer economic cooperation.[17]

Roitman, however, though conceding that efforts have been made to depart from the discredited Hispanist model in foreign policy, disputes the assertion that the PSOE government has succeeded in giving shape to a truly progressive foreign policy towards Latin America. He sees in fact a policy determined by strong United States' influence and the pro-Atlantic leanings of the PSOE's leadership. His conclusion is that the set of new policies being implemented constitute a new 'political colonialism' aimed at creating a new dependency on Spain. Spanish emphasis in democratization is 'arrogant' as it hides a desire to impose on Latin American countries the Spanish model of democratic reinsertion.[18]

Rodríguez's answer shows that though the PSOE's policies are indeed prone to verbal hyperbole, some important changes have taken place in relation to the patterns which characterized Franco's. Some of these changes are enumerated by the author as follows:

1. unequivocal statements supporting re-democratization in Latin America, and the view that it is through democracy that its problems can be solved;
2. solidarity with political organizations fighting dictatorship;
3. unequivocal support for the respect of human rights;
4. state identification through King Juan Carlos with a Spanish–Latin American identity.[19]

This rationale has no doubt been reinforced by concrete measures implemented by the last two administrations, which include specific financial support for a number of projects to foster democratic development, participation, and human rights in the area. Though in many cases these programmes can be seen as only modest contributions to a rather complex and costly enterprise, they are nevertheless attempts at providing Spain with a role, and register a shift of emphasis and intentions which cannot, and should not, go unrecorded. In some instances, these programmes have adopted a highly political profile, risking antagonism and challenges from conservative and/or dictatorial regimes in Latin America and the United States. Examples of this are the various programmes to help the development of cooperative movements in several South and Central American republics, human rights organizations and social movements in both urban and rural areas. In many instances, these are umbrella organizations which provide the main impetus for oppositional, anti-dictatorial groups. Though Spanish help is low-profile, it is nevertheless important and generally well appreciated by the sectors which benefit from it.[20]

The relationship between a democratic Spain and a foreign policy which has as its central ideological core the pursuit of democracy in Latin America is an important part of the foreign policy model taking shape under the PSOE government. This confirms, as Roberto Mesa has put it, that no country's foreign policy can be divorced from internal politics, nor from the system of relationships which characterize the dynamics of the international community of nations. Spanish foreign policy for Latin America is but a direct consequence of its profound process of re-democratization. Though the rhetorical aspects have always been present, it is in the content, not in the style, of these policies that the elements for an objective evaluation should be found.[21] Furthermore, it cannot be ignored that the new approach to Latin America is a drastic departure from the non-partisan, non-ideological policy pursued under Franco. It is no more nor less than a readjustment of Spain's position in the world, from its traditional Third Worldist standing towards an Atlantic standing, which NATO (and EEC) membership have made clearer. It reflects in fact an attempt to conciliate both positions. Policies towards the Arab world and Israel represent the other significant dimension of this readjustment, as will be seen next.

The mutual diplomatic recognition of Spain and Israel on 17 January 1986 fulfilled one of the electoral promises of the PSOE programme, which considered non-recognition as an anomaly which should be corrected. The lack of diplomatic relations between the two countries was just one aspect of the traditionally pro-Arab foreign policy pursued by the Franco regime, and not substantially altered by the transitional governments of Arias Navarro, Suárez and Calvo Sotelo. This anomaly became one of major importance once Spain embarked upon the process of democratic transition, including its bid to become a member of the European Economic Community. Spanish integration (though not to the military apparatus) into NATO during the Calvo Sotelo administration, increased the contradictions of this policy for Spain, and caused renewed pressures by other European states to achieve a 'normalization' of the situation. It was frequently pointed out that Spain was the only Western European nation not to recognize the State of Israel (though in fact the Vatican did not recognize it, and still does not). Furthermore, Israel has a comprehensive trade agreement with the EEC which grants special treatment for Israeli agricultural products, some of which would compete with Spanish products once that country became an EEC member. Not least important, there was increasing uneasiness at the anomaly of all EEC states having diplomatic relations with Israel, while Spain did not. The permanent search for a common political front by the EEC would, therefore, suffer if Spain joined without recognizing Israel.

The official announcement on diplomatic relations was the culmination of a long and painful process and, despite the official statements aimed at minimizing the potential damage to the historical Arab–Spanish friendship, revealed a significant shift in orientation and interest for Spanish foreign policy. The recognition of Israel has to be seen as part of the more Atlantic foreign policy pursued by the PSOE government, together with EEC and NATO membership, support for democracy in Latin America, and improvements of relations with the United Kingdom over Gibraltar. This is not to imply that the Atlantic leanings of this policy necessarily bring about a drastic redefinition of Spain's traditional areas of interest, nor of the generally independent thrust of its foreign policy, but that there are important changes of emphasis which could signal the beginning of more radical shifts towards 'Atlanticism' in the future.

The relations of Spain with the Arab world have always been central to its foreign policy. The isolation suffered by the Franco regime after the war (discussed in Chapter 1), with its multi-dimensional consequences, facilitated the development of a rationale for closer relations with those countries which were prepared to assist Spain. The Arab community of nations was in a special position to perform such a role: it had a deep historical association with Spain, whose culture and national identity had been influenced by centuries of Moslem occupation; geographically, Spain was the Western nation closest to the African Continent, where it had Moslem colonial enclaves until the 1970s; and, not insignificantly, Moorish troops from Spanish Morocco had played a distinctly active military role in the anti-Republican insurrection which installed General Franco in power.

Franco's first sign of friendship towards the Arabs came as early as December 1946, when he encouraged Spanish Moroccan representatives to become official delegates to the Arab League, which amounted to *de facto* recognition of that institution. At a time of intense conflict in the Middle East, the granting of recognition to the Arab League constituted a clear sign of hostility to Zionism and the Jewish national liberation movement in Palestine and, to a lesser degree, a show of antipathy to the British, the mandatory power. Franco's motivations were complex and cannot be dismissed as just pure opportunism. Anti-British, and by extension anti-colonialist, feelings played a part, as did a genuine desire to cement some kind of close relationship with peoples that had been important in shaping Spain's historical identity. True, the Jews had also been part of that heritage, but circumstances at the time were not helpful: the American Jewish community was active in mobilizing public opinion against the Franco regime, and Jews had been notable for their participation in the International Brigades fighting on the Republican side of the Civil War.[22]

Franco's *de facto* recognition of the Arab League did not go unnoticed by David Ben Gurion, then one of the most distinguished leaders of the Jewish independence movement, later to become Israel's first Prime Minister. According to reliable sources in the Israeli Foreign Office, Franco's attitude was taken as yet another token of his regime's neo-Fascist sympathies and further proof, if more were needed, of what was considered by Jewish circles as a barely disguised anti-Semitism. Arab support for the Axis powers, though in many instances more out of anti-colonialist need than pro-Nazi sympathies, further alienated any possibility of a Jewish–Spanish understanding.

Spanish diplomacy played the Arab card brilliantly in the United Nations, managing to get substantial support for its repeated bids to gain admission to the international organization. Arab support was obtained in spite of Spain's rather heavy-handed treatment of its Moroccan colonial enclave in the 1940s, which prompted a mild call by the Secretary General of the Arab League, Azzam Pasha, for Spain to try and modify its Moroccan policies. But, as Shannon Fleming points out, 'surprisingly, despite Spain's role as a colonial ruler of Moslems, the Arab states never found their new friendship with Franco terribly uncomfortable'.[23] Spain's support for the Arab cause in their fight against Israel, of course, did not go unnoticed by them.

The partition of Palestine and the creation of Israel by the United Nations in 1948 further exacerbated the poor state of Jewish–Spanish relations. It is not clear whether mutual antagonism would have prevented Israeli–Spanish diplomatic relations at that time anyway, and versions differ on who was to blame for the ultimate lack of rapport which prevented the opening of representations in Jerusalem (or Tel Aviv) and Madrid.

It is true that Franco did not grant recognition to Israel in 1948, and some researchers point out that he simply refused to do so on the face of strong pressures by the United States. Soviet support for the creation of a Jewish national homeland in Palestine, which if anything was originally more forthcoming than American support, made Franco fearful that Israel would become a pro-Soviet, Communist enclave inserted into the Moslem world with potentially serious destabilizing effects on the area.

Franco's antagonism to the new Jewish State was, at the very least, reciprocal. In 1949, Israel supported a UN resolution to retain boycott measures against Spain, while some American Jewish organizations continued reiterating bitter denunciations of his regime as having played a negative role for Jews during the Second World War. Israel's antagonism seems to have been at least as important as Franco's as a viable explanation of the non-recognition pattern. Former Spanish Foreign Secretary Fernando Morán suggested in a parliamentary debate in the Spanish Parliament that it was Israel which in fact did not want to recognize the Franco regime in 1949, and added the surprising statement that Israel's attitude 'was justified, given consideration of the kind of regime we had'.[24] Morán's statement left few doubts that it was Israel, and not Spain, that had refused to recognize the Franco regime in the 1940s and, presumably, in the 1950s.

Whoever was responsible, the end result was continued non-recognition and repeated demonstrations of mutual distrust between the two countries. Paradoxically, while in the 1945–55 period the nationalist anti-Spanish and pro-independence movement in Morocco reached a peak, this is the time when Spanish–Arab friendship consolidated. Furthermore, French problems in North Africa became acute in Algeria in the late 1950s and early 1960s, and Nationalist right-wing officers in the Spanish armed forces saw an opportunity to humiliate France, a country which, in addition to having shown consistent anti-Francoist behaviour, had also become Israel's best staunch supporter. French–Spanish disagreements over North African colonial policies merely increased the anti-French sentiments in the Spanish army, which was only too prepared to help the *colóns*, the extreme Nationalists opposing any form of independence for Algeria. Many of the more recalcitrant right-wingers involved in the organization of the anti-independence, pro-colonialist OAS movement found asylum in Spain. Many of them, however, were sent back to France on 16 October 1961, while others were sent to internal exile in the Canary Islands. At the end of the day, a reasonable relationship with France and a better one with the Moslem community of countries was seen by Franco as more important than solidarity with his French right-wing sympathizers.

From the moment of admission to the United Nations in 1955, and up to the recognition of Israel in 1986, Spain would systematically support General Assembly resolutions which in a variety of ways would sustain the Arab, while condemning the Israeli, view. This pattern reflected much more than Spanish support for the numerous resolutions aimed at protecting Palestinians' rights as individuals, consecrated anyway by the United Nations charter. In fact, Spain would be the only Western European nation to support systematically the Palestinian people's right to self-determination and a homeland, and to condemn Israeli actions to acquire, by war, Arab territories.[25]

The Yom Kippur war in 1973 brought renewed Spanish support for the Arabs. At the time, Morocco was making it increasingly clear that it had aspirations over Spanish Morocco while in the territory itself the Polisario Front was agitating in favour of independence and against both Spanish colonial status and a possible transfer to Morocco. The Israeli–Egyptian war provided Spain with an opportunity to restate its traditional support for the Arabs and regain some of the credibility lost by its continued inability to deal with its Moroccan enclave's colonial problems. In the 1967 Arab–Israeli war, the Americans had used their Spanish bases to provide a variety of logistical support for the Israelis, and the Spanish government had been unable to stop it or, some say, had been kept in ignorance about the whole episode. Well before the 1973 Yom Kippur war, the Spanish government had told the Americans that in any future confrontation between Israel and any Arab country the United States would not be allowed to use its Spanish bases to supply Israel.

The 1973 war brought dire economic consequences for Spain, as the price of petrol went up considerably, but supplies were guaranteed by the Arab nations, with which it traded almost exclusively at the time—a later diversification towards the Soviet Union would allow Spain greater flexibility. In 1969, Arab gratitude had been earned by ceding the Spanish territory of Sidi Ifni to Morocco, but the Nationalist challenge continued in Spanish Morocco, where the 267,000 sq. km. section of the Sahara controlled by Spain continued to be claimed by both the Polisario Front and Morocco.

The pressures on Spain from both the ever growing Nationalist/ Marxist Polisario Front and the Moroccans ended with the decision to abandon the colony, ceding part of its territory to Morocco and part to Mauritania, and prompting the antagonism of Polisario. The virtual partition of Spanish Sahara between Morocco and Mauritania, in February 1976, was little short of a capitulation by the Spanish State to a complex set of factors. Among these, the most relevant were: (a) fears of a deterioration of relations with the Arab world, especially the most conservative states such as Saudi Arabia, the Gulf Emirates, Jordan and Egypt, some of which provided 95 per cent of Spanish oil supplies. The more conservative Arab states were becoming increasingly preoccupied with the activities of the Polisario Front, supported by Libya and Algeria, and saw the Western Saharan conflict as a destabilizing factor in the area: (b) increasing pressure by Western Europe and the United States to settle a conflict which could create new tensions in an already troublesome area; and (c) the internal process of transition to democracy which was already under way after the death of Franco and the appointment of Juan Carlos to succeed him in 1975. Spain's political class was concentrated on the impetus towards democracy and the direction it might take and on advancing new forms of mobilization and participation (for those outside government), as well as having to cope with a substantial number of anti-democratic unknowns at the same time. A combination of all three factors produced a kind of inertia which immobilized foreign policy-designers and makers, and was not conducive to the implementation of any coherent decolonization policy for the Western Sahara.

The promise of satisfaction of the national aspirations of the Western Saharan Saharaui people would in due course create a new set of problems for the PSOE government, after the party had included in its political platform in the latest two general elections support for and identification with the struggle of Polisario. Though the PSOE commitment stopped short of outright support for Saharaui statehood, it was at least in favour of its recognition as the legitimate representative of the Western Saharan people and acceptance of the validity of its struggle for national identity. The constraints imposed by the PSOE's 'Atlanticism' soured Polisario–PSOE relations and the Saharaui movement was finally expelled from Madrid.[26] Whether this was a concession to the conservative Arab states or the United States (or both) is difficult to know.

The death of Franco in 1975 did not substantially alter Spanish perceptions of the Arab–Israeli conflict. Policies continued to be, by and large, pro-Arab and anti-Israeli, the Moroccan problem notwithstanding. Caught between the more radical Arab states (Libya, Algeria, Syria) and the more moderate ones (Saudi Arabia, the Gulf Emirates, Jordan and Egypt), and hard-pressed by the continued differences with Morocco and Mauritania over the Western Sahara, Spain opted for continuism, a policy of general identification with pan-Arabic diplomatic goals, including the Palestinian struggle for recognition of national rights and the repudiation of what it considered to be aggressive Israeli policies in the area. Fleming attributes the continuation of pro-Arabism by Spain after Franco was gone, to the following factors: '1. the inertia of an established policy; 2. the impact of Arab economic power following the 1973 Yom Kippur war; 3. the miniscule size of Spain's Jewish community (estimated at eleven thousand in 1984); and 4. Spain's desire to maintain good relations with the Arab world as a diplomatic lever against Morocco',[27] *vis-à-vis* the dispute over Ceuta and Melilla, the Spanish North African enclaves.

The transitional period under Prime Ministers Arias Navarro, Suárez and Calvo Sotelo demonstrated little, if anything, to change the view of Spanish foreign policy as essentially pro-Arab. Suárez and Calvo Sotelo allowed some form of trade to take place between Spain and Israel and informal contacts did take place at various diplomatic levels. But it was in the old-established contacts between the PSOE and the Israeli Labour party, Mapai, through the Socialist International, that the process of mutual diplomatic recognition took off.

The PSOE Secretary General and Prime Minister Felipe González had been to Israel in 1972, and subsequently a friendship developed with Israeli Labour leaders, especially Shimon Peres and Itzhaak Rabin, many years before any important member of the Spanish political class had even considered recognizing Israel. In this sense, the PSOE had been a precursor of a position which would be, later on, adopted by all Spanish political parties, with the sole exception of the Communists. On a visit to Saudi Arabia in 1984, González was asked about rumours of impending relations with Israel. The Prime Minister's answer is illustrative of the kind of motivations behind the decision to recognize Israel. 'First,' he said, 'the contacts between the Spanish Socialists and the Israeli Labour party are not new; they are part of a relationship of at least 12 or 13 years, beginning perhaps when I visited Israel in 1971 or 1972 . . .'. A summarized version of his justification for establishing diplomatic links with Israel includes the following points:

1. Spain had relationships with states, not with governments.

The central goal was to have diplomatic relations with all members of the United Nations.

2. Spain felt that it had to recognize the Jewish contribution to its history and culture, in the same way it had recognized the Arab contribution. Sefardi and Arab influences form part of today's Spain.

3. Israel's assumed pressures on the EEC to prevent Spain's membership would not alter Spain's determination to both membership and recognition of Israel. Israel, as any other country, had the right to protect its national interest as it saw fit and in this case, because of possible competition by Spanish agricultural products, it would be doing just that. There was no link between EEC membership and recognition of Israel.[28]

Mutual recognition finally came in January 1986, though approval was granted by the Spanish Cabinet on 27 December 1985.[29]

The establishment of relations between Israel and Spain was no doubt an important departure from deep-rooted patterns of diplomacy by Spain, and was followed by the upgrading of the Palestine Liberation Organization's representation in Madrid to ambassadorial level, and the granting to it of a semi-diplomatic status. This development reflects the fact that, though recognition did depart from standard pro-Arab trends, it did not fundamentally alter the core of Spanish policy for the area. The fact that some sections of society opposed recognition (especially the Spanish Communist party and organizations controlled by it) was not the main reason behind the PSOE government's caution with regard to the Arabs. The true reason can be found perhaps in the long-established pro-Arabism of the Spanish Foreign Office and the reluctance of its professional cadres to conform. It is believed that the most systematic and well-reasoned opposition to recognition came precisely from the diplomatic service itself, though younger diplomats and advisers linked to the PSOE were generally in favour.[30]

It is still too early to assess the nature of the changes in Middle Eastern policy which recognition of Israel will entail, but the mere act of challenging the long-standing Arab pretension to exclusivity shows both a desire to affirm Spanish independence and to follow a more Atlantic, and less Third Worldist, course in foreign policy. The picture is, alas, incomplete. It is in the area of defence,

NATO and Spanish–United States relations that the true nature of Spanish foreign policy will be defined in the next few years.

Notes

1. There is a large bibliography on both Peronism and Francoism. Quality varies, and the usefulness of each work will depend on what aspects the reader is interested in. General books on Peronism are: Joseph R. Barager (ed.), *Why Perón Came to Power: The Background to Peronism in Argentina*, Knopf, New York, 1968; George I. Blanksten, *Perón's Argentina*, University of Chicago Press, Chicago, Ill., 1953; S.L. Baily, *Labour, Nationalism and Politics in Argentina*, Rutgers University Press, New Brunswick, NJ, 1967. On Francoism, the following works are recommended: Juan J. Linz, 'An Authoritarian Regime: Spain', in E. Allardt and Y. Littunen (eds), *Cleavages, Ideologies and Party System*, op. cit.; and 'From Falange to Movimiento Organización: The Spanish Single Party and the Franco Regime, 1936–1968', in S.P. Huntingdon and C.H. Moore (eds), *Authoritarian One-Party Systems*, op. cit.' R. Carr and J.P. Fusi, *Spain, Dictatorship to Democracy*, George Allen and Unwin, London, 1979; J.M. Maravall, *Dictatorship and Political Dissent: Workers and Students in Franco's Spain*, Tavistock Publications, London, 1978; P. Preston, *Spain in Crisis: The Evaluation and Decline of the Franco Regime*, Harvester, Brighton, Sussex, 1966; A. de Miguel, *La Herencia del Franquismo*, Madrid, Editorial, *Cambio 16*, 1976; R. Robinson, *The Origins of Franco's Spain: The Right, The Republic and Revolution, 1931–1936*, University of Pittsburgh Press, Plymouth, PA, 1970.
2. See A. Sepúlveda Almarza, *España y América Latina: Un Estudio de Política Internacional*, Colección Estudios Latinoamericanos, CIPIE, Madrid, 1986, p. 41.
3. For a good discussion on the most important regional conflicts in Latin America, see R.A. Humphreys, *Tradition and Revolt in Latin America and Other Essays*, Weidenfeld and Nicolson, London, 1969.
4. A British role as mediating power in the Central American conflict would not have been unwelcome, according to information given to the authors by reliable sources close to the Contadora negotiating machinery. Britain's historical role in the Caribbean was seen as a positive factor, though Prime Minister Margaret Thatcher's foreign policy of unconditional support for, and identification with, President Reagan's was not deemed as encouraging. Britain's support for the United States' invasion of Grenada was seen by these sources as a devastating blow to that country's prestige and standing in both the Caribbean and Central America, thus frustrating any potential role it

could have played as mediator. Indeed, Britain itself does not see any such possibility as likely, or even desirable.

5. See O. Pinochet de la Barra, 'Algunas Reflexiones Sobre el Problema de la Antártica en el año 2000', in F. Orrego (compilador) *La Antártica y sus Recursos: Problemas Científicos, Jurídicos y Políticos*, Editorial Universitaria, Santiago de Chile, 1983.

6. For an interesting discussion, see T.O. Enders, 'La Crisis del Atlántico Sur, Antecedentes y Consecuencias', in S. Bitar and C. Moneta (compiladores), *Política Económica de Estados Unidos en América Latina: Documentos de la Administración Reagan*, Ediciones GEL, Buenos Aires, 1984.

7. Sepúlveda, op. cit., p. 42.

8. This feeling is shared by academics, diplomats, journalists and civil servants representing all shades of opinion.

9. For a thorough account of Panamanian–North American negotiations over the Panama Canal, see S.S. Rosenfeld, 'The Panama Negotiations: A Close-Run Thing', in *Foreign Affairs*, New York, October 1975, pp. 1–13.

10. See S. Gavenglio, 'Consideraciones Sobre el Retorno al Mar de Bolivia', in *Revista de Estudios Internacionales*, Madrid, July–Sept 1984, pp. 633–49. Also, H. Muñoz, 'Las Relaciones exteriores del Gabierno militar chileno', in J.C. Puig, *América Latina: Políticas exteriores comparadas*, Ediciones GEL, Buenos Aires, 1984, pp. 353–91; A. Varas, 'Política exterior y democracia en Chile', in Puig, op. cit., pp. 392–401; and A. Cole Chamorro, *145 Años de Historia política de Nicaragua*, Managua, Nicaragua, 1967.

11. F. Pike, in Cortada, op. cit., p. 181.

12. Pike, op. cit., pp. 181–211, provides a succinct, clear cut definition of Hispanism.

13. Pike, op. cit., p. 207.

14. See M. Roitman, *La Política del PSOE en América Latina*, Editorial Revolución, Madrid, 1986.

15. Roitman, op. cit., sustains this view.

16. See E.R. Rodríguez, 'Transición a la Democracia en España: Hacia una Nueva Política Iberoamericana?', in *Realidades y Posibilidades de las Relaciones entre España y América Latina en los Ochenta*, Ediciones Cultura Hispánica, ICI, Madrid, 1986, pp. 155–72.

17. See L. Yáñez-Barnuevo, 'Las Relaciones con Iberoamérica en el Horizonte 92', in *Estudios Internacionales 1983*, SEI, Madrid, 1983.

18. Roitman, op. cit.

19. Rodríguez, op. cit., p. 168.

20. See *Resumen de Programas, Programa Integral para Centro-América* and *Proyectos de Cooperación Científico-Técnica*, published by the Instituto de Cooperación Iberoamericana and the Ministerio de Asuntos Exteriores, Madrid, 1984, 1985, 1986.

21. See R. Mesa, 'La Política Exterior en la España Democrática', in *Revista de Estudios Internacionales*, no. 1, 1983, pp. 7–67. Also by the same author in the same 'Política Exterior Española'.

22. For a discussion on the Jewish contribution to the Republican side during the Spanish Civil War, see C. Schindler, 'No Pasarán: The Jews that Fought in Spain', *The Jewish Quarterly*, vol. 33, no. 3 (123), 1986, pp. 34–41.

23. Cortada, op. cit., p. 133.

24. See *Debates de las Cortes* on foreign policy, 1984, p. 3028.

25. See United Nations General Assembly, New York, *Resolutions for the 1955–1986 Period*. Andreas Papandreus' Socialist government in Greece has also adopted pro-Palestinian policies since its election to office.

26. For a discussion of Spanish relations with North Africa and the Middle East, see Shannon Fleming, 'North Africa and the Middle East', in Cortada, op. cit., pp. 121–54.

27. See Fleming, op. cit., p. 145.

28. See *Actividades, Textos y Documentos de la Política Exterior Española* (No. 36, 23.2.1984), published by the Oficina de Información Diplomática of the Spanish Foreign Office.

29. See *El País*, 5 March 1986.

30. Talks with several senior Spanish diplomats tended to confirm this view.

5

Making foreign policy: the institutional framework and the mechanisms of democratic control

The relative continuity of Spanish foreign policy has been considerably helped by the existence of a professional diplomatic apparatus with a role to play in its design and execution. Though, as has already been said, Franco personally supervised foreign policy and was responsible to an important extent for its orientation, he relied heavily on a professional body of diplomats and experts. Working mainly in the Palacio de Santa Cruz, over the years they developed the diplomatic and political expertise which would so significantly facilitate the continuity and, to a lesser extent, the consistency of foreign policy during the transition and under democracy.

The centre of foreign policy design and execution is, of course, the Ministerio de Asuntos Exteriores, also known as the Palacio de Santa Cruz. But it would be a mistake to assume that foreign policy is approached necessarily in an exclusivist, restricted way. Historically, foreign policy has been the area of politics and policy where Francoism was perhaps at its most 'open', with a reasonable degree of debate being tolerated at times, and certainly with more opportunities for public controversy than in any other area of public policy. The contradictions within the regime could not be better exemplified than with the divorce between internal and external policies. This is partly why, after the demise of the Franco regime, while internal politics changed so much, external politics did so only in terms of emphasis, though a more radical shift could be taking place currently under the PSOE government, towards a more pro-Atlantic stand.

While the main impetus came and still comes from the Palacio de Santa Cruz, the nature of foreign policy could, as in any other country, also be determined by the personality of a strong Foreign

Secretary (as in the cases of Castiella, Areilza, Oreja, Morán and Fernández Ordoñez, for example) and a variety of factors such as the state of public opinion (sounded through surveys), the media, and interest group pressures. Furthermore, not only Franco took a personal interest in foreign policy: Prime Ministers under the democratic regime have also done so, and the administrations of Adolfo Suárez and Felipe González are perhaps the most representative of this pattern.

Parliament has also become a major source of foreign policy, not just through its influential Foreign Relations Committee but also in the form of parliamentary debates whose proceedings are generally the matter of public discussion in the media, including television and also through a number of publications and specialized journals.[1] Parliamentarians see their role as one of exercising influence and trying to get policies supported by their parties implemented but, again, strong Chairpersons of the Foreign Relations Committee of the Lower Chamber will be in a position to exercise more influence than weak ones. Miguel Angel Martínez, a PSOE MP with a foreign policy interest who has been Deputy Chairperson and Chairperson of the Foreign Relations Committee of the Cámara de los Diputados, sees Parliament's role as one of both complementing existing policies and as guardian of aspects of it which are of public concern. Important foreign policy issues should consider Parliament's opinion, and Parliament should make its voice heard.[2] In this way, foreign policy under the democratic regime has become one of several general areas of government which are under continuous scrutiny.

However, the configuration of a more 'democratic' or 'progressive' foreign policy has to be considered in relative terms within the context of the traditionally closed internal political regime prevailing under Franco. It is with the inauguration of democracy that foreign policy-makers have opened up more to 'outside' considerations, though some writers still doubt that any significant progressive change has taken place. 'Foreign policy has been historically and in concept a subject which has resisted the penetration of any form of democratic control or participation', states Ramiro Brotons.[3] Furthermore, Roberto Mesa is of the opinion that the decision-making process in foreign relations has evolved from an 'aristocratic' stage, or from a civil service elitism, towards an oligarchical phase where power is concentrated amongst a few persons.[4]

The criticisms by Brotons and Mesa do take the institutions with responsibility on foreign policy in a vacuum, without giving due weight to the considerable degree of change in the Spanish regime in the last few years. In fact, Morales Moya recognizes the relativity of any analysis of this issue when he states that, 'certainly, nobody disputes the competence of the Foreign Service to carry out foreign policy'.[5] This has certainly been the case under both Franco and the democratic regime.

Morales Moya's analysis is a reflection more on the professional expertise and competence of the Spanish Foreign Service than on the democratic nature of foreign policy design and execution. The question that should be formulated here is whether it is fair to ask the Foreign Service of any country to stick to a democratic generation of its policies, or to forms of democratic control. The answer is that very probably no country in the world can afford to open up completely its foreign policy apparatus to democratic control. This fact does not preclude, however, the need for the existence of mechanisms to take into account certain democratic features such as public opinion, expert advice outside the foreign policy bureaucracy, parliamentary thinking, and legitimate pressure groups interests. In this sense, though, Mesa's criticism that the process of foreign policy decision-making in Spain has evolved from an aristocratic or elitist stage to one characterized by the concentration of powers amongst experts or/and departments is true only to a limited extent.[6] There does seem to be agreement on the fact that Franco himself retained considerable powers in foreign policy, an area which attracted him, and that an 'elitist' concentration of power developed together with the progress of Fernando Castiella's influence in the Palacio de Santa Cruz. The inauguration of the transition to democracy and, moreover, of a rather sophisticated and modern parliamentary system, however, changed the terms of reference of the foreign policy debate and also of policy decision-making, none of which can be ignored.

Among the pattern changes which have been prompted by democracy, the following ones have unavoidably affected the way in which foreign policy issues are debated and decisions taken:

1.   *A significant degree of openness on controversial foreign policy issues.* It is enough to open any Madrid, Barcelona, or even less important newspapers in a remote provincial town, to realize that the 'elitism' referred to by Mesa has given way to a healthy tendency to air

publicly important foreign policy issues. Examples abound, but the recent NATO debate, the contentious relations between Morocco and Spain, the controversy over the American bases, and the successful establishment of diplomatic relations with Israel, are fresh prototypes of a new democratic spirit around the generation of foreign policy. It would be wrong to assume that no influence has been exercised on the decision-making apparatus by the exercise of permanent and open debate. In fact, if it is accepted that Spain has left behind most of the pernicious ingredients of authoritarianism, and that the modern and democratic value-system of its political elites is reasonably imbued with and identi-fies with the new liberal democratic regime, it cannot be argued at the same time that foreign policy has remained impervious to these changes. This institutional stubbornness would require an ideo-logical vacuum that is impossible to find in a parliamentary democracy, where parties and groups compete eagerly for influ-ence and power. Ultimately, the airing of issues at the various societal levels (the media, universities, the State bureaucracy, political parties, interest groups) and the exercise of their influence throughout the means open to them make it impossible for any institution to remain free from the pressures that ensue.

2.   *The politicization of foreign policy through parliamentary scrutiny.* Though the design and execution of foreign policy has been, and still is, the almost exclusive domain of the Foreign Ministry, it would be erroneous to disregard the influence which Parliament can and does exercise in this area. Under Franco, or under the still uncertain new parliamentary institutions of the transition, it could be argued that foreign policy had been an area of interest to but a few, or that the strong personalities of Franco and Adolfo Suárez pre-empted real forms of democratic participation and/or control in the foreign policy area.

The development of a vigorous parliamentary system has ended to an important extent the relative secrecy surrounding foreign policy that existed before, though public discussion was not uncommon then anyway. The Foreign Affairs Committee of the Cámara de los Diputados has over the last five years built up considerable powers of persuasion over both the political and policy-making spheres at the Palacio de Santa Cruz and the Palacio de la Moncloa. All parties have appointed to this Committee some of their best parliamentarians, in many cases people with strong backgrounds in academia and long-standing connections in foreign affairs.[7]

3.   *The development of a critical ethos at various levels of Spanish society, especially in the sectors of the media, the trade unions and the educational/ cultural world.* It is essential to give weight to these three elements in any modern, reasonably effective democracy, complementing as they do the more traditional and generally expected role allocated to the democratic/bureaucratic institutions (Parliament, ministries, political parties, judiciary). Together with the informal instances of influence and power (issue-related interest groups—gays, women, peace, animal liberation, environment, Third World development), they constitute indispensable elements through which important currents of opinion are articulated. Put together, these are factors which have a varying, but significant, degree of influence on foreign policy. If the example of the critical role of the media is considered, for example, just a fair assessment of the Madrid daily *El País* will show the extent to which a national daily newspaper can perform considerable influence on foreign policy through its editorial policy or through first-rate international coverage and continued assessments of governmental intentions and directions on foreign policy. *Diario 16* and *ABC* confirm this pattern of highly critical media and subsequently the view that, as a whole, the media in contemporary Spain perform a more influential role than they did under Franco. As in other features of the current parliamentary system, Spain exhibits striking similarities with the older democracies of Western Europe and the existence of a solid, highly confident media system is perhaps one of the most notable of these features.

The trade-union movement is another example worth mentioning of groups outside the Palacio de Santa Cruz who can and do exercise influence on foreign policy. The fact that the two main trade-union organizations are controlled by the PSOE and the PCE is not entirely irrelevant. Furthermore, the Communist-controlled Comisiones Obreras has played an active role in organizing pressure to get certain policies implemented, as in the cases of the NATO debate and referendum (calling for a 'no' vote), the American bases in Spain (encouraging the dismantling of as many bases as possible), and diplomatic recognition of Israel (asking for the withdrawal of Israeli troops from Arab territories and Israeli acceptance of the Palestinians' rights to self-determination as a pre-condition). The Socialist-controlled UGT, though generally supportive of the government, has adopted an independent course on several issues, some of them within the foreign policy area. Leaders of UGT have used their influence, for example, to strengthen the Spanish government's actions on Nicaragua and the Contadora group, and were also important in encouraging mutual diplomatic recognition between Spain and Israel.[8] Though their influence should not be exaggerated, it is a factor of relative importance, at least in relation to certain issues.

Academia is an area in which the PSOE has been strongly represented. After all, the PSOE leadership was nurtured in the universities and in writers' and artists' associations, though always closely linked to the clandestine trade unions, which would provide the much needed mass support when the Francoist repression made it impossible to engage in open, democratic politics of any sort. Ironically, it has been in the very places were opposition to Francoism began to be organized and where it was given its meaning that criticisms of the PSOE's foreign policy have become most articulate and influential. Though, of course, the Palacio de Santa Cruz recruited, after the PSOE victory, some of the universities' best intellectuals as advisers and diplomats, others remained in academic life. These are now becoming increasingly critical of aspects of foreign policy, and it should be recognized that it would be impossible for some of their views, at least, not to have been taken on board. The writings and lectures of Roberto Mesa, Francisco Aldecoa and Marcos Roitman at the Universidad Complutense de Madrid, for example, are clear examples of informed criticism, which will no doubt eventually exercise some, as yet imprecise, influence on Spanish foreign policy. The access of Spanish academics to the national media further increases their relative weight in foreign policy-making. In addition, their expertise is required and used by the various committees in the Foreign Office and Parliament. Lately, the appointment of Julián Santa María, formerly at the Universidad Complutense and the Instituto de Investigaciones Sociológicas de la Presidencia del Gobierno, as Ambassador to Washington adds to the mounting evidence of the Spanish government's receptive stance to academic opinion and cooperation.

4. *The increasing importance of 'multilateral diplomacy'.* The growing sophistication of foreign policy-making is demonstrated by the

proliferation of organizations of various kinds, both outside and inside many countries' foreign offices. Beside the professional institutions which carry out foreign policy on behalf of governments, a host of institutions has been developing since the Second World War, sometimes belonging to larger international organizations (the United Nations, regional/continental political bodies)— a factor which significantly complicates the management of international affairs by nations. These institutions normally specialize in specific areas and over the years have acquired varying degrees of autonomy and even financial self-sufficiency. They often run their affairs independently of both governments and the larger organization to which they belong. The Economic Commission for Latin American (ECLA), UNESCO, UNISEF, and FAO are just some examples of autonomous international organizations with considerable power in this respect. Strong technocratic bureaucracies have gradually imprinted these bodies with a modernizing, seemingly politically neutral value-system, but in fact they are generally Third Worldist, developmentalist and redistributive.

The need to work with these institutions can put tremendous demands on the traditional foreign office, whose main dealings in the past have been with old-fashioned chancelleries still nostalgic about the Treaty of Versailles and the League of Nations. The democratization/modernization of Spanish society has brought about corresponding changes within the Spanish Foreign Office, which has diversified its operations accordingly. Furthermore, 'the present reality is that a considerably number of ministries invade the areas of competence of the Foreign Office. These can assume the form of overlapping of functions, even to the extent of replacing the Foreign Office in international conferences'.[9] The multilaterality of modern foreign relations, therefore, does not only bring about the need for a more professional foreign service; it also puts new demands on it, and opens the way for competition with other extensions of state power which increasingly assume foreign policy responsibilities.

The democratic changes introduced with the inauguration of the parliamentary monarchy have no doubt also brought about a number of institutional changes within the Spanish Foreign Office, so as to make it more equipped to cope with the demands of an increasing multilateral diplomacy. These changes have had to take into account the preoccupation with foreign affairs evident in the 1978 Constitution. Indeed, few modern European constitutions show such a degree of concern with foreign relations (only the Swedish Constitution could be considered more specific on this account). Though, according to some critics, the 1978 Spanish Constitution has followed the ambiguity of other constitutions in its treatment of foreign relations, an examination of it shows that it is in this fundamental charter of rights and duties that an account of the allocation of powers on foreign affairs is in fact to be found.[10] Though distributed throughout the text, the norms on foreign affairs are clear, and demonstrate a genuine concern by Spanish parliamentarians about the status of the State's international relations. Among the aspects covered by the Constitution, the most relevant are:

(a) Recognition of the participation of the Cortes in the elaboration and signature of treaties (articles 93–94);
(b) the effects of treaties on internal politics/policies (article 96.1);
(c) the intervention of the Cortes in the denunciation, and abrogation, of treaties (article 96.2);
(d) limitation of scope, style and content of international treaties to those expressly allowed by the Constitution (article 95.1);
(e) the possibility of a referendum on important issues, including sometimes those within the area of international relations (article 92).

All these points constitute important instruments of democratic control of foreign policy and give enough scope, if government so wishes, to introduce a significant degree of popular participation in foreign affairs. The relevance of these constitutional guarantees for a more open foreign policy design and execution was especially in evidence when the referendum on NATO membership was carried out in 1986. Had these articles not been written down in the 1978 Constitution, the PSOE government could have easily asked simply for parliamentary approval regarding a decision about NATO. Indeed, the government would have gained such approval without major problems. As it happened, the existence of article 87.3 of the Constitution, which more or less excludes what could be termed 'popular' or 'direct' initiatives on foreign affairs, was not invoked by the PSOE government, which preferred to stick to its original promise to consult the voters on any new proposed course on NATO.

The use of the referendum as a legitimate tool, even on foreign policy matters, is an important instrument open to governments in

Spain, with which they can challenge occasional political problems in Parliament or search for categorical public sanctioning of controversial measures. The only limitation is that the issue to be presented for popular choice has to be deemed to be of 'special importance'. Of course, anything can be of 'special importance' if the President of the government so thinks. The approval of Congress, though required, is token. As the initiative has to come exclusively from the President of the government, its use will depend as much on the prevailing political climate as on the personality of the leader of the party in government. The NATO referendum offers two contrasting examples of differing attitudes by two Heads of Governments. While in 1981 President Leopoldo Calvo Sotelo refused to submit Spain's original admission to NATO to a referendum, in 1986 Felipe González did just that, when his government decided to clarify the status of Spanish membership. Calvo Sotelo resisted all pressures to consult the populace, amidst ferocious press criticism, a national campaign of signatures, and even considerable parliamentary dissent, including that within his own party, the Union of the Democratic Centre. The temptation to repeat this behaviour was in fact evident at various levels of the PSOE structure, and in the Santa Cruz Palace, but the prevailing view was that the party had to honour its promise and risk the consequences.[11]

The potential use of the Cortes to exercise forms of democratic control of foreign policy is not, on balance, severely limited by the popular referendum. As any one-party, a democratic government will stay in power as long as it has a one-party majority in Parliament, referenda are likely to be held only if the issue in question is of such importance that direct popular sanction is considered necessary to legitimize it, reinforcing the approval that Parliament would grant anyway. A more unlikely scenario is one of a government in trouble with its own majority having to go over it, to overcome it. In any case, it is the Cortes which retains much of the bargaining power because of its constitutional faculties on treaties.

The autonomous communities and foreign policy

Articles 94 and 95 of the Constitution allow for competence in the negotiation and sanctioning of international treaties to be shared by the executive and legislative branches of government. However, there are legal instruments which diffuse and confuse these functions. The creation of autonomous regions (comunidades autonómicas) with a variety of powers, brought about by democratic rule, included a number of powers in the area of international relations. These appear on the surface to be contradicted by article 97 of the Constitution, which grants the 'government' (in its broadest meaning, and apparently not excluding Parliament) the main responsibility of foreign policy, and by article 149.1.3, which gives 'the State' exclusive competence for its execution. Closer scrutiny of the existing legislation proves this impression erroneous.

The Statute of Autonomy (Estatuto de Autonomía) for the Basque country, for example,[12] gives the autonomous region the power to ask the central government to discuss and send projects to the Cortes, if these are in any way related to the preservation of the cultural heritage and/or identity of Basque communities, or foreign nationals with a Basque background abroad.[13]

Articles 20.3 and 20.5 take this participatory power in foreign policy for the autonomous Basque region even further. They in fact give the Basque country the power to discuss and sign treaties and agreements with other countries, as granted in the Estatuto, with the only limitations established by the national constitution. The Estatuto also compels central government to inform the Basque government of any projects, treaties and agreements, including customs regulations, when these are of specific interest to the Basque country.

The Estatutos for Catalonia, Galicia, Andalusia, Cantabria, La Riojo, Valencia, Aragón, Castilla-La Mancha, Canary Islands, Extremadura, the Balearic Islands, Madrid, Castille-Léon, and the Organic Law for the reincorporation and improvement of the representative system in Navarre (*régimen foral de Navarra*), all accord wide-ranging foreign policy powers to the autonomous regions of Spain.[14] Though in all cases these powers are significantly limited by the national constitution, they nevertheless represent a form of democratic control of foreign policy with particular relevance to the autonomous regions. By granting the autonomous regions these legal powers, the State is accepting a limitation of its hitherto indiscriminate, and non-democratic, domination of foreign policy design and execution, to an extent which is quite unprecedented elsewhere. The scope of the foreign policy powers of the autonomous regions is equivalent in fact to the recognition, in principle, of the legitimacy of popular participation in that area of policy, and should not be dismissed as entirely irrelevant.

It is true that there is a degree of ambiguity regarding the foreign policy discretions of the autonomous regions, and criticisms have not been scarce because of it.[15] Ultimately, of course, these ambiguities can only be solved by resorting to the national constitutional text. But, as has been stated, the foreign policy powers of the autonomous communities 'will depend in the medium and long term on the Communities' own vitality, and on the capacity and readiness of the Central administration to absolve and to integrate initiatives and projects of mutual benefit'.[16]

The complexities of multilateral diplomacy

The increasing complexity of international relations has been exacerbated, as has been mentioned before, by the proliferation of international organizations of various kinds, most of which have been able to develop their own areas of expertise and legal discretion. The inauguration of the parliamentary monarchy in Spain made possible the adaptation of the foreign policy apparatus in Madrid to this new, highly sophisticated network of international organizations. This is a departure from patterns existing under Franco. The main problems for multilateral diplomacy under Franco were:

(a) the exclusion of Spain from the main international organizations of a regional character (European Economic Community, the Council of Europe, the North Atlantic Treaty Organization) and, up to the mid-1950s, from the United Nations and United Nations' specialized agencies;

(b) the late incorporation of Spain into the United Nations and the host of United Nations' specialized organizations, followed by reluctant acceptance by other member countries and consequent mutual distrust; and

(c) the conditioning of Spanish actions within multilateral organizations by the internal and external needs of the Franco regime, giving shape to what has been called 'unidimensionality' in foreign policy: a desperation to break up Spain's isolation and to ensure the survival of the regime, above any other considerations.

Democracy brought about considerable changes. These can be summarized as follows:

(a) the limitations of isolationism, a direct consequence of Spain's unpopularity among the family of nations involved in the anti-Fascist war, all but disappeared; 'isolation' gave way to gradual 'participation';

(b) Spain began to pursue a more active foreign policy and even become 'fashionable';

(c) it became more or less evident that Spain, though not a 'big power', could claim to be an intermediate power of regional influence, a product of the country's historical, cultural and certainly geographical configuration. The Arab countries, Africa and Latin America were to be the areas where these singularities would be more in evidence, extending a role also performed by Franco's diplomacy. In addition, pro-European policies would also develop hand-in-hand with democracy;

(d) the international/multilateral organizations seemed especially suited for democratic Spain to develop a dynamic diplomacy;

(e) the modernization of Spanish society seemed to go hand-in-hand with the kind of support that international organizations could provide. The main aim of most of these organizations is, in fact, to provide logistical, financial and planning support for the modernization of traditional, or non-modern, societies, which suited the new Spanish elites very well.

The importance of multilateral diplomacy in the contemporary world is such that no country with any pretension to influence in international relations can afford to ignore it.

The demands of multilateral diplomacy have created the need for a readaptation of the foreign policy apparatus in the Palacio de Santa Cruz. Though, as under Franco, the Ministerio de Asuntos Exteriores kept for itself and the Foreign Secretary overall control of foreign policy, a number of *ad hoc* bodies to advise, design and even execute policies have been created over the years. These bureaucratic structures, normally manned by career diplomats, work in conjunction with similar bodies in other ministries. Earlier in this chapter, reference was made to the participation in the foreign policy area of other ministerial departments; multilateral diplomacy is perhaps the area where there is more scope for inter-departmental collaboration. The Labour Ministry, for example, will be normally involved in issues on which the International Labour Organization (ILO) is involved, while the Ministry of Education and the Ministry of Culture will have to deal with any business involving UNESCO, and the Agriculture Ministry with issues involving FAO. In all these cases, the Foreign Office will always coordinate, thus maintaining overall control. Such coordination gives the Foreign Service bureaucracy greater legal powers than are on the surface apparent, such as to:

(a) communicate officially with all international organizations;
(b) appoint and brief the delegations to conferences organized by international organizations;
(c) appoint representatives to regular meetings of the various specialized working groups in international organizations;
(d) organize and brief *ad hoc* teams preparing to attend meetings, including representatives of the various ministries;
(e) channel political and/or other instructions to delegates, irres-pective of the ministry to which they belong.

The design and implementation of policies in multilateral/inter-national organizations require a rather elaborate bureaucratic struc-ture. The Spanish Foreign Office has over the years created a number of such bodies which can be grouped into two broad categories: (a) the Dirección General de Organizaciones y Con-ferencias Internacionales (Central Office for International Organizations and Conferences), with overall administrative competence in this area; and (b) several *ad hoc* departments with competence in geographical and subject areas (cultural, agri-cultural, defence, etc.).

The development of degrees of independence by these special-ized structures has been significantly affected by the devolution of international operational powers to the autonomous communities. Many of the functions now entrusted to the communities used to be within the area of control of these ministerial bodies. The incorporation of new, highly qualified technocratic cadres to the permanent staff of ministries has also contributed to the diminu-tion in quality and quantity of the powers enjoyed by the Foreign Office. The new technocracy in ministries other than Foreign

Affairs tends increasingly to question, or ignore, the traditional control over foreign relations exercised by the Palacio de Santa Cruz.[17] Multilateral diplomacy has thus provided more opportunities for controlling the Foreign Office's apparent monopoly over foreign policy. Indirectly, then, technocratic meddling from a variety of ministries and other governmental agencies is yet another mechanism of democratic control, as it further increases a certain diversification in the design and implementation of specific policies. The increasing complexity of multilateral diplomacy makes it even more likely that these participatory trends become the rule rather than the exception in future. As time passes, personalist or authoritarian models of foreign policy management will become more difficult to carry out. Consultation and technical participation in the generation of foreign policies are a *sine qua non* prerequisite of an efficient, modern Foreign Office. As will be seen next, the area of defence provides a further example of the intertwining of bureaucratic powers, with positive results in terms of democratic control on some occasions, but rather undesirable outcomes on others.

Defence, national security, and diplomacy

There is a close relationship between 'national defence' and foreign policy, and this is why in most countries there is a working relationship between the ministries in charge of both areas.

The importance of defence in Spanish foreign policy by no means necessarily singles that country out as unique among the family of nations. However, the special nature of the geo-political position of Spain creates all the conditions for a close relationship between defence and foreign policy factors.

Spain's friendship has been assiduously cultivated by the United States, precisely in recognition of the strategic role attributed to it by Western military strategists. Geographically, Spain is the bridge between Europe and Africa, borders the British enclave of Gibraltar at her African door (including substantial naval facilities), and possesses two access towns, Ceuta and Melilla, next-door to important northern African countries (Morocco, Tunisia, Algeria and Libya). Furthermore, Spanish territory is covered by American military, naval and air bases, a subject which is currently at the centre of political debate in Spain, and which will be discussed at length in this book in Chapter 7, on NATO. In addition, and as has been seen earlier, Spain has kept a historically close, friendly relationship with the Arab world and a marked antagonism towards Israel (though mutual recognition in 1986 is clearly changing this pattern), the most important ally of the United States in the Middle East. Last, but not least, Spain systematically opposed North American attempts to blockade Cuba in the 1960s and Chile in the 1970s, and in fact traded with both countries and provided various kinds of support at the peak of the United States' political and economic embargo.

It would have been impossible for Spain to stick to most, if not all, of these independent outlooks in foreign policy, at least under Franco, had it not been for the nationalist, somehow neutralist views of her military with regard to some of the most contentious issues of the Cold War. Critics can attribute this to the neo-Fascist leanings of sectors of the Spanish armed forces, an inheritance of the pro-Axis years of the Second World War. This may or may not be the case, but the paradoxical result has been that as a consequence an important Western nation has been able to formulate a foreign policy with distinctly independent features. These policies have positioned Spain considerably to the left of most other Western European countries on such issues as Third World development, South Africa, national liberation movements, Cuban—American relationships, Central America, Chile under Allende and Pinochet, decolonization, and the Middle East conflict.

The importance of the defence establishment in the formulation of foreign policy in Spain is such that the one area where the Socialist government has concentrated with unmitigated vigour in order to reform it has been the armed forces. This is not to say that the programme of 'modernization' of the armed forces has been prompted by the need to separate defence from foreign policy (indeed, the causes are as much internal as external), but one of the end results will no doubt be the modernization and political neutralization of most military structures and their isolation as a factor of undue influence on foreign policy. Perhaps the internal dimension of military powers in Spain, their traditional, even self-conscious, role as one of the pillars of the Franco regime, and the use of their repressive powers (as important as those of the two national police forces) to restrain and silence opposition have relegated to second place the more subconscious, but nevertheless tremendously important role they have performed and still perform, in foreign policy-making. They themselves have put it in no uncertain terms: 'The basic means [to sustain a policy of security, the core of any foreign policy] are two: a first step which is negotiation, in other words, diplomacy; and a second step which is more convincing and definitive, the Armed Forces, as at the end of the day the Armies are always the main instrument of foreign policy . . .'.[18]

The direct link between military attachés in Spanish embassies and the armed forces of foreign countries means that certain aspects of Spanish foreign policy can, at the discretion of the Spanish Foreign Office be redirected to the Ministry of Defence. Of course, Spain is no different from other countries, which by and large subscribe to the model of direct military-to-military links covering such matters as information on technological advances, cooperation in maneouvres, state of preparedness, and espionage matters. Where the armed forces have been historically under the control and scrutiny of civilian and democratic government, such contacts tend to be under scrupulous civilian control, be it through the foreign services, parliamentary committees or others. But where they have been historically supportive of, and involved with, an authoritarian regime, and have developed significant autonomy *vis-à-vis* the military's international links, problems can arise.

The Spanish military do perceive their role in an international context, and it is not yet clear that the democratic routines and institutions of the last ten years have in fact permeated them.[19] They have a rather broad view of their role regarding such issues as the renegotiations over the American bases, and the more general problem of the strategic importance of Spain as a Western nation with strong links with the Arab world. They also view with preoccupation the geographical proximity of Spain to Africa, and the eventual protagonism that this could create in the eventuality of a global conflict.

In general terms, the military define the concept of 'international military relations' with a specificity that cannot always be apprehended by the civilian population, who in any democratic country should control them. The suspicion also arises that the military are not completely aware, nor do they approve, of the need ultimately to submit defence matters to democratic control.

Within what they call 'specific military relations' it is possible to find considerable scope for ambiguity, and areas of foreign policy which should be primarily the political, expert or bureaucratic responsibility of civilian cadres could easily be taken over by the military.[20]

'Specific military relations' exist when the 'Spanish Armed Forces have important interests in another country, or vice versa. Normally, interest is reciprocal . . . appears then a new element, the military attaché, in charge of the military relations between the two countries . . .'.[21] Problems can develop if these military relations take place with military forces of countries with which the civilian government has no special affinity, or with which there are disagreements on matters of specific policies. The declared support by the PSOE government, for example, for the Contadora group's efforts to stabilize the Central American conflict could run into contradictions if the Spanish military maintain too close a relationship with one side, to the detriment of the other. In the specific case of Central America, this can limit what the military attaché can do, and also what the government can do, in terms of relations with the Central American armed forces, lest the political will of the government be distorted. Or, equally possible though more unlikely, the military might develop a set of relationships that run contrary to government policies on certain issues. When there are special military relations because of the existence of a treaty or a military alliance, the complications are potentially even more ominous. Pardo de Santillana writes that

the common denominator . . . in these cases . . . is of mixed committees integrated by representatives of the two countries. These committees can have a permanent status, or can have an *ad hoc* capacity. They can also be civilian—military, or exclusively military in composition . . . The Chiefs of Staff can also be in contact, and various linkage structures are established.[22]

The existence of military categories of 'friendly countries' and 'countries which are potential enemies' should not go unnoticed, especially so in a country like Spain, which has only recently shifted a hitherto non-Atlantic, somehow neutralist foreign policy towards distinctly pro-European and pro-North American policies.[23] As will be seen later the military treaties with the United States created a system of dependency of the Spanish military upon American military technology and American military training. This is not to say that the Spanish military became in any way subservient or unduly attached to United States military institutions or, even less, to United States strategic goals. The evidence in fact points out to quite the opposite: the persistence of a rather independent, equidistant outlook during the Cold War among the Spanish military. Whether this was an inheritance of the Falangist era or the genuine development of an independent political ethos is hard to say.[24]

However, the continued Spain–United States military relationship could not have passed the test of so many years without having influenced in some way at least a generation of army, air force and naval officers. The pro-NATO drive of the PSOE government was prompted, according to some military strategists, as much by the 'European vocation' of the political team in power as by the need to integrate the Spanish military into the Western defence system. In doing this the government was probably taking a gamble, though, because for purely technocratic reasons most of the military would probably favour NATO membership. But there are still ideological reservations, a kind of nostalgia for the 'old times' of Spain's 'neutrality' under Franco, which of course the United States bases disowned.

The programme of modernization of the armed forces being undertaken by the PSOE government is, according to experts, a euphemism for a massive attempt to depoliticize them. Better still, it would be the first structural scheme ever undertaken in a Western democracy to instil democratic values to the armed forces as a means to eliminate the authoritarian remnants, inherited in the Spanish case from Francoism. NATO membership is, within this context, both a scheme to make the Spanish armed forces more efficient and to take their minds off the internal political arena, making them instead share responsibility for the collective 'defence of Europe' and a modern, democratic value-system.

The modernization programme has brought about not only a reduction in military personnel but a higher degree of selectivity in the purchase of military equipment. This has resulted in a word of 'caution' from high-ranking officers who have become suspicious of the appearance of pro-disarmament tendencies in the political establishment. According to Pardo de Santillana:

This is a new subject, and a very important one at that, especially for the military, requiring deep research and continued observation, in order to be able to evaluate the consequences for national security which political decisions adopted on such a polemic issue, could have. These types of decisions are easily adopted demagogically.[25]

The uneasiness of the military when 'political' variables are introduced can be better appreciated when Pardo de Santillana states that policies to limit the acquisition of armaments and disarmament policies have a 'special politico-military character; they cannot be conceived as military relations under political control, nor as political relations with consultation of the military. The interdependence between both should be constant, close and reciprocal'.[26] The ambiguity is probably not conscious, but it is, however, present in the official text—a reflection perhaps of the increasing complexity of foreign policy when military matters are of relevance.

The participation of the military as political strategists is as debatable and controversial as the pretension of politicians to become involved in operational defence planning and execution. The line between pure politics, diplomacy and defence is unavoidably thin. But whereas this is a problem that does not need to become an obsession in countries with long-standing democratic regimes, a solid tradition of military professionalism and (at least with the evidence in hand) an apolitical general outlook, problems can arise in countries, as with Spain, whose armed forces have identified themselves with an authoritarian value-system and a dictatorial, personalist regime.

The intertwining of defence and foreign relations makes the subject a difficult one in terms of civilian—military relations. The technological specificity of defence matters creates a sense of isolation, inadequacy and ignorance in the civilian echelons of power, and a reluctant perception that these are issues better left to 'experts'. The risk of inaction, or abrogation of responsibilities, is always ominously present.

The complexity of the defence—foreign affairs relationship and the institutional influence of the defence bureaucracy on certain aspects of foreign policy are exacerbated by the strategic geographical position of Spain and the persistence of a number of issues as major factors in determining the orientations of foreign policy. The President of the current Government, Felipe González, offered ten issues as the core of Spanish defence policy when he talked to the Spanish Parliament in October 1984. These issues, however, cannot stand on their own. On the contrary, they have to be understood within the wider historical framework of Spain's importance to the Western military alliance and her equally historical reluctance to commit herself totally to such an alliance. The ten issues mentioned by González are:

1. maintenance of Spain's membership in the Atlantic Alliance:
2. Spain's non-incorporation into the integrated military organization of the Alliance;
3. the reduction of the North American military presence in Spain;
4. the reaffirmation of the non-nuclearization of Spanish territory;
5. non-adhesion, for the time being, to the Non-proliferation Treaty;
6. an interest in Spain's eventual adhesion to the West European Union, under certain conditions;
7. the definitive solution of the Gibraltar issue;
8. maintenance and reinforcement of Spain's policy within the disarmament fora;
9. continuation of Spain's policy focused towards the establishment of a network of cooperation agreements within the field of defence with other Western European countries;
10. finally, a point of exclusive Spanish domestic policy that states that the elaboration of the Joint Strategic Plan must also be included in the dialogue offered to the Spanish parliamentary parties, in order to achieve the consensus referred to above.[27]

The nature of the issues mentioned by Felipe González are all within what would generally be defined as 'security policy'. As such, it would have been unthinkable for him and his advisers not to have consulted the military. Indeed, the inclusion of such long-standing problems as Gibraltar and the American bases on Spanish territory among the ten central 'security' matters, reveals the presence of professional military advice. The strategic importance of Gibraltar in any global or regional armed conflict is historically recognized by military strategists, and certainly by Spanish military strategists.[28]

The military hand cannot be ignored, either, when more 'technical' issues are at stake. The deployment or non-deployment of intermediate ballistic systems in Western Europe, controlled by the United States, is one such issue. However, to pretend that this is purely a security matter where exclusively operational aspects are involved would be a mistake. Indeed, this is a highly political issue and one where the civilian exercise of democratic control would be more than justified.

The Spanish military are, according to reliable information, eager to secure the installation of an intermediate ballistic system in Western Europe, and the participation of Spain is not ruled out. This would, however, run contrary to the anti-nuclear policy of the present Spanish government, though there have been several signs of a shift lately. 'Theoretical' studies on the use of nuclear armaments have been carried out by the military in Spain, according to Defence Minister, Narcis Serra. He denied that these exercises would in any way be construed as training in the use of tactical nuclear weapons and revealed that the first military texts on the use of atomic armament in Spain dated back to 1956. The ambiguity of the current position is not helped by statements that contradict one another, however, as when Serra himself added that he contemplated the development of all defence systems, faced with the dangers of hypothetical chemical or atomic aggressions: 'I do not believe they will ever come, but we have to be prepared'.[29] Furthermore, press reports in 1986 and 1987 have shown increasing preoccupation by the Spanish government *vis-à-vis* the nuclear issue. In most cases these reports have confirmed that the non-signature of the Non-proliferation Treaty (known as the Tatlelolco agreement) by Spain symbolizes that country's confidence in terms of atomic technology. Western analysts agree that Spain's decision not to exclude itself from its status as a potential member of the exclusive atomic club of nations is prompted by two main factors: (a) her possession of the technology necessary to produce nuclear armaments; and (b) the pressures by the military establishment on politicians not to abrogate that potential by becoming a member of the Non-proliferation Treaty (NPT).[30] The latest information suggests, though, that the NPT will be signed by Spain after all. A new change of heart, however, can not be discounted.

Spain's reluctance to guarantee a non-nuclear future is in sharp contrast to her declared goals regarding the non-nuclear character of the Spanish territory, and the potential conflict this position could create with the United States. This dichotomy reflects the dual civilian–military nature of security policy and the unavoidable contradictions that will develop from time to time. According to experts quoted by the reputable Spanish daily, *El País*: 'North American ships with nuclear arms routinely make stops at Spanish ports'. The information only confirmed what has been known for years: that the United States has used several Spanish ports for stopovers by North American military ships, especially at Palma de Mallorca, Málaga, Cádiz and Benidorm, all of them important tourist spots. According to extremely reliable sources, the wording of the referendum specifically left the door open for the American ships to use Spanish ports even when they were carrying nuclear weapons: 'The President of the Government did not want to find himself in the same position as the socialist government of New Zealand, when it forbade the use of New Zealand by United States' ships carrying nuclear weapons'.[31]

The authorization to allow nuclear-armed and nuclear-propelled ships to use Spanish ports is the prerogative of a mixed civilian–military committee made up of both Spanish and North American representatives, being the ideal set-up for the exercise of military influence. The 'technical' character of such operations is likely to deter civilian members from using their discretionary powers. The Joint Committee for Political, Military and Administrative matters (Comité Conjunto para Asuntos Políticos, Militares y Administrativos—CCPMA) is perhaps the most important of all the *ad hoc*, civilian–military, Spanish–North American institutions created to oversee and control the complex, mixed defence and security system in which the two countries are partners. The Committee also controls the use of Spanish air space by foreign, especially North American, military aircraft, and the facilities offered by and to the North American military, naval, and air-force bases. The fact that there are two Spanish members and two North American members is indicative of the weight given to the foreign counterpart by the Spanish government. Furthermore, the Committee is not normally subjected to direct parliamentary (or parliamentary committee) control, and its decisions would not normally even go on to consultation with the President of the government, though it is likely that, at least in some cases, the Defence and/or the Foreign Secretary would be in some way involved.[32]

The initial Socialist promise to study sympathetically the possible signature of the NPT, included in the electoral platform of 1982, has been alternately ignored and recognized. After confirming his government's intention to sign the treaty (on the occasion of his first parliamentary address) Felipe González' position changed only one year later, when the government informed the Cortes (in October 1983) that 'this problem requires a great dose of caution'.[33] The reason given was that signature of the treaty would limit Spain's possible manufacture and acquisition of nuclear propelled naval equipment. Clearly, this change of policy was motivated at least as much by military planning as by political expedience. Some cynical point of view put to this author by an unexpected source was that the change of heart was a clear-cut case of military pressure on the government, and one that no government could afford to resist.[34] In this way, the Spanish Parliament was excluded from practising any form of democratic control on such an important policy issue, and the military were able to exercise significant influence on the shape of a very important aspect of foreign policy.

The announcement by the government of its intention to become a member of the NPT, made at the beginning of 1987, registers yet another shift in policy which only confirms the delicate interplay between military influence and civilian control of defence matters. It is thought that military fears of possible limitations to Spain's atomic potential by signing the treaty were weakened by a careful process of clarification. After all, there are numerous aspects of atomic activities which can still be carried out under the NPT.

Notes

1. See *Revista de Estudios Internacionales*, vol. 5, no. 1, Jan.–March 1984. Also, *Leviatán (Revista de Hechos e Ideas)*, Summer 1984, Il Época, no. 16, and *Afers Internacionals*, Autumn–Winter 1985.
2. Miguel Angel Martínez, MP, in interview with B. Pollack, 1984.
3. See Antonio Morales Moya, 'Relaciones Internacionales y Función Diplomática en la Historia Contemporánea' (quoting Antonio Remiro Brotons), in *Documentación Administrativa*, 205, Julio–Septiembre 1985, p.46. A detailed discussion of the State's functions in foreign policy is provided by Antonio Remiro Brotons, *La Acción Exterior del Estado*, Tecnos, Madrid, 1984.
4. Roberto Mesa, quoted by A. Morales Moya, op.cit., p. 46.
5. See ICI, *Realidades y Posibilidades de las Relaciones entre España y América Latina en los Ochenta*, Ediciones Cultura Hispánica, Madrid, 1986.
6. Mesa, quoted by Morales Moya, op.cit., p. 46.

7. Examples worth mentioning are those of Javier Rupérez, Manuel Medina and Miguel Angel Martínez, among others.

8. There had been contacts and links of various kinds between the Spanish Socialist-controlled trade union, UGT, and the Israeli united trade union organization, Histadrut, for many years before diplomatic relations were formally established between Spain and Israel. The Socialist International provided additional opportunities for high-level contacts between members of the PSOE and the Israeli Mapai party. Furthermore, a close friendship is said to have developed between Felipe González and Shimon Peres during the years of shared experiences within the Socialist International. González visited Israel long before his party was a serious contender for power in Spain, and certainly when relations between the two countries were far from good.

9. Mesa, quoted by Morales Moya, op.cit., p. 47.

10. A critical view on the limitations of foreign policy design is put forward by Antonio Remiro Brotons in 'El Poder del Estado', *Documentación Administrativa*, 205, op.cit., pp. 53–90.

11. Conversations between B. Pollack and Juan Domingo Yánez, Ángel Viñas, Manuel Medina, Miguel Angel Martínez and Julián Santa María in 1984 and 1986.

12. Ley Orgánica (Organic Law) 3/18, December 1979.

13. Article 6.5 of the Estatuto de Autonomía para el País Vasco, Ley Orgánica, 3–18 December 1979.

14. Tomás Solis Gragera, 'El Poder Exterior y las Comunidades Autónomas', in *Documentación Administrativa*, op.cit., pp. 91–118.

15. See A. Remiro Brotons and T.Solis Gragera, *Documentación Administrativa*, op.cit.

16. A. Remiro Brotons, quoted by T. Solis Gragera, op.cit., p. 117.

17. See Francisco Villar Ortíz de Urbina, 'Diplomacia Multilateral y Servicio Exterior', in *Documentación Administrativa*, op.cit., pp. 119–28.

18. José Ramón Pardo de Santillana y Coloma, former Chief of Staff of the defence establishment, in 'Seguridad Nacional y Diplomacia', *Documentación Administrativa*, op.cit., pp. 205–17.

19. There is a large list of books and articles on the subject. For recommended titles, see B.Pollack and J.Taylor, 'The Transition to Democracy in Portugal and Spain', *British Journal of Political Science*, vol. 14, 1983, pp. 209–42.

20. The term 'specific military relations' is a category coined by General José Ramón Pardo de Santillana y Coloma in 'Seguridad Nacional . . .', op.cit.

21. Op.cit., p. 207.

22. Op.cit., p. 208.

23. Pardo de Santillana y Coloma, op.cit.

24. Confidential talks with navy and army officers, Madrid, 1984 and

1986.

25. J.R. Pardo de Santillana y Coloma, *Documentación Administrativa*, op.cit., p. 212. 'Se presta a concesiones para la galeria' has been translated to English as 'are easily adopted demagogically'.

26. Op.cit., p. 212.

27. Informal talks with a senior defence adviser, 1984.

28. Gibraltar appeared to be one of the most important issues for future foreign policy, according to some high-ranking military officers interviewed by B. Pollack in 1984. This priority had not changed substantially in mid-1986, when the PSOE was re-elected to form a government with a substantial, if reduced, overall majority. Strategic considerations seemed to be one of the motivations (i.e. the role of Spain as a power of regional influence), but nationalism, and particularly a pervasive anti-British feeling, were at least as important.

29. *El País*, 2 February 1987.

30. *El País*, 1 February 1987. This issue includes an extensive report on Spain's nuclear potential.

31. *El País*, 2 February 1987.

32. According to *El País*, as recently as 1986, the CCPMA authorized the use of Spanish ports by seven American nuclear ships, the Hyman G. Rickover, Tinosa and Number One submarines; the John F. Kennedy and Nimitz aircraft carriers; and the South Carolina and Bainbridge Cruisers (*El País*, 2 February 1987).

33. *El País*, 1 February 1987.

34. This version was generally confirmed to B. Pollack by reliable military and diplomatic sources in Madrid.

6

Democracy, modernity and foreign policy: Spain and Europe

After the transition to democracy, Spain's accession to the European Economic Community in January 1986 is probably the most significant event in recent Spanish history. The 'Europeanization' of Spain has had, and will continue to have, profound implications for a country which for nearly forty years was considered by many to be the 'sick man of Europe'. The acceptance of Spain into the European Community signalled not only the end of the years of isolation of Spain from Europe, but also the final victory of modern Spain over traditional Spain.

The modern/traditional dichotomy has been a persistent feature of Spanish society since the eighteenth Century.[1] One of the paradoxes of this fundamental cleavage was that many of the liberal reformists of the early nineteenth Century identified with and aided the occupation forces of post-revolutionary France. Modernization and the destruction of the traditionalist order was equated with enforcing rationalization via the Napoleonic code. One lasting consequence of this 'collaboration' was that modernization became associated with Europeanization, often articulated as alien and *contra España* (against Spain) by the traditionalists. Thus the conservatism of the old order was often shrouded in appeals to nationalism against the internationalist 'conspiratorial' modernizers. This societal dichotomy was characteristic of the internal conflicts throughout the nineteenth and twentieth Centuries, with the antagonism between the two value-systems ultimately erupting in the confrontation of the 1930s.

The modernizing value-system articulated by the Republican forces—mainly the working class and its political allies at the time, the new, incipient urban middle class and the intelligentsia—put forward a programme for the radical transformation of the traditionalist Spain of the 1930s: secularization of society, agrarian reform, state education, political pluralism and, given the internationalist context then prevailing, anti-Fascism. The presentation of such a value-system was, however, ultimately to delegitimize the Republican regime because of the resistance of important sectors of Spanish society and the state, i.e. the landed aristocracy, the Catholic Church and the military. Without the acquiescence of at least the latter two of these groups, no government could have survived in the 1930s. The Civil War of 1936–9 resulted in the victory and imposition of an ultra-nationalist, traditionalist, authoritarian, anti-participatory, Catholic-integralist value-system.

The success of the traditionalists and the defeat of the modernizers in the Civil War were the consequences of complex historical factors and here we intend to outline just one which we consider pertinent to our discussion of the development of Spanish society and its relations with Europe. Whilst international circumstances were unfavourable to the Republic, perhaps the most important reason for explaining why the internalization of a liberal democratic value-system did not succeed in the Spain of the 1930s was the dichotomous evolution of Spanish society.[2]

The failure to achieve equilibrium in the spheres of economic, social and political development was another of the defining features of Spanish society up until 1977. This was manifestly evident during the period of the Second Republic, the political superstructure of which was far in advance of the sociological and economic configuration of Spain at that time. Although economic modernization and industrialization had achieved considerable impetus during the years of General Primo de Rivera's dictatorship, in 1930, on the eve of the Republic, Spain remained primarily an agrarian society, albeit with a nascent industrial bourgeoisie and proletariat.[3] The reformist governments of the Second Republic, with the exclusion of the conservative backlash of the *bienio negra* (black biennium), unleashed a wave of popular expectation which the new regime was incapable of realizing. The political polarization and general anarchy that marked the years of the Republic were partly a consequence of the process of modernization itself. Huntington has termed such a situation, where social, economic and political demands outstrip the process of institutionalization, 'Mass Praetorianism'.[4] In a situation of mass praetorianism, 'social forces confront each other nakedly; no political institutions are recognised or accepted as legitimate intermediaries to moderate group conflict . . . Each group employs means which reflect its particular nature and capabilities: the wealthy bribe; students' riot; workers' strike; and the military coup'.[5] *El Alzamiento* (the uprising of the rebel officers in 1936) resulted from a situation of political overload in a period of hegemonic crisis. The new social forces were not sufficiently strong or cohesive to provide both the socio-economic base and the moral and political authority to legitimize a democratic, modernizing value-system. Likewise, the military were no longer capable of domination by consent, either passive or active.

From the outset, the newly constructed authoritarian state was riven with contradictions, and throughout the years of the dictator-ship the traditionalist modernist dichotomy was to acquire com-plex, often contradictory and paradoxical dimensions. After 1939, modernization, which had for so long been anathema to the traditionalists, was increasingly adopted not only by the opposition but also by significant elements within the regime itself. In fact there developed a series of competing 'ideologies of modernization' during the Francoist era that we shall label: (1) non-democratic—nationalist; (2) non-democratic–internationalist; and (3) democratic—internationalist.

The democratic—internationalist project of modernization was one which sought the 'total' modernization of Spanish society, economic modernization within the framework of a modern, democratic, pluralist political framework, and integration into the post-war international community and specifically, after 1957, into the European community. This position was adopted by the main anti-regime opposition, although not exclusively, throughout most of the period of the dictatorship. In the latter years of the old regime, many of what Linz has termed the 'within regime opposi-tion' advocated a similar project of modernization.[6] The non-democratic projects sought to restrict modernization to the purely economic sphere without extending to social and political life generally. Such projects, emanating from within the regime, differed solely in the approach to be taken to achieve economic modernization, and particularly over the necessity or desirability of Spain's participation in the international economic community. The two opposing nationalist—internationalist perspectives can be identified with the two major phases in the political economy of Francoism. The nationalist experiment corresponded to the period of autarky from the end of the Civil War to the early 1950s, and the internationalist project began with the economic liberalization of the late 1950s. The brief intervening period was one of ambiguity and readjustment.

The adoption of autarky was partly a consequence of the disarticulation of world markets during the conflict of 1930–45, and later as a result of the international ostracism and isolation of the regime by the international community. Apart from having to make a virtue of necessity, there is no doubt that the following of autarkic policies was also a conscious political decision by the Franco regime.[7] The *Estado Nuevo* (new state) sought to foment national independence, coupled to a particular view of capitalist development, via a policy of import substitution industrialization. Economic protectionism in the form of high tariffs and quantitative restrictions on imports, together with state intervention, via the Instituto Nacional de Industria (the National Institute for Industry, INI), was intended to promote rapid industrialization. This non-democratic model of modernization also had an important political goal, i.e. to solidify a social base of support for the traditionalist regime. This was to be achieved by integrating the nascent capitalist elite with the old Latifundista elite. In this way the regime sought to overcome 'the contradiction between the city and the countryside that threatened the political vitality of the oligarchy.'[8] This aristo-capitalist elite, along with that other bastion of Franco-ism, the military, was intended to play a leading role in the economic modernization of the country by managing the INI and controlling the firms attached to it.

By 1950, the failure of this nationalist experiment was self-evident. The adoption of autarky had not promoted industrial development. The protective tariffs and the interventions of the INI had merely served the interests of the agro-capitalist oligarchy. Monopolistic control of the economy by these sectors had in fact acted as a restraint on development: guaranteed markets had stifled technological innovation and capital accumulation. Thus by the end of this period Spain remained both agriculturally and industrially backward.[9] Indeed, the defining feature of the autarkic period was 'capitalist stagnation without democracy'.[10]

By the mid-1950s, the stranglehold of the model of development based on autarky had considerably weakened so that by the following decade it was possible to talk of a 'Spanish miracle'. The basis for this 'miracle' was a result of both exogenous and endogenous developments. The most important external factor was that with the rise of the Cold War the total isolation of the regime was finally ended. The search by the United States for anti-Communist allies led to the signing of an agreement between Spain and the United States in 1953. In return for allowing the establishment of US military bases in Spain, the Francoist regime received over one billion dollars of aid over a period of eight years (see Chapter 7). Whilst the ending of isolation and the influx of foreign aid acted as an external catalyst on Spanish economic development, as important, if not more so, was the changing balance of power that was occurring in the Francoist coalition which culminated in a distinct shift in the regime's 'ideology of modernization'.

The beginnings of this change can be traced to the waning of the influence of the Falangists, with their notion of 'splendid isolation', who were becoming increasingly marginalized, and the rise of the Opus Dei technocrats. After the government reshuffle of February 1957, three members of Opus Dei (Alberto Ullastres, Mariano Navarro Rubio and Laureano López Rodó) held key positions in economic affairs as Ministers of Commerce, Hacienda (taxation and budget) and Planning respectively. Other like-minded technocrats occupied other important posts.[11] The failure of autarky had convinced the new ministers that the keynote to economic modernization was the liberalization of the Spanish economy and its integration into the international economy. Most important in respect of the latter was the interest generated in the technocratic circles by the creation of the European Economic Community. Although in 1959 exports only accounted for 4 per cent of Spain's GNP, Europe was considered as an important market for Spain, as it absorbed approximately one-quarter of such exports.[12] Furthermore, Europe was considered as a natural source of much-needed foreign technology and investment. Between 1958 and 1959, the first move towards 'opening up' to Europe were undertaken. Spain joined the International Monetary Fund (IMF), the International Bank for Reconstruction and Development (World Bank) and the Organization for European Economic Cooperation (OEEC), now the Organization for Economic Cooperation and Development (OECD). Furthermore, measures undertaken by the new technocratic administration, beginning with the Stabilization Plan of 1959, greatly facilitated the inflow of foreign multinational capital.

The liberalization and modernization of the economy proposed by the technocrats were not intended by the regime to be extended to the political structures of authoritarianism—organic democracy.

It was within this context of attempting to promote a non-demo-cratic–internationalist modernization programme that the first overtures to the EEC were made. In February 1962, the Spanish Minister for Foreign Affairs, Fernando María Castiella y Maíz, submitted a petition to the Council of Ministers with a view to forming an association between Spain and the EEC. This was proposed as the first step toward full integration into the Community. This application was rebuffed by the EEC not on the basis of economic criteria but because Spain did not fulfil the political requirements set out in the European Parliament's Birklebach report of 15 January 1962, which clearly stipulated that 'states whose governments do not have democratic legitimization and whose people do not participate in government decisions, either directly or through fully elected representatives, cannot aspire to be admitted into the circle of peoples which forms the European communities'.[13] Although the regime's lack of democratic credentials barred the way to Spain acquiring full or even associate membership, a preferential agreement was arrived at in 1970, which served to further the economic interaction between Spain and the EEC countries. Throughout the 1960s, Europe had remained of primordial importance in terms of the geographical distribution of Spain's trading patterns. Between 1960 and 1970, imports from the EEC increased from 25.2 per cent to 49.3 per cent of total imports. In the same period, Spanish exports to the EEC, although showing a quantitative decrease, reflected the process of development that was occurring in their changing qualitative nature. Agricultural exports decreased dramatically in percentage terms of total exports, whilst there was a marked increase in the export of machinery and transport from 2.0 per cent in 1961 to 14.7 per cent in 1970.[14] Between 1970, after the signing of the preferential agreement, and 1973, Spain's trading figures with the EEC countries increased from 109,930 million pta. to 240,000 million pesetas, whilst Spain's exports underwent a similar increase with the total value rising from 60,336 million pta. to 144,729 million pta.[15] The importance of the 1970 agreement was clearly stated by the Spanish Foreign Minister at the time, Gregorio López Bravo. Spain, he declared, had taken the decision 'to place its roots in Europe: our destiny is decided'.[16] The internationalist project of modernization undertaken under the auspices of the Opus Dei technocrats had indeed served to deepen the economic Europeanization of Spain. However, López Bravo's proclamation in 1970 that Spain's destiny was decided was somewhat premature, or perhaps prophetical; the one remaining obstacle to Spain firmly placing its roots in Europe remained the very nature of the Franco regime. Although the Francoist modernizers had opened the door to Europe, it would need a process of internal *apertura* (opening) before Spain could fully realize its true potential in Europe. Paradoxically, the foundations for such an opening, which the Francoists sought to prevent at all costs, were laid during the very process of economic modernization initiated by the old regime.

The modernization programme of the technocrats was to have a profound effect on the internal configuration of Spanish society. Indeed, the changes that occurred in the 1960s and 1970s so altered the sociological and economic structures of the country that the circumstances that had prevailed throughout the period of autarky up to the mid−1950s were no longer applicable. The demographic pattern of Spain had changed from being a largely rural one to a predominantly urban one. Spain had been transformed into an industrial society with a national bourgeoisie and proletariat, and the growth of the service sector had also increased the importance of the *Capas Medias* (middle sectors) in the social structure. The quantitative and qualitative economic progress experienced during the 1960s and 1970s had produced a not insubstantial increase in the level of affluence of many sectors of Spanish society.[17] This relative affluence that accompanied the 'Decade of Development', 1959−69, initially provided the authoritarian regime with a degree of legitimacy, as it was seen to be providing the goods. Such legitimacy was, however, superficial in that it was based on the passive consent of a population denied any participation in the decision-making process. Paradoxically, Francoism, which had appealed to the 'spiritual' values of traditional Spain during its 'crusade' in the 1930s, had by the 1960s become dependent upon the growth of a materialist ethos of capitalist consumerism. Although never relinquising its traditionalist value-system, Francoism now sought 'to elevate development, and economic growth, to an official state philosophy'.[18]

Ultimately, however, the acute transformation that had occurred in the social and economic structures served to highlight the severe limits of socio-political modernization. The dichotomous nature of Spanish society had thus been inverted during the years following the defeat of the Second Republic. Whereas in the Spain of the 1930s political structures had in many ways been far in advance of social and economic developments, by 1970 the authoritarian political system was manifestly lagging behind the socio-economic evolution of the country. The rapid transformation that had occurred since 1950 had promoted the development of the very social forces that would eventually reject the legitimacy of the regime. Furthermore, the contradictions of non-democratic modernization was to rupture the social and political coalition that had provided the foundation for the regime. Organic democracy, vertical sindicalism, catholic integralism and the Movimiento were increasingly considered as residual, and detrimental, to the modernization and Europeanization of Spain, both within and without the regime. This global rejection of the legitimacy of the authoritarian regime was reinforced by the negative attitude of the European Community *vis-à-vis* Spain's application to become an integral part of the EEC.

The technocratic project of modernization undertaken by the Franco regime explicitly excluded the necessity for political change; thus an attempt was made to depoliticize the interaction between Spain and Europe.[19] Parallel to this regime-initiated project of modernization/Europeanization, there evolved a democratic–internationalist option. For the anti-regime opposition, the idea of Europeanization was equated with more than economic modernization, and it would also entail a fundamental transformation of the socio-political order. This particular 'pro-European option in Francoist Spain signified a negation of the values postulated by the regime'.[20] From the opposition's perspective, progress regarding Spain's incorporation into Europe was unattainable under the Franco regime and could only be achieved by the dismantling of the authoritarian system.[21]

The new-found affluence of the 1960s did not halt the growth of the internal opposition during these years. Indeed, the limited political changes that had been undertaken by the government in its attempt to gain international respectability and further its application to become part of the European Community only served to accelerate the development of the anti-regime opposition. Changes in the laws regulating labour relations aided the resurgence of an independent working-class movement. The changes relating to collective bargaining and the structure of the official trade unions were considered necessary by the technocrats in order to decentralize the bargaining process and to allow for the development of a dynamic capitalist economy. One undesirable consequence, from the regime's point of view, was that such changes also heralded the emergence of an initially spontaneous, but later organized, labour opposition in the form of the Comisiones Obreras (Workers' Commissions). Relaxing of the laws on press censorship also fomented opposition and dissent, while the reporting of strikes and unrest occurring throughout Spain helped lessen the sense of isolation of opposition groups. The international respectability that the regime sought to promote by such superficial reforms was, however, undermined by the constant resort to repression when dissent was carried too far. The most pressing internal problem for the regime was the rise of the militant Basque nationalist organization Euzkadi Ta Azkatasuna (ETA, Basque Nation and Liberty), which had embarked upon an armed struggle against the Spanish state in the early 1960s. States of emergency and show trials followed in the wake of ETA activity. By the early 1970s, Spain had thus become once again the pariah of Western Europe. The final break came with the withdrawal of European ambassadors from Spain after the execution of five 'terrorists' in 1975. This international protest not only isolated the regime, but it also served to confirm that so long as the authoritarian system remained intact Spain would be unable to fulfill her European vocation.

By the time of Franco's death in November 1975, the opposition, i.e. those who sought a political solution other than *continuismo*, consisted of a broad *de facto* coalition of heterogeneous social and political forces. What the diverse sectors of this coalition had in common was a modern, as opposed to a traditional, outlook of society. Whilst there existed differences on specific issues, the coalition was united in their determination to rid Spain of its authoritarian political system. The heterogeneity of the anti-regime opposition would ultimately lead to the realization that a *ruptura pactada* (negotiated break) with modernizers from within the regime was the only viable means of obtaining their objective. Thus the confrontation between modernity and tradition acquired a new significance, contributing to the development of a broad centrist social/political bloc whose main ethos would be modernization and Europeanization, the two terms in this case being synonymous.

Following the transition to democracy, the consensus of political opinion regarding the future of Spain's relations with Europe was revealed during the period of the first democratically elected

Cortes for forty years. On 28 July 1977, some six weeks after being elected to office, the centrist UCD government submitted a formal application for full membership of the EEC and formal negotiations were opened on 5 February 1979. The positions of the other three main national parties represented in the Cortes, the conservative coalition (CD) and the two parties of the left, the Eurocommunist PCE and the socialist PSOE, were in complete accord with the government regarding Spain's accession to the EEC. There was total agreement that no economically viable or politically suitable alternative to the European Community existed. It was accepted that the Spanish economy was inextricably linked to the Community and, furthermore, that accession would be considered by the Spanish people as a display of international political support for the new democratic regime. There was, however, a divergence of opinion between the parties as to the goals to be pursued and the long-term direction of the European Community. The UCD and CD did not seek to alter the basic capitalist nature of the Community. The parties of the left, on the other hand, viewed the transformation of the Community itself as a long-term objective. The PSOE proclaimed that, in alliance with its socialist partners in Europe, it would work for a 'democratic, socialist and non-imperialist Europe'. The PCE, which had accepted the EEC since its adoption of Eurocommunism in the early 1970s, argued that it was necessary to transform 'the present character of the Community, dominated by the large monopolies'.[22]

With the restoration of democracy in 1977, Spain had satisfied the political requirements stipulated by the European Parliament as fundamental prerequisites for membership of the Community. Thus in April, with the process of democratization well under way, the European Parliament had given unanimous support for Spain's accession to the EEC. However, despite the expectations of most Spaniards that incorporation into the Community would be carried out relatively quickly, the negotiations started in 1979 proved to be both protracted and difficult.[23] Whereas during the dictatorship the Community had rebuffed Spain, ostensibly for political reasons, the assessment of democratic Spain's application appeared to be based chiefly on economic criteria. This was particularly disturbing to the Spanish modernizers, who, especially after the attempted coup of 1981, had considered membership as a means of helping to consolidate the fledgeling democracy. Successive Spanish administrations pursued the negotiations with attempts to iron out the economic difficulties relating to Spain's accession.

The principal point of contention in the negotiations was over the period of adaptation to be allowed for Spain's agricultural and industrial products. Spain sought a short period of adaptation for her relatively competitive agricultural goods, whilst seeking to protect her vulnerable industrial activity by procuring a lengthier period for the dismantling of the protective tariffs that had existed since the pre-democratic era.[24] Other major problems related to fishing, the free movement of labour (at the time there were approximately 500,000 Spanish migrants in EEC countries), and financial and budgetary matters. It was Spain's main trading partner in the EEC, France, originally an ardent proponent of extending the 'Latin bloc' within the Community, that was to present the most obdurate opposition to extending the boundaries of the Community. The political opposition to Spain's entry was spread across the political spectrum in France, from the far right to the French Communist party (PCF).[25] President Giscard d'Estaing was in fact responsible for the deadlock in negotiations which lasted almost twelve months between 1980 and 1981. Following the victory of François Mitterrand in the French presidential elections of 1981, the negotiations once again gradually gained momentum but it was not until 1983 that any real progress was made. At a meeting of the European Council in June to discuss future Community finances, the allocation of budget contributions assumed Spanish and Portuguese membership.[26]

Although the impasse regarding Spain's entry into the EEC was a consequence of economic difficulties, after 1983 the negotiations acquired an added political dimension. The question of Spain remaining in the NATO alliance, which it had joined in 1981, was a major issue of political debate within the country. This debate intensified following the Socialist government's volte-face in 1983, when it declared that it was now in favour of remaining in the alliance (see Chapter 7). On 13 September 1984, three months before the 30th Congress of the PSOE, at which the PSOE leadership sought also to reverse the party's position *vis-à-vis* NATO, the ten EEC foreign ministers met in Dublin at an extraordinary meeting called to discuss future negotiations with Spain. At this meeting it was decided that Spanish accession was not merely an 'economic' affair. The ministers expressed their concern that any further delays in reaching an agreement at the negotiations would have a negative effect upon the forthcoming PSOE conference, and would possibly undermine the 'positive position' that the Socialists had now adopted toward the alliance. It was thus agreed to put forward a comprehensive package that would form the basis for Spain's definite integration into the Community.[27] It was after this meeting that the moves towards Spain's full membership of the EEC gathered momentum; the accession treaty was signed nine months later on 12 June 1985 and Spain, together with Portugal, joined the ranks of the EEC on 1 January 1986. The European vocation of the democratic-modernizers had been realized.

Since the death of General Franco in 1975 and throughout the period of negotiations regarding Spain's accession, the economic importance of its relations with the European Community had steadily increased. By 1983, the EEC countries provided outlets for approximately half of Spain's exports, the total value of which had increased from 196.8 million pta. in 1975 to 1,323.6 million pta. in 1983. Although imports from the EEC remained stable during this period at about one-third of total imports, it was significant that 64 per cent of imported capital goods emanated from the Community. The major trading partners in the EEC were France and the Federal Republic of Germany, which, in 1984, supplied 25.7 per cent and 29.6 per cent of Spain's imports from the EEC and received 30.6 per cent and 19.5 per cent of Spain's exports to the Community, respectively. Furthermore, since 1975 Spain had become increasingly reliant on the EEC countries as a source of foreign investment. Whereas in 1975 the United States supplied 40.6 per cent of foreign investment and the EEC 35.6 per cent, by 1983 the figures were 11.7 and 51 per cent respectively. As it was with trade, so it was with investment, France and the Federal Republic of Germany accounting for almost a third of total investment.[28] Thus, at the time of Spain's accession to the European Community, the economic importance of the EEC for Spanish trade and development was beyond dispute. There was, as all political parties had accepted, no viable economic alternative to full integration into Europe.

Although an avid supporter of Spain's integration into the European Community, the PSOE, as the party of government at the time of accession, was forthright in warning the Spanish people that entry into the EEC should not be considered as a panacea for all the economic problems facing the country.[29] On the contrary, as Prime Minister González pointed out on the eve of

Spain's entry, in the short term at least 'integration into Europe is likely to be a harsh blow'.[30] Apart from having to face the worst international recession since the 1930s along with the rest of her European partners, Spain also had the task of coming to terms with the added problem of the economic legacy of the Franco regime.

Whilst Spain had emerged as a major ranking industrial country by the 1970s, the unprecedented growth rates that had accompanied the Francoist modernization programme of the 1960s had not tackled the fundamental structural problems of the Spanish economy. The 'miracle' had been largely based on the development of basic industries such as shipbuilding and steel production. The problems of dependence on such industries were accentuated because of the failure fully to appreciate the impact that the rise in oil prices after 1973 would have on production costs.

Another problem facing the democratic regime was the increase in labour costs since 1977. The corporatist nature of labour relations under the old regime, even taking into account the changes that had occurred after 1958, meant that the Sindicatos Verticales had been in effect agencies of political, social and economic control of the working class, denying as it did the independent organization of the labour movement. Thus, the competitiveness of Spanish industry under the dictatorship had been based on relatively low labour costs rather than high per capita production levels.

Compounding these problems was the high level of dependence on foreign capital and investment, and the lack of indigenous investment in research and development that would have enabled the economy to overcome problems caused by technological change and economic readjustment. Restrictions on foreign investment were virtually eliminated from most sectors of the economy in 1963, which amounted to an 'open door' policy towards foreign/multinational capital.[31] By the end of 1973, 202 of the largest 500 firms operating in Spain were wholly or largely dependent upon foreign/multinational capital. The principal source of this investment was the United States, although European companies were becoming increasingly involved in certain sectors of the economy. The encroachment of foreign/multinational capital, operating through direct investment and the introduction of technology, penetrated virtually all branches of industrial production in Spain. Foreign firms predominated in the following sectors: mining, iron, steel and metal production, chemicals and pharmaceuticals, plastics, rubber and tyre production, paint, industrial, agricultural, commercial and private vehicles, office machinery, telephone equipment, electro-domestic appliances, natural and synthetic fibres, glass and foodstuffs.[32] Parallel to this foreign-owned or controlled sector of the economy, similar monopolistic concerns were owned by the Spanish state in the form of INI. The latter, as a consequence of the inefficiency that tends to accompany undemocratic bureaucratic structures, tended toward inefficiency and lacked innovation, which was exacerbated by the retention of protective tariffs that had remained intact despite the general liberalization of the economy. Furthermore, whilst dominated by foreign and state monopolies, the economy was also characterized by its acute dichotomous nature, with a large number of small and medium-sized firms. Private non-monopoly capital was concentrated in this sector and accounted for the employment of the overwhelming majority of the economically active population, with less than 22 per cent of all firms employing workforces of over 500 people.

The structural dependence of the Spanish economy upon foreign/multinational capital and technology was reinforced by insufficient national resources being devoted to research and development. At 0.34 per cent of GNP ($7 per capita) in 1974, Spain's expenditure on research and development was far less than other European countries. Figures for the Federal Republic of Germany and the United Kingdom in the same year were 1.5 per cent ($20 per capita) and 2.2 per cent ($33 per capita).[33] By the 1970s, critics of the complacency of the national bourgeoisie and the Spanish state were predicting that this would lead to 'a growing technological dependency linking important sectors of the economy to the penetration and control of foreign investment, a process which might favour this generation of Spanish capitalists, but which in the long term would precipitate the colonization of our economy'.[34]

Thus, since the mid-—1970s the Spanish economy has had to cope with these extra burdens, as well as international recession; consequently, the economic problems facing the country since the transition to democracy have been more acute than those of most other European countries. The years since 1975 have seen minimal economic growth, and in 1980 zero growth. The inbuilt structural weaknesses of the economy have become manifest during the last decade. The overmanned, inefficient basic industries went into irreversible decline with the onset of the recession and the subsequent decline in both internal and external markets. Domestic demand for steel fell by more than 25 per cent between 1983 and 1984, production of metal products, shipbuilding and motor vehicles fell by 7.5 per cent, 14.4 per cent and 49.5 per cent respectively.[35] When the Socialist government took office in December 1982, growth of GDP was around 2 per cent, inflation stood at 14 per cent and unemployment 16 per cent. The extent of Spain's economic problems provoked Prime Minister González to declare that 'Spain needed forty years of socialism to compensate for the forty years of Francoism'.[36]

The above statement by Prime Minister González notwithstanding, the electoral triumph of the PSOE in 1982 was not a step towards four decades of socialism but rather one more along the path of modernization. The absolute majority gained by the PSOE was not a consequence of their having proposed a socialist transformation of Spanish society but rather of having adopted a programme of rational modern capitalism. Since 1977, the PSOE had discarded any vestige of its Marxist past and taken up the moderate centrist position previously occupied by the UCD. In effect, by 1982, the PSOE had been transformed into the political *portavoz* (spokesperson) of the ethos of democratic modernization that had permeated much of Spanish society. It was modernization rather than socialism that was to become the principal motto of the PSOE in government. This has been clearly reflected in the economic policies of the government over the past five years. From the outset one of the fundamental goals in the government's economic strategy was to rationalize Spanish industry to increase its international competitiveness in anticipation of EEC membership. This was to be achieved by cutting back on spare capacity, reduction in labour costs and the repealing of laws relating to employment security. Apart from the streamlining of basic industries in the state sector, this policy of industrial modernization was intended to promote the development of more technologically advanced industries, with the aim of transforming the industrial infrastructure of the country from a labour-intensive to a capital-intensive system of production.[37]

Thus, even before Spain's accession to the EEC, the Socialist administration had initiated many domestic economic reforms that were considered necessary to promote industrial modernization. The government's commitment to industrial modernization has not been without its critics. Primarily, the rationalization of the

144 Spain and Europe

traditional industries has meant that the commitment of the Socialists to create 800,000 jobs by 1986 has been abandoned, and furthermore it has in fact resulted in an even higher rate of unemployment. At its present level of 27 per cent of the economically active population, this is the highest unemployment rate amongst the OECD countries.

The government's policy of shifting economic priorities towards capital-intensive production has also resulted in significant problems. Apart from the fact that this is unlikely to compensate for job losses, it has also deepened the problem of economic dependency. Even with the dismantling of the political structures of authoritarianism, the long-standing reluctance of Spanish entrepreneurs to invest in research and development has persisted. This has accentuated the Spanish industry's reliance upon the importation of foreign/multinational, now chiefly European, technology. For example, in the first eight months of 1984, foreign investment in Spanish firms amounted to $650 million, a 40 per cent increase over the previous year.[38]

In the context of the problems of promoting national industrial development, another major aspect of the PSOE's modernization programme may be considered. Since coming to power the government has persistently refused to promote further state intervention in the economy. Nationalization has been spurned by the PSOE government, preferring instead to pursue a neo-liberal version of 'free market socialism', relying on the initiative of the private sector, an initiative that has evidently not been forthcoming from within the ranks of the national bourgeoisie. One critic of the government has suggested that

industrial strategy has to take into account that private initiative cannot cope adequately in our present condition. This is not a new phenomenon in Spain . . . Even under Franco the initiative to develop basic industries had to be undertaken by the State . . . Private initiative has no role to play . . . It has to be accepted that in a country such as ours development and true modernization demand a planning of resources that only the State is capable of carrying out.[39]

Since accession to the EEC the future of Spanish industry remains uncertain. Although the terms of the treaty will also have a profound effect on other sectors of the economy, especially agriculture and fishing, its most important consequences will probably be seen in the future model of industrialization and modernization in Spain. Spanish industrialists generally agree that entry into the EEC will allow Spain to play an important role in the construction of a united Europe; however, as the director of the economic section of the Confederación Española de Organizaciones Empresariales (CEOE, Spanish Employers' Association) stated shortly after the signing of the accession treaty, 'there are many fears about the impact of entry into the European market.'[40] A similar concern was displayed by Panero Florez, the president of the Confederación Española de Pequeñas y Medianas Empresas (CEPYME, Association of Small and Medium Enterprises), who confessed that 'the small firm is scared of Europe'.[41] The dismantling of protective tariff barriers over the next seven years, in accordance with the terms of the treaty, will result in Spanish industry facing stiff competition from more modern cost-effective European firms. Despite the programme of rationalization undertaken by the present government, it is quite likely that certain sectors of industry in Spain will be unable to weather the 'shock' of entry into the EEC. Most importantly, given the problem of generating indigenous investment, coupled to the government's modernization plan, it may be that those enterprises most able to adapt to the increase in competition will be those that are increasingly penetrated, and dominated, by foreign/multinational capital.

The realization of the democratic−internationalist project of modernization, under the auspices of the PSOE government, may thus eventually reveal one of the greatest paradoxes in democratic Spain's search to fulfil her European vocation. Whilst there can be no doubt that Spain's economic and political future will be articulated via a European forum, it may also be the case that the particular pattern of modernization adopted by the present government will considerably weaken the position of Spain *vis-à-vis* her European partners. As we have pointed out above, the acceptance of the free market may be tantamount to accepting that Spain's integration into Europe will be accompanied by an increased structural dependency upon the inflow of EEC capital and technology. Whilst incorporation into the Community has confirmed the victory of modern Spain over traditional Spain, there has also been a degree of continuity. The failure to promote a viable strategy for the internal generation of investment and innovation has remained, and may conclude with the Spanish economy becoming a relative satellite to the rest of Europe. Spain may not so much have entered Europe as Europe will have taken over Spain. Apart from the important implications for internal economic development, this may also have profound consequences in terms of Spain's wider foreign policy initiatives.

One of the guiding principals of the PSOE's foreign policy in 1982 was a commitment to developing an autonomous international perspective, rejecting the global bipolar military divisions. This 'autonomy' was considered essential to maintaining and enhancing Spain's 'special relationships' with the Arab world and Latin America. Such policies would allow Spain to play a positive role, despite the constraints of her status as a *potencia media* (middle-ranking power), in redefining the agenda of international politics. Spain would thus be able to contribute to relocating the axis of global formations away from the confrontational East–West divide to one of cooperation between North and South. Entry into the EEC was not considered as prejudical to this vocation; indeed it was perceived as a positive advantage.

By the time of Spain's accession to the European Community, the PSOE had revised its position on the existing global military divisions, and more importantly on Spain's role within that divide. The relationship between Spain's process of modernization, her European vocation, and participation in the NATO alliance, discussed in the following chapter, are perhaps the most outwardly manifest indications of the limits that have been imposed upon the formulation of an autonomous foreign policy as a direct consequence of the dependent nature of her inclusion within the EEC.

Notes

1. On the tradition versus modernity cleavage in Spanish society, see B. Pollack and J. Grugel, 'Opposition in Contemporary Spain: Tradition against Modernity', in E. Kolinsky (ed.), *Opposition in Western Europe*, Croom Helm and European Centre for Political Studies, London, 1986.
2. On the nature of Spain's development, see 'El Caso Español: la Diacronia Estructural de la Modernización', in *Anuario Político Español, 1969*, Cuadernos para el Diálogo, Madrid, 1970.
3. J. Harrison, *An Economic History of Modern Spain*, Manchester University Press, Manchester, 1978, p. 129.
4. See S. Huntington, *Political Order in Changing Societies*, Yale University Press, New Haven, 1968.

5. op. cit., p. 196.

6. J.Linz, 'Opposition to and Under an Authoritarian Regime', op. cit.

7. Harrison, op. cit., p. 153.

8. C. Moya Valganon, 'Las Elites Económicas y el Desarrollo Español', in *La España de los Años 70: Vol. 1, La Sociedad,* S.del Campo, (ed.), Editorial Moneda y Credito, Madrid, 1972.

9. Tamamés R., *Estructura Económica de España,* Alianza Editorial, Madrid, 1985, p. 154.

10. J. M. Maravall, *El Desarrollo Económico y la Clase Obrera,* Ariel, Barcelona, 1970, p. 19.

11. On Opus Dei, see D. Artiques, *El Opus Dei en España: Su Evolución Ideológica y Política,* Ruedo Ibérico, Paris, 1968.

12 B. Watson, 'Economic Adjustments of Modern Spain with Reference to EEC Membership', in *Spain and Portugal,* Thunderbird Graduate School of International Management, Glendale, Arizona, November 1972, p. 1.

13. Quoted in G.N.J. Perry, *Spanish Foreign Policy and the European European Community* (unpublished B.Soc. Sc. thesis), University of Birmingham, 1985, p. 11.

14. *Informe Económico del Banco de Bilbao.*

15. Tamamés, op. cit. p. 252.

16. Quoted in E.M. Baklanoff, *La Transformación Económica de España y Portugal,* Espasa-Calpe, S.A., Madrid, 1980, p. 116.

17. On the quantitative economic growth of Spain in the 1960s, see report of the Comisaría del Plan de Desarrollo, Boletín Oficial del Estado, Madrid, 1971.

18. J.P. Fusi, Introduction to 'De la Dictadura a La Democracia: Desarrollismo, Crísis y Transición (1959–1977)', *Historia,* Year VIII, Extra, February 1983, p. 6.

19. F. Morán, 'La Opción Europea en el Marco de la Política Exterior Española', *Afers Internacionals,* Barcelona, 1983, p. 54.

20. F. Morán, *Una Política Exterior para España,* Editorial Planeta, Barcelona, 1980, p. 293.

21. Morán, op. cit., p. 289.

22. On the position of the different parties on the EEC, and other foreign policy issues, see R. Mesa, 'La Política Exterior en la España Democrática,' *Revista de Estudios Internacionales,* vol. 3, no. 1., Jan.–March 1982.

23. This optimism was expressed regularly in newspapers of different political persuasions.

24. Extebank, Banco Exterior de España, *Monthly Economic Report,* Madrid, April 1984, p. 2.

25. The Spanish PCE condemned the attitude of the PCF. It is possible that this was a cynical political tactic on the part of the French Communists to gain votes in the rural South.

26. Tamamés, op. cit., p. 254.
27. *El País*, 12 September 1984.
28. Souces: *Informe Anual Sobre Comercio Exterior*, Madrid, Ministerio de Hacienda, 1984; *Boletin de Informaciones Comerciales Españolas*, no. 1923, 1983; *Informe del Banco de Bilbao; Eurostats*.
29. Morán, *Una Política Exterior*, op. cit., p. 290.
30. Felipe González, quoted in S.Carrillo, *España en Europa?*, Conferencia en el Club Siglo XXI, Madrid, December 1985.
31. Baklanoff, op. cit., p. 73.
32. Tamamés, op. cit., pp. 182–5.
33. D. Valcarcel, and J.M. Girones, 'La Investigación en España', *Revista de Occidente*, vol. 3, no. 1, November 1975.
34. The 'Group of 27', quoted in Baklanoff, p. 87.
35. *Irish Times*, 17 July 1985.
36. J. Hooper, *The Spaniards*, Penguin, Harmondsworth, 1986.
37. *Cambio 16*, 4 July 1983.
38. *The Economist*, 27 October 1984, p. 24.
39. Carrillo, op. cit., pp. 6–7.
40. *Irish Times*, 17 July 1985
41. Quoted in Carrillo, op. cit., p. 4.

Democracy, Modernity and Foreign Policy: Spain and NATO

The mass consensus which accompanied Spain's integration into the European Economic Community was not similarly demonstrated regarding the question of the country's participation in the North Atlantic Treaty Organization. Whilst the majority of Spaniards were convinced that entry into the economic and political structures of Western Europe was essential to the modernization of Spain, they remained sceptical that integration into the military structures of the West would have any tangible benefits. Consequently, between 1977 and 1986, the issue of national defence was to divide the political class and the Spanish people generally. Preston and Smyth have pointed out the paradoxical situation existing during these years.[1] Whilst Spanish accession to the EEC enjoyed overwhelming popular support within Spain, this met with fierce resistance from within the EEC itself (see Chapter 6). Conversely, the eagerness displayed by the member states of NATO to accept Spain's entry into the alliance was firmly rejected by a significant section of the Spanish people.[2] A poll undertaken by the Centro de Investigaciones Sociológicas in September 1981 revealed that 43 per cent were against Spain joining NATO, while only 13 per cent were in favour.[3]

Despite this paradoxical climate of national and international opinion, or perhaps, as we shall see later, because of it, on 30 May 1982 Spain became the sixteenth member of the Atlantic Alliance, the first addition to either of the military blocs in over a quarter of a century. The decision taken by the then incumbent UCD government of Leopoldo Calvo Sotelo to secure Spain's adhesion to the military alliance, and the method utilized to achieve it, resulted in what has undoubtedly been one of the most polemical political debates to arise in the country since the transition to democracy, a polemic which, despite the endorsement of Spain's continued participation in NATO via a national referendum held on 12 March 1986, is far from over.

Essential to an understanding of the controversy that has surrounded Spanish security policy under the present democratic regime is the legacy bestowed upon it by its authoritarian predecessor, and particularly the 'peculiar relationship' that the Franco regime had cultivated with the United States.[4] Spanish–United States relations during the Franco era have been considered in an earlier chapter of this book; here we shall merely recapitulate some aspects of that relationship pertinent to comprehending security policy in Spain since 1977.

Generally isolated from the international community after the defeat of the Axis powers, the Francoist regime had been excluded from the process of European reconstruction and the material benefits of the Marshall Plan. The pariah status imposed upon the regime, coupled with its ideological commitment to autarkic economic policies, meant that by the beginning of the 1950s the economic situation in Spain was critical and the future of Francoism uncertain. The authoritarian regime desperately required international aid to ensure its survival. This isolation was considerably lessened with the onset of the Cold War, when the anti-Communist credentials of the Francoist regime and Spain's geopolitical position were considered by the United States as more important than its authoritarian nature. The unsuccessful attempts by the United States to have Spain included in NATO, not least because of the opposition of most of the West European member states, was offset by the Pact of Madrid between the major NATO powers and the dictatorial regime signed in September 1953. The 'pact' involved three bilateral agreements on Defence, Mutual Defence and Economic Aid. Although the latter provided the Franco regime with a source of investment and trade, the terms of the agreement were far less favourable than other European countries had received through the Marshall Plan. Furthermore, 30 per cent of the total aid received by the Spanish government during the first ten-year period of the pact was earmarked for defence.[5] However, it is most likely that this solution was favoured by Franco as a 'delightful alternative' as he regarded NATO as a 'nest of liberals that would contaminate his state'.[6]

These bilateral agreements were important for a number of reasons. Primarily, the massive aid grants received by the regime enabled it to overcome the temporary crisis, although its long-term

economic stability was perhaps more dependent upon the fundamental changes in economic policy that were undertaken in the
following years. The abandoning of autarky and the development
of a dynamic free market economy under the auspices of the
Opus Dei *technocrati* were, however, dependent upon the
re-establishment of relations with the international community and
the influx of much-needed foreign investment. Thus, the ending
of Spain's isolation in 1953 and United States' pressure upon
its allies to normalize relations with Spain provided the foundation for the economic 'miracle' of the 1960s. Paradoxically, the
process of economic development set in motion at this time, whilst
allowing for the stabilization of the regime, also, as we have
outlined in the previous chapter, held the seeds of its eventual
decline.

The bilateral agreements were also of exceptional importance
because of the consequences they would have for Spanish security
policy. After 1953 the United States was ostensibly the pillar of
Spain's defence requirements. Throughout the 1960s, Spain was
among the top ten countries receiving military aid from the United
States, and the sixth largest purchaser of US military hardware.
Furthermore, the agreements not only heralded the end of Spain's
international isolation but also of its tradition of neutrality. Despite
having been excluded from NATO, by allowing for the installation
of United States' naval and air bases on Spanish territory, the Pact
of Madrid effectively incorporated Spain into the military defence
system of the West. This fact obviously did not go unnoticed in the
Soviet Union, especially following the renegotiation of the treaty in
1963 which permitted the entry of Polaris and later Poseidon
submarines to the naval base in Rota, and the storing of strategic
nuclear weapons at Torrejón, on the outskirts of Madrid. In March
1986, a Soviet specialist on the United States, commenting on the
military bases in Spain during the Franco era, stated that 'the
presence of nuclear arms at the Spanish bases was taken into
account by the USSR'.[7]

Despite the inclusion of a mutual defence agreement, the Pact of
Madrid also seriously undermined the autonomy of Spanish
security policy. It would appear from the secret pacts that accompanied these agreements that Franco was determined to secure
United States aid at almost any cost to national security and
national sovereignty.[8] One outstanding example is the 'additional
clause' to paragraph two of Article III of the defence agreement of

1953, which remained in force from the signing of the agreement until 1970, and which remained secret until after the transition to democracy. This clause deals with the utilization of the bases at times when Communist aggression threatens the security of the West' and, less specifically, at times 'of emergency'. In his analysis of this secret clause, Viñas concludes that this was in effect a blank cheque for the United States regarding the bases in Spain, allowing Washington to take the initiative in acts of reprisal, with no obligation to Spain and her head of state than the passing-on of information in their possession regarding the imminent 'aggression' or 'threat' and the intention of counteracting it by means of attack. On the other hand, Spain was not guaranteed assistance from the United States in the event of an attack on Spanish territory, colonies or protectorates.[9]

Although the above-mentioned 'additional clause' was abrogated during the renegotiated agreements of 6 August 1970, and further improvements in Spain's position realized via the treaty of friendship and cooperation which replaced it on 24 January 1976, which included the agreement to remove United States' nuclear missiles from Spain,[10] the fundamental imbalance between the two signatories remained intact throughout the entire period of dictatorship.

In sum, the defining characteristics of Spain's security policy under the authoritarian regime were on the whole negative. The erosion of Spain's sovereignty, as a consequence of the fundamental imbalance in the agreements with the United States, meant that whilst there existed the possibility of becoming embroiled in a generalized East—West conflict, there was no guarantee of support in the case of reprisals against Spanish territory or during conflict within a scenario peculiarly threatening to Spain. Following the decolonization of the Sahara, the major threat emanated from the Moroccan claim to Spain's enclaves in North Africa (Ceuta and Melilla). Furthermore, since 1953 Spain had become increasingly dependent upon the United States. These particular problems of Spanish security arising from almost four decades of authoritarian rule would have to be confronted by policy-makers under the democratic regime installed in 1977.

With the collapse of the old authoritarian order and the restoration of democracy, the political objections to Spain's accession to NATO were removed. Although the strategic problems of United States' policy-makers had been partly resolved by the bilateral agreements of 1953, the important geo-strategic position of Spain meant that her incorporation into NATO remained a fundamental foreign policy objective for the United States and her Western allies.[11]

As pointed out at the beginning of this chapter, the enthusiasm displayed by the fifteen member states toward democratic Spain's potential integration into NATO was not replicated within the country itself. The militant anti-NATO feelings held by many Spaniards reflected both the strength of a traditional neutralist outlook and reticence at becoming involved in a global bipolar military/political division. But there was also a positive correlation between the negative attitude towards the alliance and an intense, often visceral, anti-Americanism. Although this was more prevalent amongst Socialist and Communist supporters, it was by no means limited to those on the left. The hypernationalism of the far right often revealed overtones of anti-American as well as anti-Soviet hysteria, reflecting the anti-capitalist and anti-Communist rhetoric of the 'pure' Falangism of José Antonio Primo de Rivera. Moreover, there existed a solid bloc of Spanish opinion stretching across the political spectrum that maintained a deep mistrust of the United States and, by extension, NATO. In May 1985, when opinion polls still revealed a substantial majority opposed to continued membership of NATO, 64 per cent of Spaniards disagreed with the view that the United States was a true and loyal friend of Spain.[12] This was manifest in the hostile demonstrations that greeted President Reagan during his visit to the country later that same month.

In the eyes of many Spaniards, the United States had been responsible for propping up the old authoritarian regime since the agreements of 1953. Furthermore, the commitment of the Reagan administration to Spain's new democracy was questioned as a consequence of statements made by Secretary of State Alexander Haig when the future of the democratic regime was threatened in February 1981. Also the cultural bonds of *Hispanidad* coloured the Spanish people's perception of United States' policy *vis-à-vis* Latin America. The findings of the above-mentioned opinion poll in 1985 showed that an overwhelming majority believed that Spain should attempt to further the cause of peace in crisis-torn Central America, although 62 per cent believed that this was dependent upon United States' policy in the area.[13] The Reagan administration's policy in Central America, for example, and backing for the

Contras in Nicaragua, were considered unjust and aggressive and are clearly unpopular with most Spaniards.

Thus the majority of the Spanish people were totally opposed to integration into a military alliance in which the United States was considered to be the commanding force. It was within the context of this paradoxical situation that the convoluted internal debate on Spain's entry into, and after May 1982 remaining in, the alliance took place.

The 'peculiar relationship' with the United States and the consequent problem of reformulating an effective policy for national security was not the only legacy bestowed upon Spain's democratic regime by its authoritarian predecessor. In the previous chapter we considered the problems of political and economic modernization facing the new democracy as it sought to achieve its 'European vocation'. In the following pages we shall focus our attention on the process by which these issues became an integral part of the redefinition of security policy between 1977 and 1986.

Following the death of Franco, the question of Spain joining the alliance was officially broached for the first time by the government of Carlos Arias Navarro on 28 January 1976, some four days after the signing of the treaty of friendship and cooperation.[14] The restrictive process of *apertura* attempted by his government was, however, rejected by the Spanish people and Arias was forced to resign. Even had domestic opposition to this attempt at *continuismo* failed, it is highly unlikely that the NATO member states, including the United States, would have looked favourably upon an application from the government to join the alliance. The Western powers were particularly concerned that anything less than outright democratization might intensify the level of mass mobilization and increase the likelihood of the success of the Spanish left-wing strategy at that time, of effecting a *ruptura democrática* (democratic break) and the setting-up of a provisional government that would include both Socialists and Communists. Such a radicalization of events in Spain might jeopardize the geo-political and geo-strategic interests of the West in the area. These fears were, however, allayed by the successful formulation of a transition 'from above' under the guidance of King Juan Carlos and Arias's replacement, Adolfo Suárez, which led to the holding of the first democratic elections in forty years on 15 June 1977.

The first two governments of the new regime were formed by the UCD under the premiership of Suárez. From the outset, both

Suárez and his party advocated the eventual incorporation of Spain into NATO. But it would be mistaken to conclude, as some commentators have, that this was conceived as a priority item of policy.[15] The major priority tasks of the Suárez government had been concerned chiefly with domestic affairs—above all the consolidation of the democratic system. Foreign policy was basically considered as an extension of this overriding concern, with the primary goal of obtaining international support for the new regime, and with high priority given to Spain's application for EEC membership. Suárez himself categorically stated that NATO membership was not one of the 'fourteen priorities' of his government.[16] Although the UCD had clearly stated its support for entry into NATO, this theme was not mentioned in the party's electoral campaign in 1977 nor did it form part of the government's programme afterwards.[17] It was during the period of Suárez's second term of office that the subject of NATO was raised in numerous parliamentary debates, beginning with his investiture speech on 30 March 1979. The declarations that emanated initially from the government merely repeated, however, the UCD's advocacy of Spain eventually joining the alliance, and that the timing and form of such participation would be decided after the matter had been thoroughly debated in Parliament.[18] It is generally agreed that it was not until the Summer of 1980 that the first concrete statement regarding the timing of Spain's incorporation into NATO was made by Foreign Minister Marcelino Oreja. In a declaration to a Madrid newspaper, Oreja not merely reiterated the commitment to taking Spain into NATO but specified, to the surprise of the country at large, that such integration would be carried out within the lifetime of the government.[19] The timing of this statement coincided with the increasing difficulties facing the country in its application to the EEC following the attempt by France to impede the enlargement of the community. Given the priority that it had placed on accession to the EEC, Oreja clarified the government's position by insisting that participation in the alliance would be dependent on progress regarding the Spanish application to join the European Community.

Apart from his preoccupation with domestic affairs, Suárez had been hesitant in promoting the cause of Spain's entry into NATO for a number of reasons. He feared that participation in the alliance would be detrimental to the special relationship that Spain had with both Latin American and the Arab countries. Also, it has been claimed, he was wary of pursuing a policy that would be internally divisive and break the general political consensus on foreign policy that had hitherto existed.[20] Whilst the pronouncement of Oreja may have been a tactical move to undermine French obstructionism,[21] it is important to note that the first specific statement regarding Spain's imminent application to join the alliance was linked to other foreign policy objectives and in particular Spain's accession to the EEC. The 'matriculation' with NATO and membership of the European Community was to become a decisive issue in the debate surrounding Spain's entry into the alliance.

The resignation of Suárez in early 1981 meant that it fell to his successor, Leopoldo Calvo Sotelo, to set in motion the process by which Spain would become part of the alliance. Following Oreja, Calvo Sotelo viewed NATO membership as a natural extension of Spain's integration into the European Community. However, the main justification for his government's decision to adhere to the treaty emphasized the geo-strategic position occupied by Spain which, according to Calvo Sotelo, meant that Spain could not adopt a neutralist policy.[22] The impact of the abortive coup at the time of the new premier's investiture was to add to the list of reasons put forward in favour of joining the alliance. Whereas the problems facing Spain over her application to join the EEC had linked the NATO issue with wider foreign policy goals, the attempted coup of 23 February ('23-F' as it is commonly known in Spain) firmly wedded, in the minds of some, the internal political situation to the question of joining the alliance.

There was much uncertainty as to how the armed forces would react to the process of democratization that had been set in motion following the death of their *Generalisimo* in November 1975. As the chief bulwark of the Francoist system, the military had been ideologically saturated by the anti-liberal, anti-democratic value-system of the old regime. The virtually closed institution of the Spanish armed forces had remained practically unaffected by the movement toward national reconciliation that had gradually permeated Spanish civil society and certain state institutions throughout the last twenty years of the dictatorship. Throughout the Francoist era the armed forces had been almost completely cut off from progressive, modernizing sectors of Spanish society and remained the staunchest defenders of the traditional order. The fear of many was that the military would intervene in the political process to ensure that Francoism would continue without Franco.

The threat of *golpismo* hung over the young democracy like the sword of Damocles.

The events of '23-F' brought into relief the necessity of accelerating the transformation of the armed forces from a backward-looking institution prone to intervention in domestic politics to a modern professional body loyal to the Consitution whose prime concern would be the defence of national territory against external aggression. Many advocates of Spain's integration into NATO, including Calvo Sotelo, would argue after '23-F' that participation in the alliance was conducive to the democratization of the armed forces.[23] This would promote their technical modernization and also help to erode their traditionalist collective mentality. Thus, one adherent to this thesis has stated that 'contact with the non-political officers of countries in which democracy has long been taken for granted, along with technical modernization, is bound to foster a steady increase in professionalism'.[24] Critics of this thesis have claimed that it is fundamentally flawed in two respects: it is both ahistorical and deterministic. Since the signing of the Washington treaty in 1948, the history of certain member states of NATO, and indeed of the organization itself, tends to undermine the claim made in the preamble to the treaty that the signatories sought to 'safeguard the freedom, common heritage and civilization of their peoples, founded on the principles of democracy, individual liberty and the rule of law'.[25] Historical facts, opponents claimed, speak for themselves. Portugal, under the authoritarian regime of Salazar, was admitted as a founder member of the treaty in 1949. The inclusion of Greece and Turkey in the alliance in 1952 has not prevented the military from periodically taking power in those countries. In fact, the coup of the colonels in Greece in April 1967 was executed via the utilization of the Prometheus Plan—a counter-subversion plan elaborated by NATO itself. More recently, in January 1985, the Greek authorities had cause to register a serious complaint with the military committee of the alliance. Exercises undertaken at the NATO defence college in Rome had included the simulation of a *coup d'état* by the Greek military, with the aid of foreign agents, following a hypothetical left-wing election victory.[26] It was therefore argued, with apparent justification, that Spain's participation in NATO would not of itself guarantee the stability of the democratic regime. This view was given added credence by the response of the United States' Secretary of State Alexander Haig to the attempted coup in

February 1981. The events at '23-F' were, according to Haig, an 'internal Spanish affair'. With apparent disregard for the above-mentioned events, premier Calvo Sotelo boldly affirmed that 'entry into NATO will kill at birth any attempted coup'.[27]

By the time of Spain's entry to NATO in May 1982, apart from matters relating solely to defence, Spanish security policy had been inextricably linked to the consolidation of democracy and the achievement of foreign policy objectives, namely Spain's accession to the EEC.

Within the main opposition party, the PSOE, the debate over defence policy was intense as a consequence of the substantial degree of support within the party for a neutralist option. The position eventually adopted by the PSOE was to be influenced, however, by the argument that the practicable alternatives were limited by the country's existing relationship to the Western defence system as a consequence of the bilateral accords with the United States. The formulation of a socialist foreign policy would therefore have to be defined within the context of such limitations. The most influential contribution to socialist foreign policy at this time was Fernando Morán's *Una Política Exterior Para España: Una Alternativa Socialista*. In his discussion of the most appropriate defence policy for Spain, and with specific reference to the issues of NATO and the treaty with the United States, Morán insists that the matter be considered objectively rather than ideologically.[28]

Primarily Morán critically assesses a number of theoretical neutralist options. The Utopian—pacifist position of renouncing national self-defence is rejected as both impossible and undesirable. Non-aligned neutralism is dismissed as a *Tercer Mundista* (Third Worldist) approach and is likewise unsuitable for Spain. The defining characteristics of the member states of the non-aligned movement (non-Western European, ex-colonial developing countries) does not correspond to the social, economic, cultural or political reality of Spain. The national precedents for neutrality have a particular resonance amongst the Spanish people; Morán argues, however, that such a tradition of neutrality by Spain at times of international conflict (1914—18 and 1939—45) is no longer applicable as it was a consequence of specific historical circumstances, when the theatres of war were still relatively restricted. The contemporary situation is totally different with the high level of sophistication and destructive power of modern warfare technology making it highly unlikely that Spanish territory would not be affected in a future global conflict. Regarding the possibility of neutrality recognized by international law, Morán, in agreement with the UCD, maintained that this also is no real alternative for Spain. Juridical neutrality is ultimately dependent not only upon a country's desire for neutrality but also upon the respect for such neutrality by other nations and particularly the superpowers. Most important in determining a country's ability to adopt such a position is its geographical and geo-political position. The important geo-strategic position of Spain means that such neutrality would almost certainly be violated at times of conflict.[29]

Having discounted the various proposals for Spanish neutrality, Morán also discounts NATO membership as an appropriate defence policy option.[30] The influence of Morán's criticisms and rejection of NATO was evident in the foreign policy resolutions passed by the PSOE at its 29th congress in October 1981.[31] The positions adopted by the Socialists, reflecting the arguments put forward by Morán, were succinctly formulated in a PSOE propaganda document which intended to 'explain to the country what NATO is and (the PSOEs) attitude toward it'.[32]

From the outset the PSOE made it clear that it was not opposed to NATO *per se* but rather to Spain's integration into the organization. Furthermore, this opposition was not based on ideological conviction but, following the advice of Morán, it resulted from an objective consideration of how both Spanish national interests and the cause of world peace would best be served.

The conclusion reached by the PSOE leadership was that no clear or appreciable advantages were to be gained by Spain becoming a member of NATO. Primarily, national security would not be enhanced, as Article 6 of the treaty excludes North Africa: the most likely areas of conflict for Spain, Ceuta and Melilla, are not therefore covered by the treaty. As a member of the alliance Spain would, however, be drawn into any global conflict. Participation in the alliance would also increase the likelihood of nuclear weapons being installed on Spanish territory which would be a retrograde step, as Spain had been non-nuclear since 1979.

Spain's entry into the alliance would undermine the development of an autonomous foreign policy as it would tie Spain to a military alliance in which the United States occupied a hegemonic position. Thus Spain's dependence upon the United States would increase rather than diminish. The PSOE rejected the argument that Spain's integration into NATO was tied up with

EEC membership; there was no perceived connection between the two organizations, and the cases of Ireland and Norway were pointed to as examples.

The cause of world peace would not be enhanced as the relative balance between the two blocs would be disturbed, thereby raising international tensions. In its opposition to NATO, the PSOE was adamant that this did not signify a rejection of Spain's role in Western defence. The Spanish liberal democratic regime was inextricably linked to the West and would have to play its part in defence of the shared values of pluralism and liberty. This role was, however, already being fulfilled via the bilateral treaty with the United States. The retention, and renegotiation, of this treaty would enable Spain to continue playing its part in Western defence and also allow it a degree of autonomy that would not be possible in NATO. It is perhaps important to note here that whilst the PSOE rejected Spain's participation in NATO, it had explicitly accepted participation in the existing global political and military divisions, unlike its neutralist anti-Nato ally, the PCE, which also called for the unconditional removal of all United States' bases.[33]

Finally, regarding the impact on domestic affairs, the Socialists maintained that the consolidation of the democratic regime was in no way related to Spain's entry into the alliance. Concern was expressed, on the other hand, that the decision of the UCD government to procure Spain's membership via a simple parliamentary majority would in fact have a profoundly divisive and destabilizing effect within the country. The UCD had broken the political consensus on foreign policy that had existed since 1977.[34]

It was the breakdown of this consensus, and the apparent gulf between the position of the government and the wishes of the majority of Spaniards, that precipitated the PSOE's demand, supported by the PCE, that the issue be put to the electorate in the form of a referendum. This demand was premised on the provision of Article 92.1 of the 1978 Constitution which states that 'political decisions of special importance may be submitted to a consultative referendum of all citizens'.

The ensuing debate over the holding of the referendum was as virulent as that over NATO. The government's position, upheld by the council of state, was that constitutionally it was not obliged to hold a referendum. Furthermore, such a consultation would set a dangerous precedent and undermine the authority of Parliament. International repercussions were also feared, as no other country had ever put the issue to a referendum. With the growth of the peace movements in Western Europe, concern was expressed that a referendum in Spain may set off a chain reaction with demands for popular consultation in other NATO member states. The government's rejection of extra-parliamentary consultation ultimately prevailed after a congressional vote of 172 to 142 in favour of its position. Thus, Spain's application for membership, which led to its integration into the alliance in May 1982, was affected by a simple majority vote in Parliament. The polemic did not, however, stop there. The PSOE had promised, if it gained government office at the subsequent elections, that it would still submit the issue to a referendum.

The process of Spain's entry into NATO initiated by Calvo Sotelo was to take place in two phases: first with regard to the 'political' structure of the alliance, which would then be followed by full military integration. The negotiations regarding the latter were, however, interrupted by internal political developments. The disintegration of the UCD was gathering momentum and the Calvo Sotelo government was forced to bring forward the general election, originally scheduled for 1983, to October 1982.

The PSOE was swept to power in the general elections of 1982, gaining over 48 per cent of the popular vote and an absolute majority in the Congress of Deputies. Within a week of taking office, the newly appointed Foreign Minister, Fernando Morán, announced that the government was to freeze the integration of Spain into the military structure of NATO. The government announced its intention of undertaking a careful study of Spain's continued participation in the alliance after which the promised referendum, which had been one of its firmest pledges during the election campaign, would be held.

In 1982, whilst in opposition, the PSOE had been the most vociferous opponent to Spain's adhesion to NATO. By 1983, after some twelve months in office, the Socialist government had revised its position as did later the party at its 30th Congress in December 1984. When the referendum was eventually held in March 1986, the PSOE was convinced that it was of paramount importance that the country remained in the alliance and called upon the electorate to both comprehend and support this position. How and why had the PSOE reached this conclusion?

The traditional posture of the Spanish socialists *vis-à-vis* NATO appeared to many, not least other Western European Socialist parties such as the German SPD, as incompatible with the otherwise moderate 'Euro-socialism' embraced by the party. This view was shared by some Spanish Socialists who as early as 1978, even prior to the UCD's first definite commitment to integration, argued that the PSOE should align itself with its sister parties in Europe on the issue. It was argued that such a position would give Spanish socialism more credibility within the eyes of its European partners and with the Spanish electorate as a potential alternative government.[35] Given the state of Spanish public opinion regarding NATO membership in 1978 and the overwhelming victory of the PSOE in 1982 on a platform which included support for Spain's withdrawal from the alliance, the latter argument need not be considered further. That other Western European Socialist parties preferred a PSOE committed to NATO was evident both from the 'fraternal pressure' that they brought to bear on the Spanish Socialist leadership, prior to 1983, to modify its position toward the alliance, and the support given to the PSOE during the referendum in 1986.[36] It would, however, be a mistake to consider the eventual volte-face of the PSOE as a mere consequence of its having opted for a security policy that was part of a wider Euro-socialist foreign policy common to sister parties in Western Europe.

In a study of the foreign policy positions of Western European Socialist parties it was concluded that whilst multilateral cooperation exists between such parties this does not constitute a homogeneous system. The formulation of foreign policy by Western European Socialist parties is influenced, if not determined, by five major internal variables—which may differ markedly from country to country.[37] Although the PSOE was not included in the abovementioned study, a consideration of these variables in the Spanish context may be useful in attempting to explain both the pragmatism of, and room for manoeuvre open to, the PSOE on the NATO issue.

1.   *The strength of the national Communist party*

The level of electoral support for the national Communist party may well influence Socialist foreign policy. If the national Communist party has a significant degree of support thereby constituting an electoral threat to, or potential coalition partner with, the Socialists, the foreign policy decisions of the latter may be formulated under certain pressure from the left. In Spain this has not proved to be the case.

During the period of the transition to democracy it was widely believed, and feared—both nationally and internationally by many—that the PCE would emerge as a major political force, and in all likelihood the hegemonic party of the left, in post-Franco Spain. The premises for this supposition was the prestige and following the Communists had gained as the most consistent and best-organized opposition force to the old regime. Between 1977 and 1982, however, the PCE failed to make any impact upon the electorate and had virtually paled to insignificance on the national political scene within five years of loyal existence. By 1982, the PCE's share of the vote had been reduced to 4 per cent and the PSOE, with 48 per cent and an overall majority in Congress, had incontrovertibly consolidated its position as the principal party of the left. The Communists' search for political space within the pluralist democratic system had demonstrably failed. Although the PCE's lack of success was due to a number of factors, we shall only outline the two that are relevant to the themes developed in this and the previous chapter.[38]

Of significant importance in determining which of the two parties of the left would emerge as hegemonic in democratic Spain was the international, and more specifically the European, dimension. Modernization, as pointed out in the previous chapter, was inextricably linked to Europeanization. Spanish aspirations to shed any vestiges of its authoritarian past and to cast off the old Francoist notion that 'Spain is different', coupled with the country's impending integration into the European Community, worked against the PCE, despite its acceptance of the EEC. Communism, regardless of its 'Euro' prefix, and the peculiar case of the Italian Communist party notwithstanding, was considered as an outmoded and archaic political movement, whilst social democracy was perceived as the most appropriate and legitimate mode of leftist expression in the European context. Another possible explanation for the failure of the PCE is that any display of substantial support for the Communists was hindered by the fear that this would provoke a traditionalist backlash and increase the likelihood of military intervention to thwart the modernization of Spanish society. After all, one of the fundamental 'justifications' for the military rebellion that had resulted in four decades of authoritarian rule had been the insurgents' crusade to save the country from 'Communism'. Furthermore, during the transition to democracy, the military, even the more liberal and democratic among them, had vehemently opposed Suárez' legalization of the PCE.

When the Socialists came to power in 1982, the PCE, although retaining a power base in the trade-union movement, had been confined to the margins of Spanish politics. Communism posed no electoral threat to the PSOE and with a substantial overall majority in the Cortes the Socialists are not dependent upon PCE support.

Thus the PCE, which had been the Socialists' main ally in opposing Spain's entry into NATO and supported putting the issue to a referendum, was by 1982 in no position to bring pressure to bear upon the government when it reformulated its policy position *vis-à-vis* the alliance.

2.   *The degree of ideological commitment of the Socialist party*

The level of commitment of a particular Socialist party to Marxist ideology may influence its perception of international affairs. The less ideologically oriented a Socialist party, the more likely it is to tend toward pragmatism. The history of the Spanish Socialist Workers' party is an interesting case in this respect. The PSOE, founded in 1879 by Pablo Iglesias, was conceived as a non-establishment, virulently anti-bourgeois party. For the following hundred years the party was self-defined as a Marxist, class-based mass organization which totally rejected the capitalist system.[39] In 1976 at the party's 27th Congress, the first to be held in Spain since the defeat of the Second Republic, the PSOE emerged as the most radical and openly Marxist of the Western European Socialist parties. In 1979, after some three years of legal existence, this position had been totally reversed with the rapid transformation of the PSOE into one of the most moderate Socialist parties in Western Europe.[40] This process of deradicalization was, however, already under way during the party's clandestine existence under the old regime.

Throughout most of its underground existence the PSOE remained committed to the re-establishment of a republic as the only legitimate form of government, and to socialism as the most appropriate socio-economic system, but the changing patterns of social and economic development that occurred from the mid-1950s on brought about the gradual but distinct shift in this allegiance. Important groups within the PSOE were prompted to abandon the old emotional issues of republic versus monarchy and socialism versus capitalism and to adopt a different, more realistic, one of democracy versus dictatorship. During this period of the transition to democracy the static ideological commitments of the

PSOE were increasingly abandoned. The fundamental and most immediate societal/political dichotomy was perceived as being between traditionalists and modernizers, i.e. those who wanted to maintain, and after 1977 restore, the old order and those who sought the social, economic and political modernization of Spanish society. Neither constitutional monarchy nor capitalism were considered by the rejuvenated PSOE as inherently alien, or prejudicial, to such a model of modernization. Since the transition to democracy the PSOE had thus been transformed from a radical, extremely ideological, party into a moderate, highly pragmatic one. This was evident in the cautious electoral programme of the PSOE in 1982, which revealed the obvious shift of the party towards the political centre. The orthodox economic policies pursued by the Socialists (see previous chapter) have demonstrated the non-existence of a socialist ideological commitment and indicate the degree of flexibility and pragmatism of the administration.

The moderation and pragmatism displayed by the Spanish Socialist party on domestic issues could, if necessary, be transferred to foreign policy. An example of this would be the recognition of Israel by the present administration. In connection with security policy it has to be recalled that the PSOE had never stated its opposition to Spain's entry into NATO on ideological grounds; thus a pragmatic U-turn on the issue might easily be shrouded in terms of 'objective considerations'.

3. *The impact of internal factionalism within the Socialist party*
The degree of internal factionalism within a Socialist party may obscure the formulation of a coherent foreign policy. Also the existence of a strong left-wing faction may radicalize policy positions. In the case of the PSOE, the process of deradicalization outlined above was accompanied by the increasing domination of the leadership over the party rank-and-file and the relative isolation of the more radical faction, the *Sector Crítico* (critical sector). In the years immediately following the transition to democracy, the *críticos* emerged as a powerful force within the party, gaining considerable support at the PSOE's 28th Congress held in May 1979. The ensuing crisis within the party following González's tactical, and short-lived, resignation as party leader led to the holding of an extraordinary congress in October of the same year. This congress reaffirmed the position of the leadership which had been defeated at the previous congress, and heralded the decline

of the *críticos* who had put forward radical alternatives to the moderate policies expounded by González. By 1979, the formulation of policy was therefore firmly under the control of a moderate–pragmatic leadership without any serious challenge from radical factions within the party.[41] González's domination of the party and the waning of radical influence within the rank-and-file greatly facilitated the party's U-turn on NATO at its 30th Congress in December 1984.[42]

4.   *Links between the Socialist party and trade unions*

The stronger the links between Socialist party and trade unions, and more importantly the greater the strength and national importance of the unions, the more significant the impact of the latter will be on foreign policy decisions. But the degree of trade-union influence on, or disagreement with, the security policies of Western European Socialist parties, or governments, is not generally significant anyway.

Since the dismantling of the Francoist state-controlled Sindicatos Verticales (vertical unions), and the legalization of independent trade unions in 1976, one of the main features of the Spanish trade-union movement has been its relative ineffectiveness. The level of trade-union affiliation, at 13 per cent of the total workforce, is one of the lowest in Europe. Apart from the effect that almost forty years of having been denied basic trade-union rights might have had upon Spanish workers, this weakness is partly explained by the fact that the transition to democracy coincided with the onset of a general economic crisis. Whilst many other European trade unions had consolidated their positions at times of economic expansion and full employment, the newly emergent Spanish unions were confronted with economic decline and rising unemployment. The trade unions in Spain have been further weakened by political divisions. Smaller religious and regional unions apart, organized labour in Spain is dominated by two major trade-union federations, the General Workers' Union (Union General de Trabajadores, UGT) and the Workers Commissions (Comisiones Obreras, CC.00). The former is linked to the PSOE whilst the leadership of the latter is predominantly Communist. These political differences have produced grave difficulties in attempts to promote a common Labour front *vis-à-vis* government policies that have not always coincided with the interest of Spanish workers. Although there have been short-lived *ad hoc* agreements between the two organizations, the fundamental ideological and strategic differences between them ruled out any prospect of coherent united action. The political rivalry between the two main trade unions was manifest also at an international level, with the UGT firmly opposed to CC.00's application to join the European Trade Union Confederation.[43] Thus, the general weakness of organized labour in Spain was compounded by political divisions.

The Communist-led Workers' Commissions, which have adopted an opposing posture towards the Socialist government, has had virtually no influence upon government policy. Given the links existing between the UGT and PSOE, the former has given critical support to the present administration. However, representing a meagre 6 per cent of the work force, the pressure which the UGT has been able to bring to bear on government policy has also been minimal. Thus the policy decisions of the Socialist government have been formulated, revised or reversed without the need to convince or appease a strong labour movement. The centrist, pragmatic positions of the PSOE have appealed to the multi-class broad centre which is a defining feature of the Spanish electorate and is therefore not dependent upon the support of organized labour. Again, this eased the government's task regarding NATO as both CC.OO and UGT had adopted policies opposed to Spain remaining in the alliance.[44] UGT, however, suffocated the recognition of Israel.

5. *The national economic environment*

The economic condition of a particular country will also be a decisive factor in influencing, if not determining, the foreign policy of a Socialist party. As we have dealt in some detail with this matter in the previous chapter, it is sufficient to reiterate here that since the 1950s the Spanish economy had been opened up to the penetration of, and had become dependent upon, foreign multinational capital. The programme of technological modernization undertaken by the present Socialist administration has served to deepen that dependency.

Given that major technological and capital inflows emanate from member states of NATO and the EEC, it is not inconceivable that the PSOE government's reconsideration of Spain's participation in the alliance was influenced by 'external pressures'. Indeed, as is shown below, the government itself virtually admitted as much during the period leading up to the referendum. Whereas the four aforementioned internal political factors facilitated the government's U-turn on NATO, it was perhaps this final internal economic factor which determined that it was undertaken in the first place.

The explanation that was put forward by the PSOE leadership for the government's volte-face was a curious mixture of old and new arguments. Continuity, it was claimed, lay in the guiding principles behind Socialist policy, i.e. that they sought to formulate a defence policy which would both guarantee Spain's security and sovereignty and effectively contribute to the cause of world peace. The government's objective consideration had, however, led them to reassess and reformulate previous policy decisions. The argument was simple: in opposition the PSOE had not had access to all the relevant information and thus honest mistakes were made; with the experience and benefits of being in government they had been able to analyse more fully the repercussions that Spain's remaining in, or leaving, NATO would have on security and foreign policy.[45] The overall conclusion reached by the PSOE leadership was stated in no uncertain terms by the Minister for Defence, Narcis Serra. To leave NATO now, affirmed Serra, would be a historical irresponsibility.[46]

Between 1983 and the holding of the referendum some three years later, the specific reasons put forward for this change of heart were many and varied. In contradiction to the arguments set out in 1982, the PSOE now accepted that Spanish territorial security would be better safeguarded by remaining in NATO. More emphasis was placed on the geo-strategic importance of Spain in the case of East–West conflict. Remaining in NATO would also strengthen Spain's position *vis-à-vis* the United States in negotiations over the future of the American bases. Likewise, it would strengthen the 'European pillar' at NATO.[47] Rather than leave the alliance, it was necessary 'to work from within NATO in order to ensure that the European nations are masters of their own destiny without submitting themselves to the interests of Washington'.[48] Another of the key points of Socialist opposition to joining NATO had been that it would disturb the existing equilibrium between the two blocs. Now it was argued that to leave the alliance would also have destabilizing consequences as it would alter the status quo. The domestic political situation would also be affected by a decision to quit the alliance, although it was never explicitly stated. During the referendum campaign, veiled references to the political instability that would ensue if Spain withdrew from the alliance tied the issue of NATO to the consolidation of democracy.

The main argument put forward by the government was that remaining in NATO was a fundamental prerequisite for the modernization of the country. If Spain was to play the role of a modern European nation it also had to accept its responsibilities towards the international community of which it professed to be part. Thus Spanish Socialists maintained that the project of industrial and technological modernization that they had initiated, and that was absolutely essential to overcoming Spain's economic difficulties, was conditional upon the country accepting this definition of its role in the Western defence system. The process of modernization was itself dependent upon access to foreign technology and investment from both Western Europe (principally France and the Federal Republic of Germany) and the United States.[49] Contrary to previous positions, the government explicitly stated that, although there was no legal connection, Spain's accession to the EEC was *de facto* inextricably linked to remaining in NATO. In short, to leave the alliance would be detrimental to the national interest. In effect, the PSOE had adopted virtually wholesale the views that had previously been expounded by the centrist UCD government.

Aware of the extent of public opinion opposed to Spain remaining in the alliance, which the PSOE had itself played a major role in fermenting prior to 1982, the government stressed that whilst it did not want to renounce the treaty, Spain's continued participation would be dependent upon certain provisos. These provisos were that: (1) Spain would not be incorporated into NATO's military command structure; (2) the military presence of the United States on Spanish territory would be reduced; and (3) nuclear weapons would not be stored or deployed in Spain.

It was by means of this approach to integration, which received the sanction of the Secretary General of NATO, Lord Carrington, that the government hoped to sweeten what was for many Spaniards a bitter pill to swallow. Although there had been a significant reduction in the projected 'no' vote, from 52 per cent in October 1984 to 34 per cent in February 1986, right up to the eve of the referendum opinion polls predicted a defeat for the government.[50]

Despite the apparent scepticism displayed by the Spanish people about the advantages of remaining in the alliance, and confounding the pollsters, the government's position was ultimately endorsed on the day of the referendum. Fifty two per cent of those who voted opted to stay in the alliance whilst 39 per cent opposed. With an abstention rate of 40 per cent, the figures in terms of the total electorate were 32 per cent and 24 per cent respectively.[51]

It might, however, be wrong to view the victory of the government as indicative of a radical shift of public opinion in favour of Spain remaining in NATO. Although impossible to calculate, it is quite likely that a substantial proportion of those who abstained did so not from habit, or following the advice of the conservative opposition party Alianza Popular (Popular Alliance) but because they were PSOE voters who could not bring themselves to vote against their government. Also the two umbrella organizations that campaigned against Spain's continued participation in the alliance, the Coordinadora Estatal de Organizaciones Pacifistas and the Plataforma Cívica Para la Salida de España de la Otan, managed to bring together many diverse political and social movements, with the number of 'no' votes cast reaching nearly 7 million.

The Socialist government had, however, managed to convince a sufficient section of the electorate to turn the tide of opinion and snatch victory from the jaws of defeat. Judging from opinion polls (although their findings might be questioned, given the outcome of the referendum itself), this was not due to the *à la carte* approach of the government. A majority of Spaniards did not believe that the conditions that the government had placed upon remaining in NATO would in fact be fulfilled. Fifty per cent thought that Spain would eventually be fully incorporated into the alliance's military structure; 56 per cent believed that nuclear weapons would be installed on Spanish territory; and 57 per cent doubted that the United States' military presence would be reduced as a consequence of Spain remaining in NATO.[52] This display of scepticism by the Spanish electorate was not perhaps without foundation.

(1) *Integration into NATO's military structures*
Until 1966 there was no actual division between NATO's civil and military organizations. It was only when Charles de Gaulle called into question the future of France's participation in the alliance that the allies sought a formula that would appease the French and hold NATO together. By this formula France was able to abandon the military structure of the alliance. It was to the French mode of participation that the Spanish government often alluded when it

was claimed that Spain likewise would not participate in the military structures of the alliance. Spain, however, unlike France, is represented in the highest military authority of the alliance—the Military Committee. Furthermore, Spain also participates in the following agencies in NATO's military structure: Advisory Group for Aerospace Research and Development (GARD); NATO Training Group (NATO Training) Military Agency for Standardization (MAS); NATO Electronic Warfare Advisory Committee (NEWAC); Military Committee Meteorological Group (MGMC); and the NATO Defense College (NADEFCOL).

The example of Spain's participation in NADEFCOL is perhaps indicative of the uncertainty surrounding the future role of Spain in the military organizations of NATO. The origins of NADEFCOL emanated from a speech made by General Eisenhower to the NATO Standing Group in 1951.[53] The establishment of a NATO Defense College was necessary, according to Eisenhower,

for the training of individuals who will be needed to serve in key capacities in NATO organizations . . . Its students should consist of carefully selected officers of the military services, probably of the grade of colonel or equivalent, who are considered of suitable calibre for later assignments to key NATO military posts.[54]

The ambiguity of Spain's position towards the military organizations of NATO, coupled to the government's hesitancy to make public the memorandum regarding Spain's mode of participation, heightened the suspicions of the opposition that Spain has been integrated into the military structures by the 'back door'.[55]

(2) *Spain and the deployment of nuclear weapons*
The question of whether Spain will remain non-nuclear is also debatable. The pronouncement of government ministers in favour of the nuclear strategy of both the United States and NATO has cast a shadow of doubt over their commitment to a non-nuclear Spain. During a visit to Bonn in May 1983, the Prime Minister expressed his understanding of, and agreement with, NATO's decision to deploy Pershing II and cruise missiles in Europe.[56] At a meeting of the European members of NATO on 12 December 1985, Francisco Fernández Ordóñez, who had replaced Fernando Morán as Foreign Minister, stated his support for the Strategic Defense Initiative (SDI). SDI, he affirmed, 'is from Spain's point of view an instrument for peace'.[57]

Furthermore, whilst the treaty of Friendship and Cooperation signed in 1976 prohibited the installation or storing of nuclear weapons on Spanish territory, it also stipulated that this could be reversed in the future if the Spanish government so desired. Also it has been pointed out that despite this prohibition it is in fact extremely difficult for the Spanish authorities to verify if United States' nuclear submarines are still utilizing the naval base at Rota.[58]

(3)   *The reduction of the United States' military presence*

Whether the government will be able to reach a working agreement with the United States to reduce the level of United States' forces and military hardware based on Spanish territory is also uncertain. At present there are approximately 12,000 United States' troops stationed at the bases. Spain is thus one of the Pentagon's major host countries in Europe. Only the Federal Republic of Germany, Great Britain and Italy have a greater United States' military presence. Some 3,600 of the United States' military personnel are stationed at Torrejón, which is the headquarters of the Sixteenth Air Division. The base at Zaragoza, which was expanded in 1970 as a substitute for the base in Wheelus, Libya, houses a special section for United States' bombers integrated into NATO. The base at Morom, near to Seville, is mainly used as a back up to naval operations at Rota. Rota itself is of exceptional logistical importance to the United States, as it plays a fundamental role in the Mediterranean operations of the Sixth Fleet, and as such has a manning level of over 5,000.

The intention of the Socialist government to reduce the United States' military presence in Spain was first officially pronounced in Prime Minister Gonzalez's famous Decalogue in 1984. On 12 May 1986, two months after the referendum, the Spanish Junior Minister for Defence, Eduardo Serra, met with representatives of the United States' government. Whilst the official reason for Serra's visit was to discuss arms sales between the two countries, he also emphasized that the political situation in Spain required a 'new attitude' on the part of the United States regarding the bases. The Spanish government made it clear that it was seeking a substantial reduction in the number of United States' troops based at Zaragoza and the complete 'de-Americanization' of the Torrejón air base, with Spanish military personnel and aircraft replacing the existing United States' forces.[59] In December 1985, a joint Spanish–United

States Communiqué announced that negotiations to renew the treaty of Friendship, Defence and Cooperation (which in July 1982 had replaced the previous treaty of 1976) would begin in July 1986. The Communiqué further stated that one of the objectives of these negotiations would be 'to adjust the United States military presence to the level that is deemed necessary'.[60] From the outset, however, the negotiations have proved to be tense and difficult, with the United States accusing Spain of non-cooperation and lacking a 'sufficiently constructive' attitude, and the offers of the United States being rejected in turn by Madrid as 'merely cosmetic and insufficient'.[61] The main point of contention has been over the future of the seventy-two F16 bombers stationed at Torrejón. Whereas the Spanish government insisted upon the F16s being removed from Spanish territory, the United States' Defense Secretary Caspar Weinberger maintained that it was essential to the Pentagon's strategic planning that they remain.

Having accepted Spain's participation in the alliance, the major problem for a Spanish Socialist government committed to reducing the United States' military presence is, as pointed out by Rafael Luis Bardaji of the International Institute for Strategic Studies, to identify which of the United States' forces based in Spain are integral to NATO's defence system and which are solely serving the global interests of the United States.[62] This is likely to prove a difficult task and may impede any substantial reduction of United States personnel on Spanish territory.

Finally, it has to be pointed out that, in accordance with the Spanish Constitution, the referendum of March 1986 was 'consultative' and is not therefore binding upon the present, or perhaps more importantly a future, government. Despite the apparent hegemonic position of the PSOE, the possibility of a future non-Socialist government cannot altogether be excluded. Thus the conditions stipulated by the Socialists for Spain's continued participation in the alliance will not necessarily be accepted by a future administration.

Apart from the government's expert manipulation of the media[63] and the confusion that surrounded the 'surrealistic' nature of the referendum itself,[64] it was claimed, with some justification by those who had campaigned for Spain to leave NATO, that the government victory was based on a *voto de miedo* (vote of fear). The Spanish people, it was argued, had supported the government's position not because of any perceived positive advantages for national security, but rather because the government had instilled a sense of foreboding in the country about potentially dire economic consequences if Spain withdrew from the alliance.[65] In a country with the highest level of unemployment in Western Europe, the mere suggestion or suspicion that the economic situation would deteriorate as a consequence of withdrawal would have had far-reaching affects on people's voting intentions.[66]

Perhaps most important in explaining the government's victory in the referendum was, however, its ability successfully to package the shift in policy as being absolutely essential to the modernization of Spanish society. Between the election of 1982 and the referendum of 1986, the Socialist government succeeded in convincing a majority of those that voted, that internal modernization and Europeanization were inextricably linked to participation in NATO. Arguably, the 'ideology of modernization', rather than the question of national security, was the determining factor in explaining both the PSOE government's U-turn and the endorsement it received in 1986. Withdrawal from NATO viewed from this perspective would have meant 'missing the train into the twenty-first century'.[67] In an interview twelve months after Spain had decided to remain in NATO, the Deputy Prime Minister Alfonso Guerra triumphantly claimed that in five years the Socialist government had achieved its goals of securing 'democratic stability, salvaging the economy and the ending of international isolation'.[68] Whether the goals of national and international security that they also sought to enhance have been achieved by Spain's participation in NATO remains to be seen.

Notes

1. See P. Preston and D. Smyth, *Spain, the EEC and NATO*, Routledge and Kegan Paul, London, 1984.
2. Preston and Smyth, op. cit., pp. 1–2.
3. See J.M. Arija, 'Los Españoles y la Otan', *Ideas para la Democracia*, no. 1, Madrid, 1984.
4. A.Viñas, 'Política Económica y Política de Defensa', *Sistema*, no. 56, September 1983.
5. See Lorca y Calatava, 'Las Resoluciones Ecónomicas, España–Estados Unidos', *Boletín de Informaciones Comerciales Españolas*, no. 1993, Madrid, June 1985.
6. D. Reinado, 'Los Bases U.S.A.', *Mundo Obrero*, 6 March 1986.

7. *El País*, 3 March 1986.
8. See A. Viñas, *Los Pactos Secretos de Franco con Estados Unidos*, Ediciones Grijalbo, Barcelona, 1981.
9. Viñas, op. cit., p. 197.
10. The terms of this treaty also stipulated that if it so wished the Spanish government could reverse this decision in the future.
11. On the geo-strategic importance of Spain, see S. Menual, 'The Geo-strategic Importance of the Iberian Peninsula', Conflict Studies, no. 133, Institute for the Study of Conflict, London 1981; and E. Barbe, 'La Región Mediterránea' ((1): 'El Flanco Sur de La OTAN'), *Afers Internacionals* Centro d'Informacio i Documentacio Internationals a Barcelona, Barcelona, Spring 1984.
12. *El País*, 5 May 1985.
13. Ibid.
14. See Carlos Arias Navarro, *Hacia una Plenitud Democrática: Discurso Pronunciado en el Pleno de las Cortes Españolas el 28 de Enero de 1976*, Ediciones del Movimiento, Madrid, 1976.
15. W.T. Salisbury, 'Spain's Foreign Policy', in T.D. Lancaster and G. Provost (eds.), *Politics and Change in Spain*, Praeger, New York, 1985, p. 212.
16. F. Morán, *Una Política Exterior para España*, Planeta, Barcelona, 1980.
17. Indeed, the issue of NATO did not appear in the programme of any party in 1972. On the subject, see Marquina Barrio Antonio, 'Defensa y Seguridad en las programas de los Partidos Políticos', in *España qué Defensa*, Instituto de Cuestiones Internacionales, Madrid, 1981, pp. 215–30.
18. See 'Discurso de Investidura de Adolfo Suárez, 30/3/1979', in *España y la OTAN*, Secretaría de Relaciones Internacionales, Madrid, August 1981.
19. *El País*, 15 June 1980.
20. See F. González, 'Discurso del Presidente del Gobierno Sobre La Paz y La Seguridad', Madrid, February 1985.
21. This is the view of Preston and Smyth, op. cit., p. 72.
22. See 'Discurso de Investidura', Referencias a la Politica Exterior de 18 Febrero de 1984', in *España y la OTAN*.
23. *El País*, 16 February, 1986.
24. A.Gooch, 'A Surrealistic Referendum: Spain and NATO', *Government and Opposition*, vol. 21, no. 3, 1986.
25. *The North Atlantic Treaty Organization*, NATO Information Service, Brussels, 1981, p. 264.
26. *El País*, 16 February 1986.
27. Quoted in Preston and Smyth, op. cit., p. 18.
28. Morán, op. cit., p. 119.
29. Morán, op. cit., pp. 80–8.
30. Morán, op. cit., pp. 88–114.

31. See 'Resoluciones del XXIX Congreso del Partido Socialista Obrero Español,' 21–24 de Octubre de 1981. *Política Exterior e Internacional*, in A. del Arenal and F. Aldercón (eds.), *España y la OTAN: Textos y Documentos*, Editorial Tecnos, Madrid, 1986.

32. See '50 Preguntas Sobre la OTAN', (October 1981) in Arenal and Aldercon, op. cit., p. 314.

33. For the PCE's position on NATO, see *Programa Electoral del Partido Comunista de España*, 15–16 September 1982, p. 46.

34. '50 Preguntas', in Arenal and Aldercón, op. cit., pp. 314–30.

35. *El País*, 2 December, 1978.

36. Ibid.

37. See W.J. Feld (ed.), *The Foreign Policy of West European Socialist Parties*, Praeger, New York, 1978, pp. 145–47.

38. For a detailed account of the rise and decline of the PCE, see E.L. Mujal, *Communism and Political Change in Spain*, Indiana University Press, Bloomington, 1983.

39. See B. Pollack, *Factions in the Spanish Socialist Workers Party: The Case of the 1979 Extraordinary Congress* (unpublished) 1980.

40. On the social democratization of the PSOE, see D. Shore, 'Two Transitions: Democratization and the Evolution of the Spanish Socialist Left', *West European Politics*, vol. 8, no. 1, January 1985.

41. B. Pollack, op. cit., pp. 1–19.

42. On the relationship between the deradicalization of the PSOE and its consequences for the U-turn of 1983–84, see R.F. Neld, *The Spanish Socialist Workers Party and NATO*, (unpublished M.Soc.Sc. thesis), University of Birmingham, 1981.

43. B. Barnouin, *The European Labour Movement and European Integration*, Francis Pinter, London, 1986, p. 38.

44. For a succinct account of the history of the Spanish labour movement since the Civil War, see J. Setein, *El Movimiento Obrero y el Sindicalismo de Clase en España (1939–1981)*, Ediciones de la Torre, Madrid, 1982.

45. F. González in *Cambio 16*, 10 March 1986.

46. *El País*, 20 January 1985.

47. González, *Política de Paz*, op. cit., p. 47.

48. PSOE document, quoted in V. Fisas Arnengal, *Una Alternativa a la Politica de Defensa en España*, Editorial Fontamara, Barcelona, 1985.

49. *El País*, 20 January 1985.

50. *El País*, 9 February 1986.

51. *El País*, 17 March 1986.

52. *El País*, 9 February 1986.

53. The Standing Group was disbanded in 1966 and its functions transferred to the Military Committee.

54. *The North Atlantic Treaty Organization*, op. cit., (Barcelona) pp. 248–9.

55. *Interviu*, 8 October 1986.

56. *El País*, 4 May 1983.

57. *El País*, 16 December 1985.
58. *Mundo Obrero*, 6 March 1986, p. 17. As was shown earlier in this book, several bases have in fact been used by American nuclear vessels.
59. *El País*, 19 May 1986.
60. *El País*, 15 December 1985.
61. *El País*, 4 April 1986.
62. *El País*, ibid.
63. *El País*, 13 March 1986
64. Surrealist in the sense that the PSOE, which had been one of the most ardent opponents of entry now advocated voting to remain in the alliance, whilst the consistently pro-Atlanticist Alianza Popular called for abstention as it disagreed with the necessity of holding a referendum on the issue. See Gooch, op. cit., p. 300.
65. This was stressed by Prime Minister González three days before the referendum.
66. The possible impact that the fear of deterioration in the economic sphere might have had upon sectors of the Spanish population was observed by one of the authors in Cornella del LLobregat, Barcelona. Although Catalunya voted 'no', in certain industrialized areas support for the government's position increased dramatically and in working-class *barrios* most affected by unemployment the 'yes' vote was often in the majority.
67. F. González, quoted in *The Observer*, 16 March 1986.
68. *El País*, 19 April 1987.

Bibliography

Archives

Chile: Cámara de Diputados de la República de Chile, *Debates Parlamentarios*, 1946–7.

_____ Foreign Office, 1970–3.

_____ *Federal Republic of Germany*: German Foreign Office, *Documents on German Foreign Policy, 1918–1945*, Series D, Vol. III, *The Spanish Civil War*.

_____ *Great Britain*: *Public Records Office*, London, 2299/75/41.

House of Commons, *Debates*, Hansard, London.

Spain: Comisaria del Plan de Desarrollo, *Reporte*, Boletín Oficial del Estado, Madrid, 1971.

_____ Cortes Españolas, *Debates*, Madrid.

_____ *Estatuto de Autonomía del País Vasco*, Ley Orgánica, 3–8 December 1979.

_____ Instituto de Cooperación Iberoamericana (ICI), *Realidades y posibilidades de las Relaciones entre España y América Latina en los Ochenta*, Ediciones Cultura Hispánica, Madrid, 1986.

_____ Instituto de Cooperación Iberoamerica (ICI), *Resumen de Programas Previstos para 1984*, internal document, Madrid, 1984.

_____ Ministerio de Asuntos Exteriores, *Archivos Generales*, Madrid, 1940–2.

_____ Ministerio de Hacienda, *Informe Anual Sobre Comercio Exterior*, Madrid, 1984.

_____ Oficina de Información Diplomática, Ministerio de Asuntos Exteriores, *Actividades, Textos y Documentos de Política Externa Española*, No. 36, Madrid, 23 February 1984.

United Nations: *General Assembly, Debates*, New York, 1945–55.

United States: Department of State, *Documents: The War Years, 1940*, vol. 9, Washington DC, 1956.

_____ House of Representatives, *Debates, 1946–7*, Washington DC.

Periodicals and newspapers

ABC, Madrid, 1940–60, 1975–85.
Los Angeles Times, California.
Arriba (Falangist newspaper),
Cambio 16, (national weekly magazine), 1970–86.
Daily Telegraph, London,
Diario de Barcelona,
Diario 16, (national daily newspaper),
Economist, London, 1980–6.
Excelsior, Mexico City.
Gramma, Havana, Cuba, 1963–6, 1986.
L'Humanité (French Communist party newspaper), 1970–1.
Interviu, Barcelona, 1986.
Irish Times, Dublin, 1985.
Investia, Moscow.
Jewish Chronicle, 1945–55.
Leviatán, 'Revista de Hechos e Ideas', 1984.
Guardian, Manchester.
Le Monde, Paris.
Mundo Obrero, 1986.
New York Times, 1946–86.
El País, Madrid, 1978–87.
Pueblo, (Falangist newspaper), 1970–6.
Revista Ercilla, Santiago, Chile, 1946–7.
Revista de Estudios Internacionales, 1984.
Times, London.
Trud, Moscow.
Washington Post, Washington DC.
L'Unitá (official Italiam Communist party daily newspaper), 1970–1.
Ya.

Articles: journals and books

Arija, J.M., 'Los Españoles y la OTAN', in *Ideas Para la Democracia*, no. 1, Madrid, 1984.

Barbe, E., 'La Región Mediterránea (1): El Flanco Sur de la OTAN', *Afers Internacionales*, Barcelona, Spring 1984.

Boletin de Informaciones Comerciales Españolas, no. 1923, Madrid 1983.

Bonet, Pilar, 'La Fascinación Soviética por España', *El País*, Madrid, 16 May 1984.

Bru, C., 'España entre Dos Tratados', *Leviatán*, II Epoca, no. 17, Autumn 1984, pp. 69–80.

Bueno, J.M., 'Política de Seguridad Española', *Leviatán*, II Epoca, no. 17,

Autumn 1984, pp. 35–46.

Cuadernos Para el Diálogo, 'El Caso Español: la Diacronía Estructural de la Modernización, in *Anuario Político Español 1969*, Madrid, 1970.

Flemming, Shannon, 'North Africa and the Middle East', in J.W. Cortada (ed.), *Spain in the Twentieth century: Essays on Spanish Diplomacy, 1898– 1978*, Aldwych Press, London, 1980.

Fusi, J.P., Introduction to 'De la Dictadura a la Democracía, Desarrollismo, Crísis y Transición (1959–1977)', *Historia*, vol. 8, Extra, February 1983.

Gavenglio, S., 'Consideraciones sobre el Retorno del Mar a Bolivia', *Revista de Estudios Internacionles*, Madrid, July–Sept. 1984, pp. 633–49.

Germani, G., 'Political Socialization in Fascist Regimes: Italy and Spain', in S. P. Huntington and C. H. Moore (eds.), *Authoritarian One Party Systems*, Basic Books, New York, 1970.

Gooch, A., 'A Surrealistic Referendum: Spain and the NATO', *Government and Opposition*, vol. 21, no. 3, 1986, pp. 300–16.

Halstead, C.R., 'Spanish Foreign Policy, 1936–1978', in J.W. Cortada (ed.), *Spain in the Twentieth Century: Essays on Spanish Diplomacy, 1898–1978*, Aldwych Press, London, 1980.

Kettle-Williams, J., 'The Birth of the Peace Movement in Spain: An Introductory Note', *Journal of Area Studies*, no. 9, Spring 1984, pp. 42–3.

Linz, Juan J., 'An Authoritarian Regime: Spain', in E. Allardt and Y. Littunen (eds.), *Cleavages, Ideologies and Party Systems*, Free Press, New York, 1964.

_____ 'From Falange to Movimiento-Organización: the Spanish single party and the Franco Regime, 1936–1968', in S.P. Huntington and C.H. Moore (eds.), *Authoritarian One Party Systems*, Basic Books, New York, 1970.

_____ 'Opposition under An Authoritarian Regime: The Case of Spain', in R.A. Dahl (ed.), *Regimes and Opposition*, Yale University Press, New Haven, 1974.

Lorca y Calatava, 'Las Resoluciones Económicas España–Estados Unidos', *Boletín de Informaciones Comerciales Españolas*, no. 1993, Madrid, June 1985.

Mangas Martín, A., 'El Referendum sobre la OTAN y la Denuncia del Tratado del Atlántico Norte', *Revista de Estudios Internacionales*, no. 3, July–Sept. 1984, pp. 651–61.

Marquina Barrios, Antonio, 'Defensa y Seguridad en los Programas de los Partidos Políticos', in *España que Defensa*, Instituto de Cuestiones Internacionales, Madrid, 1981, pp. 215–30.

Maravall, José M., 'Political Cleavages in Spain and the 1979 General Election', *Government and Opposition*, vol. 14, 1979, pp. 299–317.

_____ 'Spain, Eurocommunism and Socialism', *Political Studies*, vol. 27, 1979, pp. 218–35.

Menual, S., 'The Geostrategic Importance of the Iberian peninsula', *Conflict Studies*, no. 133, London, 1981.

Mesa, R., 'La Política Exterior en la España Democrática', *Revista de Estudios Internacionales*, no. 1, 1983, pp. 7—67.

Morales Moya, Antonio, 'Relaciones Internacionales y Función Diplomática en la Historia Contemporánea', *Documentación Administrativa*, no. 205, 1985, p. 46.

Morán, F., 'Cuatro Años Cumplidos: España a Punto, 1982—1986. Balance de una Gestión, PSOE, 1986', *Leviatán*, no. 16, 1984, pp. 7—20.

_____ 'La Opción Europea en el Marco de la Política Exterior Española', *Afers Internacionales*, Barcelona, 1983.

Moya V.C., 'Las Élites Económicas y el Desarrollo Español', in S. del Campo (ed.), *España en los Años 70: vol. 1, La Sociedad*, Editorial Moneda y Crédito, Madrid, 1972.

Muñoz, H., 'Las Relaciones Exteriores del Gobierno Militar Chileno', in J.C. Puig (ed.), *América Latina: Políticas Exteriores Comparadas*, Ediciones GEL, Buenos Aires, 1984, pp. 353—91.

Oliart, A., 'España y la Alianza Atlántica: Una Opción para Nuestra Política de Defensa', *Revista de Política Comparada*, no. 6, Autumn 1981, pp. 11–29.

Panes, E., 'OTAN: de Entrada No, No', *Leviatán*, II Epoca, no. 12. Autumn 1984, pp. 47—58.

Pardo de Santillana y Coloma, José Ramón, 'Seguridad Nacional y Diplomacia', *Documentación Administrativa*, no. 205, 1985, pp. 205—17.

Pollack, B., 'The 1982 Spanish General Elections and Beyond', *Parliamentary Affairs*, vol. 36, no. 2, 1983, pp. 201—17.

_____ 'Spain: From Corporate State to Parliamentary Democracy', *Parliamentary Affairs*, vol. 36, 1978, pp. 52—66.

Pollack, B., and Grugel, J., 'Opposition in Contemporary Spain: Tradition against Modernity', in E. Kolinky (ed.), *Opposition in Western Europe*, Croom Helm and European Centre for Political Studies, London, 1986.

Pollack, B. and Taylor, J., 'The Transition to Democracy in Portugal and Spain', *British Journal of Political Science*, vol. 13, 1983, pp. 209—42.

Reinado, D., 'Las Bases U.S.A.', *Mundo Obrero*, 6 March 1986.

Rodríguez, E.R., 'Transición a la Democracia en España: Hacia una Nueva Política Iberoamericana?', in *Realidades y Posibilidades de las Relaciones entre España y América Latina en los Ochenta*, Ediciones Cultura Hispánica ICI, Madrid, 1986, pp. 155—72.

Rosenfeld, S.S., 'The Panamá Negotiations: a Close-run Thing', *Foreign Affairs*, October 1975, pp. 1—13.

Salas Lopez, F. de, 'El Proceso de Integración de España en la OTAN', *Revista de Estudios Internacionales*, vol. 3, no. 1, Jan.—March., 1982.

Salisbury, W.T., 'Spain's Foreign Policy', in T.D. Lancaster and G. Provost (eds.), *Politics and Change in Spain*, Praeger, New York, 1985.

Santesmases, A., 'PSOE y OTAN', *Leviatán*, II Epoca, no. 17, Autumn 1984, pp. 59—68.

Schindler, C., 'No Pasarán: the Jews that Fought in Spain', *Jewish Quarterly*, vol. 33, no. 123, 1986, pp. 34–41.

_____ 'Secretaría de Relaciones Internacionales, 'Adolfo Suarez, Discurso de Investidura, 30/3/1979', in *España en la OTAN*, Madrid, 1981.

Shore, D., 'Two Transitions: Democratization and the Evolution of the Spanish Socialist Left', *West European Politics*, vol. 8, no. 1, January 1985.

Solis Gragera, Tomás., 'El Poder Exterior y las Comunidades Autónomas', *Documentación Administrativa*, no. 205, 1985, pp. 91–118.

Story, J., 'Spanish Political Parties: Before and After the Election', *Government and Opposition*, vol. 12, 1977, pp. 473–93.

Valcárcel, D. and Girones, J.M., 'La Investigación en España', *Revista de Occidente*, vol. 3, no. 1, November 1975.

Varas, A., 'Política Exterior y Democracia en Chile', in J.C. Puig (ed.), *América Latina: Políticas Exteriores Comparadas*.

Villar Ortiz de Urbina, Francisco, 'Diplomacia Multilateral y Servicio Exterior', *Documentación Administrativa*, no. 205, 1985, pp. 119–28.

Viñas, Á., 'Coordenadas de la Política de Seguridad Española', *Leviatán*, II Epoca, no. 17, Autumn 1984, pp. 7–34.

_____ 'Economía de la Defensa y Defensa Económica: Una Propuesta Reconceptualizadora', *Revista de Estudios Políticos (Nueva Epoca)*, no. 37, Jan.–Feb. 1981, pp. 25–42.

_____ 'Este–Oeste, Norte–Sur y Europa Occidental', *Leviatán*, II Epoca, no. 16, Summer 1984, pp. 65–79.

_____ 'Estrategia Nacional y Entorno Exterior: El Caso de España', *Revista de Estudios Internacionales*, vol. 5, no. 1, Jan.–Mar. 1984, pp. 73–101.

_____ 'Política Económica y Política de Defensa', *Sistema*, no. 56, September 1983.

_____ 'Spain and the United States and NATO', in C. Abel and N. Torrents (eds.), *Spain: Conditional Democracy*, Croom Helm, London, 1984.

Watson, B., 'Economic Adjustments of Modern Spain with Reference to EEC Membership', in *Spain and Portugal*, Thunderbird Graduate School of International Management, Glendale, Ariz., 1972.

Yáñez Barrionuevo, L., 'Las Relaciones con Iberoamérica', in *Estudios Internacionales 1983*, SEI, Madrid, 1983.

Books

Alba, V., *Transition in Spain: From Franco to Democracy*, Transition Books, New Brunswick, NJ, 1978.

Alianza Popular, *Los Aliados Dentro de la OTAN*, Publicaciones de Alianza Popular, Madrid, 1984.

Amsden, J., *Collective Bargaining and Class Struggle in Spain*, Weidenfeld & Nicholson, London, 1972.

Arango, R., *The Spanish Political System: Franco's Legacy*, Westview Press, Boulder, Colo., 1978.

Arenal, A. del and Aldercón, F. (eds.), *España y la OTAN: Textos y Documentos*, Tecnos, Madrid, 1986.

Arias Navarro, Carlos, *Hacia una Plenitud Democrática*, Discurso Pronunciado en el Pleno de las Cortes Españolas el 28 de Enero de 1976, Ediciones del Movimiento, Madrid, 1976.

Armero, J.M., *La Política Exterior de Franco*, Planeta, Barcelona, 1978.

Artiques, D., *El Opus Dei: Se Evolución Ideológica y Política*, Ruedo Ibérico, Paris, 1968.

Baily, S.L., *Labour, Nationalism and Politics in Argentina*, Rutgers University Press, New Brunswick, NJ, 1967.

Baklanoff, E.M., *La Transformación Económica de España y Portugal*, Espasa-Calpe, Madrid, 1980.

Baraguer, Joseph R., (ed.), *Why Perón Came to Power: The Background to Peronism in Argentina*, Knopf, New York, 1968.

Barnouin, B., *The European Labour Movement and European Integration*, Frances Pinter, London, 1986.

Blankstein, George I., *Perón's Argentina*, University of Chicago Press, Chicago, 1953.

Brennan, G., *The Spanish Labyrinth*, Cambridge University Press, Cambridge, 1950.

Brotons, Antonio Remiro, *La Acción Exterior del Estado*, Tecnos, Madrid, 1984.

Carr, R., and Fusi, J.P., *Spain: Dictatorship to Democracy*, Allen & Unwin, London, 1979.

Carrillo, S., *España en Europa?*, Conferencia en el Club Siglo XXI, Madrid, December 1985.

——— *La Ruptura Democrática*, La Gaya Ciencia, Barcelona, 1976.

Chamorro, A. Cole, *145 Años de Historia Política de Nicaragua*, Managua, Nicaragua, 1967.

Cortada, J.W., *Two Nations over Time: Spain and the United States 1776–1977*, Greenwood Press, London, 1978.

Coverdale, F.F., *The Political Transformation of Spain under Franco*, Praeger, New York, 1979.

Díaz, E., *Pensamiento Español*, Cuadernos para el Diálogo, Madrid, 1974.

Feld, W.J. (ed.), *The Foreign Policy of the West European Socialist Parties*, Praeger, New York, 1978.

Fisas Arnengal, V., *Una Alternativa a la Política de Defensa en España*, Editorial Fontanara, Barcelona, 1985.

González, Felipe, *Discurso del Presidente del Gobierno Sobre la Paz y la Seguridad*, Madrid, February 1985.

González, S., *España Neutral*, Gráficas Espejo, Madrid, 1947.

Halstead, C.R., *The United States and the Spanish Question*, unpublished Master's thesis, University of Virginia, 1953.

Harrison, J., *An Economic History of Modern Spain*, Manchester University Press, Manchester, 1978.

Hoare, S., *Embajador ante Franco en Misión Especial*, Sedaway, 1977.

Holborn, H., *A History of Modern Germany*, Eyre & Spottiswoode, London, 1969.

Hooper, J., *The Spaniards*, Penguin, Harmondsworth, 1986.

Humphreys, R.A., *Tradition and revolt in Latin America and other essays*. Weidenfeld & Nicholson, London, 1969.

Huntington, S., *Political Order in Changing Societies*, Yale University Press, New Haven, 1968.

Klepak, H.P., *Spain: NATO or Neutrality?*, Centre for International Relations, Queens University, Ontario, 1980.

Lancaster, T.D., and Provost, G., *Politics and Change in Spain*, Praeger, New York, 1985.

Lacquer, W., *Fascism*. University of California Press, Berkeley, 1976.

Lleonart, A.J., *España y la ONU: I (1945–1946) y II (1947): Estudio Introductivo y Corpus Documental*, Consejo Superior de Investigaciones Científicas, Madrid, 1983.

Maravall, J.M., *El Desarrollo Económico y la Clase Obrera*, Ariel, Barcelona, 1970.

_____ *Dictatorship and Political Dissent: Workers and Students in Franco's Spain*, Tavistock Publications, London, 1978.

_____ *The Transition to Democracy in Spain*, Croom Helm, London, 1982.

Mesa Garrido, Roberto and Luzarraga, Francisco Aldecoa, *Apuntes del Curso sobre Política Exterior Española*, Facultad de Ciencias Políticas y Sociología, Departamento de Relaciones Internacionales, Universidad Complutense, Madrid.

Miguel, A. de., *La Herencia del Franquismo*, Editorial, *Cambio 16*, Madrid, 1976.

Minet, G., Siotis, J., and Tsakaloyannis, P. (eds.), *The Mediterranean Challenge: Spain, Greece and Community Politics*, European Research Centre, University of Sussex, Falmer, 1981.

Minter, W., Schmitter, P. and Payne, S., *A History of Spain and Portugal*, University of Wisconsin Press, Madison, 1973.

Morán, Fernando, Foreword in J.M. Armero, *La Política Exterior de Franco*, Planeta, Barcelona, 1978.

_____ *Una Política Exterior para España*, Planeta, Barcelona, 1980.

Mujal, E.L., *Communism and Political Change in Spain*, Indiana University Press, Bloomington, 1983.

Neld, R.F., *The Spanish Socialist Workers Party and NATO*, unpublished M.Soc. Sc. thesis, University of Birmingham, 1981.

NATO Information Service, *The North Atlantic Treaty Organization*, Brussels, 1981.

Paniagua, Javier F., *La Ordenación del Capitalismo Avanzado en España, 1957–1963*, Anagrama, Barcelona, 1977.

Partido Comunista de España, *Programa Electoral del Partido Comunista de España*, 15—16 September 1982.

Payne, S.G., *Falange*, University of California Press, Stanford, 1961.

Perry, G.N.J., *Spanish Foreign Policy and the European Community*, unpublished B.Soc. Sc. thesis, University of Birmingham, 1985.

Pinochet de la Barra, Oscar, 'Algunas Reflexiones sobre el Problema de la Antártida en el Año 2000', in F. Orrego (ed.), *La Antártida y Sus Recursos: Problemas Científicos, Jurídicos y Políticos*, Editorial Universitaria, Santiago de Chile, 1983.

Pollack, B., *Factions in the Spanish Socialist Workers Party: The Case of 1979 Extraordinary Congress*, unpublished paper to the Workshop on Factionalism in the Political Parties of Western Europe, European Consortium for Political Research, Florence, 1980.

Poulantzas, N., *The Crisis of the Dictatorships: Portugal, Spain and Greece*, New Left Books, London, 1976.

Preston, Paul (ed.), *Spain in Crisis: The Evolution and Decline of the Franco Regime*, Harvester, Brighton, 1976.

—— and Smyth, D., *Spain, the EEC and NATO*, Routledge & Kegan Paul, London, 1984.

Robinson, R., *The Origins of Franco's Spain: The Right, the Republic and Revolution, 1931—1936*, University of Pittsburg Press, Plymouth, 1970.

Roitman, M., *La política del PSOE en América Latina*, Editorial Revolución, Madrid, 1986.

Rubottom, R.R. and Carter-Murphy, J., *Spain and the United States since World War Two*, Praeger, New York, 1984.

Ruperez, Javier, *España en la OTAN, Relato Parcial*, Plaza y Ginés, Barcelona, 1986.

Rushworth, J. (ed.), *Spain, Portugal and the European Community*, University Association for Contemporary European Studies, London, 1979.

Sampedro, J.L. and Payne, J.A. (eds.), *The Enlargement of the European Community: Case Studies of Greece, Portugal and Spain*, Macmillan, London, 1983.

Secretaría de Relaciones Internacionales, *Dossier: España en la OTAN*, Madrid, 1981.

Supúlveda Almarza, A., *España y América Latina: Un Estudio de Política Internacional*, CIPIE (Colección Estudios Latinoamericanos), Madrid, 1986.

Serrano Suñer, Ramón., *Memorias*, Barcelona, 1977.

Setein, J., *El Movimiento Obrero y el Sindicalismo de Clases en España (1939—1981)*, Ediciones de la Torre, Madrid, 1982.

Tamamés, R., *Estructura Económica de España*, Alianza Editorial, Madrid, 1985.

Taylor, A.J.P., *Europe: Grandeur and Decline*, Penguin, Harmondsworth, 1967.

Thomas, H., *The Spanish Civil War*, Harper and Row, New York, 1963.

United Nations, General Assembly, *Resolutions (for the 1955—86 period)*, New York.

United States, Department of State, *The Spanish Government and the Axis*, Washington, DC, 1946.

Vásquez Montalbán, M., *La Penetración Americana en España, Cuadernos para el Diálogo*, Madrid, 1974.

Vicens Vivés, J., *Aproximación a la Historia de España*, Editorial Vicens Vivés, Barcelona, 1978.

Vilar, S., *La Naturaleza del Franquismo*, Ediciones Península, Barcelona, 1977.

Viñas, Angel, *Los Pactos Secretos de Franco con Estados Unidos: Bases, Ayuda Económica, Recortes de Soberanía*, Grijalbo, Barcelona, 1981.

Further recommended bibliography

AAS—IEPALA, *Sáhara: La Traición*, Madrid, 1980.

Abella Ramallo, Carlos, *El Sáhara Español: Estudio Actual y Espíritu de Colaboración Funcional*, Memoria de la Escuela Diplomática, Madrid, 1966.

Aguirre de Cárcer, Rodrigo, *El Sáhara Español—Colonia—Provincia—Autodeterminación*, Memoria de la Escuela Diplomática, Madrid, 1976.

Assidon, Elsa, *Sáhara Occidental: Un Enjeu pour le Nord-Ouest Africain*, Maspera, Paris, 1978.

Association des Amis de la R. A. S. D., *Dossier de Sahara Occidental*, Paris.

Azzuz, Mohamed Ibn., 'Por que Reivindicamos Río de Oro?', *Magrib 9*, Rabat, 1966.

Barbier, Maurice, *Le Conflit du Sáhara Occidental*, L'Harmattan, Paris, 1982.

Barros, Raimundo, 'Comunidad Económica Europea: La Incertidumbre Compartida', *Revista Estudios Internacionales*, Santiago de Chile, July—Sept. 1984, pp. 378—400.

Bitar, Sergio and Moneta, Carlos (eds.), *Política Económica de Estados Unidos en América Latina: Documentos de la Administración Reagan*, Editorial G.E.L., Buenos Aires, 1984.

Carbajal Gárate, José Ignacio, *La Cuestión del Sáhara Español en Naciones Unidas*, Memoria de la Escuela Diplomática, Madrid, 1970.

Carrillo Salcedo, Juan Antonio, 'La Posición de España Respecto de la Cuestión del Sáhara Occidental: De la Declaración de Principios de Madrid al Comunicado Conjunto Hispano—Argelino', *Política Internacional*, Madrid, no. 163, 1979.

Colloqué de Massy, *Sáhara Occidental: Un Peuple et Ses Droits*, 1—2 April 1978, L'Harmattan, Paris, 1978.

Comité de Relaciones Exteriores del Frente Polisario, *Sáhara Occidental: La Lucha del Pueblo Sarahuí*, Madrid, 1979.

Cortada, James W., *A Bibliographic Guide to Spanish Diplomatic History*,

1460–1977, Greenwood Press, Westport and London, 1987.

Criado, Ramón, *Sáhara: Pasión y Muerte de un Sueño Colonial*, Ruedo Ibérico, Paris, 1977.

Enders, T. O., 'La Crisis del Atlántico Sur, Antecedentes y Consecuencias', in S. Bitar and C. Moneta (eds.), *Política Económica de Estados Unidos en América Latina: Documentos de la Administración Reagan*, Ed. G. E. L., Buenos Aires, 1984.

Fassi, Allal El, *Livre Rouge*, Peretti, Tánger, 1961.

───── *La vérité sur les Frontières Marocaines*, Peretti, Tánger, 1961.

Foreign Affairs Committee, London, *Gibraltar: The Situation on Gibraltar and United Kingdom Relations with Spain: Seventh Report from the Foreign Affairs Committee, Session 1980–81* (together with Appendices, the Proceedings of the Committee relating to the Report, and the Minutes of Evidence taken before the Committee with Appendices), HMSO, London, 1981.

Franck, Thomas M., 'The Stealing of the Sahara', *American Journal of International Law*, vol. 70, no. 4, October 1976.

García Figueras, Tomás, *La Acción Africana de España en Torno al 98 (1860–1912)*, Ed. C.S.I.C., Madrid, 1966.

García i Segura, Caterina, 'La Política Exterior del PSOE durant la Transición Política Española: De la Clandestinitat a la Constitución?', *Revista CIDOB d'Afers Internacionals*, Barcelona, no. 7, 1985, pp. 47–66.

Gaudio, Attilio, *Le Dossier du Sahara Occidental*, Nouvelles Editions Latines, Paris, 1978.

───── *Sahara Espagnol: Fin d'un Mythe Colonial?*, Arrisala, Rabat, 1975.

Gómez Molleda, María Dolores, *Los Reformadores de la España Contemporánea*, Ed. C.S.I.C., Madrid, 1981.

Goytisolo, Juan., *El Problema del Sáhara*, Anagrama, Barcelona, 1979.

Grabendorff, Wolf and Roett Riordan (eds.), *América Latina: Europa Occidental y Estados Unidos: Un Nuevo Triángulo Atlántico?*, Ed. G.E.L., Buenos Aires, 1984.

Granda, Germán and García y García, José Luis, 'La Cooperación para el Desarrollo de las Comunidades Europeas y Sus Relaciones con América Latina: un Reto Para España', *Revista Estudios Internacionales*, Santiago de Chile, July–Sept. 1984, pp. 401–13.

Hilton, Stanley E., 'América Latina y Europa Occidental, 1880–1945: La Dimensión Política', in Wolf Grabendorff and Riordan Roett (eds.), *América Latina, Europa Occidental y Estados Unidos: Un Nuevo Triángulo Atlántico*, Ed. G.E.L., Buenos Aires, 1984.

Husson, Philipe, 'La Question des Frontiéres du Maroc', *S. G. du Gouvernement, D. de la Documentation*, Paris, 1960.

Instituto para la Integración de América Latina, *Integración Latinoamericana*, Revista Mensual del INTAL, Buenos Aires.

Jacquier, Bernard, 'L'Autodetermination de Sahara Espagnol', *Revue Générale de Droit International Public*, Paris, July–Sept. 1974.

Jover, José María, *Política, Diplomacia y Humanismo Popular en la España del*

Siglo XIX, Ediciones Turner, Madrid, 1976.

Laroui, Abdallah, *L'Algérie et le Sahara Marocain*, Serar, Casablanca, 1976.

Lazrak, Rachid, *Le Contentieux Territorial entre le Maroc et L'Espagne*, Dar el Kitab, Casablanca, 1974.

López Bravo, Gregorio, 'Perspectiva de las Relaciones Internacionales en la Presente Década', *Revista Diplomacia*, Santiago de Chile, no. 23, 1982, pp. 22–9.

Lopezarias, Germán and Lama, César de la, *Morir en el Sáhara*, A.Q. Ediciones, Bilbao, 1975.

M.A.E., *Livre Blanc sur la Mauritanie*, Rabat, 1960.

M.A.E., *Sáhara Occidental: Exposé Écrit du Gouvernement Espagnol*, Madrid, 1975.

M.A.E., *Sáhara Occidental: Informations et Documents que Présente le Gouvernement Espagnol à la Cour Conformément au Deuxième Paragraphe de la Résolution 3292 (XXIX) de l'Assemblée Générale des Nations Unies*, vol., 7 Madrid, 1975.

Maestre, Juan, *El Sáhara en la Crisis de Marruecos España*, Akal, Madrid, 1975.

Martínez Lage, Santiago, *España Ante el Movimiento Descolonizador en las Naciones Unidas: La Práctica Española en Materia de Descolonización*, Memoria de la Escuela Diplomática, Madrid, 1972.

Meréndez del Valle, Emilio, *Sáhara Español: Una Descolonización Tardía'*, *Cuadernos para el Diálogo*, Los Suplementos, no. 68, Madrid, 1975.

Mercer, John, *Spanish Sahara*, George Allen & Unwin, London, 1976.

Mesa, Roberto, *Teoría y Práctica de las Relaciones Internacionales*, Editorial Taurus, Madrid, 1977.

Miské, Ahmed-Baba, *Front Polisario. L'Âme d'un Peuple*, Rupture, Paris, 1978.

Mousset, Albert, *L'Espagne dans la Politique Mondiale*, Éditions Bossard, Paris, 1923.

Potemkim, V.P. *et al*, *Historia de la Diplomacia*, Editorial Grijalbo, Mexico City, 1966.

Price, David Lynn, 'Morocco and the Sahara: Conflict and Development', *Conflict Studies*, no. 88, 1977.

República Islámica de Mauritania y el Reino de Marruecos, Libro Verde Mauritano, 1960.

Revouvin, Pierre, *Historia de la Relaciones Internacionales*, Aguilar, Madrid, 1969.

Rezette, Robert, *Le Sáhara Occidental et les Frontières Marocaines*, Nouvelles editions Latines, Paris, 1975.

Salas, Jesús, *Intervención Extranjera en la Guerra de España*, Editora Nacional, Madrid, 1975.

Salom Costa, Julio., *España en la Europa de Bismark: La Política Exterior de Cánovas*, Editorial C.S.I.C., Madrid, 1967.

Sandoval y Goig, Fernando, *Sáhara: Abandono o Traición?*, Fuerza

Nueva, Madrid, 1980.

Santos, Alberto, 'Le Basculement vers le Sud de la Politique de Défense de l'Espagne', *Revista CIDOB d'Afers Internacionales*, Barcelona, no. 7, 1985, pp. 23–46.

Segura Palomares, Juan, *El Sáhara, Razón de una Sinrazón*, Acervo, Barcelona, 1976.

Sepúlveda Almarza, Alberto., *España y América Latina: Un Estudio de Política Internacional* (Cuaderno CIPIE, no. 14), CIPIE, Madrid, 1985.

Thompson, V. and Adloff, R., *The Western Saharans: Background to Conflict*, Narnes and Noble, New York, 1980.

Trout, Frank E., *Morocco's Saharan Frontiers*, Droz, Geneva, 1969.

United Nations, Dept. of Political Affairs, Trusteeship and Decolonization, *The Question of Western Sahara at the United Nations: Decolonization*, New York, 1980.

Varios autores, *Sáhara, Sáhara*, Bilbao, 1976.

Vilar, Juan B., *El Sáhara Español*, Sedmay, Madrid, 1977.

Villar, Francisco, *El Proceso de la Autodeterminación del Sáhara*, Prólogo de Fernando Morán, Fernando Torres Editor, Valencia, 1982.

Viñas, Angel, *La Alemania Nazi y el 18 de Julio*, Alianza Universidad, Madrid, 1977.

———— 'Relaciones Hispano-Norteamericanas en Materias de Seguridad', *Estudios Internacionales 1984*, Sociedad de Estudios Internacionales, Madrid, 1985.

Whitaker, Arthur P., *Spain and the Defense of the West: Ally and Liability*, Harper Bros., New York, 1961.

Wirth, Rafael and Balaguer, Soledad, *Frente Polisario: La Ultima Guerrilla*, Laia, Barcelona, 1976.

Yata, Ali., *La Sahara Occidental Marocain*, Al Bayane, Rabat, 1973.

Index